5/26/11

The Tainted Gift

The Tainted Gift

THE DISEASE METHOD OF FRONTIER EXPANSION

Barbara Alice Mann

NATIVE AMERICA: YESTERDAY AND TODAY
Bruce E. Johansen, Series Editor

PRAEGER
An Imprint of ABC-CLIO, LLC

A B C 🔶 C L I O

Santa Barbara, California • Denver, Colorado • Oxford, England

Library of Congress Cataloging-in-Publication Data

Mann, Barbara Alice, 1947–
    The tainted gift : the disease method of frontier expansion / Barbara Alice Mann.
        p. cm. — (Native America: yesterday and today)
    Includes bibliographical references and index.
    ISBN 978-0-313-35338-3 (hardcover : alk. paper) — ISBN 978-0-313-35339-0 (ebook)
    1. Indians of North America—Diseases.   2. Communicable diseases—West (U.S.)—
Transmission.   3. Disease management—West (U.S.)—History.   4. Medical policy—
United States—History—Sources.   5. Public health—Government policy—United
States—History—Sources.   I. Title.
    E98.D6M36   2009
    362.1'08997—dc22   2009016642

13   12   11   10   09   1   2   3   4   5

This book is also available on the World Wide Web as an eBook.
Visit www.abc-clio.com for details.

ABC-CLIO, LLC
130 Cremona Drive, P.O. Box 1911
Santa Barbara, California 93116-1911

This book is printed on acid-free paper ●

Manufactured in the United States of America

Ohio Cherokee Ballad

"Come here, my little Indian friend,"
The soldier said to me
"I know what's good for you—
Just you wait and see."

"See the pretty blankets;
see the color blue.
I got them at the smallpox ward
a gift from me to you."

Now, see the little children
with scabs and running sores.
They all have the smallpox;
they're dying by the score.

Given to Barbara Alice Mann by Barbara Crandell
Ohio Bird Clan Cherokee
Taken from her family papers, *circa* 1910

for Ward Churchill

Contents

∼

Foreword

~

*T*he *Tainted Gift: The Disease Method of Frontier Expansion* examines long-standing Native American allegations that disease was knowingly and deliberately spread as part of the immigrants' intent to reduce Native peoples in North America and ease land seizure. Dr. Barbara Alice Mann has selected four instances to determine what degree of evidentiary support exists for such assertions: an asserted exchange of smallpox-laced blankets at Fort Pitt in 1763; the 1832 Choctaw Removal; a smallpox epidemic on the High Plains in 1837; and the 1847 allegations of the poisoning of the Cayuses in Oregon. She examines documentary and traditional evidence, without preconceived ideas. Her findings reveal a damning degree of complicity in all four cases. In other words, natural pathogens and sometimes, European medicines, were used as deliberate weapons in the battle for the land, often with what an attorney might deem malice aforethought.

Going through primary sources is the scutwork of historians and thus sometimes evaded. Far from evading the scutwork, however, Dr. Mann's work provides a rare, incisive analysis of primary sources scattered among records that are often incomplete, unorganized, and un-indexed, compiled by people who had little interest in documenting the horrors in which they participated. Sometimes, as Mann points out, records were deliberately mangled to facilitate fraud. The convenience of future historians was not considered.

Later document sanitation almost certainly occurred around the 1763 smallpox distribution out of Fort Pitt examined in chapter 1. Mann tracks down and puts into context extant, high-level documents and memos that allude to now-missing letters and reports. Just as importantly, she finds previously overlooked Fort Pitt journals that unequivocally demonstrate that the smallpox distribution was a deliberate act, later commended by high British officials. She also presents Ohio oral traditions published in 1912 that corroborate the events portrayed in those fort records.

In chapter 2, Mann's analysis clearly indicates that officials realized that they were marching the Choctaws into cholera and smallpox epidemics during the 1832 Removal. Here and elsewhere, Dr. Mann's work is searing—and revelatory in its detail and sweep. Mann's work provides a window on the debates engaged in by the conductors of Removal: We can listen to bureaucrats debate whether Choctaws on Removal, heading into areas where smallpox was epidemic, should be vaccinated for the disease, considering the expense.

Cholera, or "The Blue Death," struck (as Mann says) like "an atomic bomb," a new kind of plague not known before, in the midst of other, no less deadly, but more familiar maladies, such as smallpox. As the disease spread, merchants and others balked at quarantines that would impede commerce and cost them money. Time and again, ships became disease vectors, as cholera was carried from Eurasia across the Atlantic to the U.S. East Coast, and then into the interior. Many of the passengers, who usually bathed rarely, if at all, spread infection in their feces. Once the disease reached Native peoples, who had no immunity, it spread like fire through tinder—aggravated by the stresses of forced migration. The 1832 cholera pandemic coincided with Jackson's initial Removals, just as the Choctaws were being forced westward. The dangers were ignored; government contractors often were paid per capita, and a dead Indian, whose body could be left at roadside, cost less to feed and transport than a live one.

On steamboats, Indians were packed 600 or more per vessel, creating perfect conditions for the wildfire spread of diseases. Contractors saved money this way, too. Observers at the scene described the inhumane conditions—Mann paints the wrenching picture: standing-room only, with no space (not to mention privacy) to relieve oneself. On land, they were force-marched, barefoot in all weather, underfed often rancid meat (more savings for the contractors). Army officers who protested the cruel conditions were curtly told to shut up. Natives who complained of disease were told they were being superstitious.

Chapter 3, on the 1837 epidemic that mauled the Mandans and other High-Plains peoples, is an especial tour de force, in which Dr. Mann deconstructs not only a thicket of conflicting (and sometimes intentionally falsified) primary sources, but also a gaggle of secondary sources that constitute the generally accepted version of these events that most people read today.

Combing primary sources, and critiquing the secondary literature, Dr. Mann acutely questions the general assumption that Indians stole infected blankets and spread smallpox themselves during a "drunken frolic." In addition, she establishes that smallpox aboard the merchant ship *St. Peter's* was much more severe than many later accounts admitted, and that several people died en route of the infection. In addition, she has traced the origin of the epidemic to blankets and other trade cloth transmitted by a trader, Jim Beckwourth, a mixed-blood Euro-African, who was well known to his contemporaries.

In chapter 4, Dr. Mann similarly digs deeply into long-ignored documents, both in French and in English, about the deaths of Marcus and Narcissa Whitman, to differentiate the actual events in Oregon Territory from the myth of martyrdom that encrusts the subject today. From the first, the Cayuses claimed that Dr. Whitman had been deliberately poisoning them, a charge that only accelerated with the advent of a measles epidemic in 1847. To date, those charges have been waved off as "Indian superstition," but Dr. Mann's careful reconstruction of the medicine of the day and the death rates around Whitman's mission sheds a new light on the uncomfortable discussion.

In addition to the deliberate dissemination of disease, in these four cases, Dr. Mann describes some of the most wretched and wrenching racist cant I have ever seen, as various contemporary non-Indian observers seemed to enjoy watching Indians die horribly of smallpox, dehumanizing "The Other" as a pretext for taking the Other's land. In the end, pathogens become weapons of war utilized willingly by various traders, Indian agents, and military personnel to rid themselves of human obstructions to conquest.

Where the spread of disease was not utilized intentionally, its potency was often ignored, because admitting the problem would have been a threat to traders' profits. The crew of the *St. Peter's* knew without a doubt, for example, that the cargo of their ship had infected people on board by the time, sailing northwestward, that they reached Council Bluffs, opposite Omaha, on the Missouri River. At that point, they should have turned around, returned to St. Louis, quarantined the infected people, and burned the ship to its waterline. Instead, money talked, and the ship continued upriver with hemorrhagic smallpox on board, to ignite the 1837 epidemic.

Mann compares the mindset of Indian Removal to the German concept of *lebensraum*. The comparison will be uncomfortably close for many American readers, some of whom will swallow hard when they learn that Removal, like *lebensraum,* was advanced as a final solution as well as a cover for one group's thirst for another's land. For "steamboats," read "cattle cars." By reading Andrew Jackson's speeches, we learn how he justified the many trails of tears as the U.S. government's inevitable historical favor to the original inhabitants of North America.

A roaming people ("settlers") thus rationalized their eviction on the assumption that Native peoples (some of whom had occupied the same territories for several thousand years) were without roots in the land. The percentage of the Cherokees who died on the Trail of Tears was similar (one quarter) to the death rate of Polish people during World War II. Another World War II analogy could be the Death March of Bataan.

Courage is required to look such history in the face—especially when the history is ours, and the ashes of the afflicted lie under our feet.

Bruce E. Johansen
Series Editor

Introduction

I am no fan of introductions, at least, not of what they have dwindled down to in standard historical books: a bland outline of what is in the pages to follow. It seems to me that, if someone wants to know what my book is about, then she should read it. The table of contents and index can always be perused for clues. If neither provides insight into what the book is about, then either I am, or the reader is, an idiot.

Publishers do not seem to agree with me on this, but then again, I was also advised not to title this work *The Gift of Disease*, lest an erstwhile cataloguer shelve it in the self-help section of the bookstore. I successfully resisted that effort to tinker with my title, but then, marketing got into the act, determining that, as a title, *The Gift of Disease*, was "too academic." I suspect that the real purpose of neutering the title to *The Tainted Gift* was to soften the settler agency strongly implied by *The Gift of Disease*.

All right, pay attention: This book is about awful facts of American history. It is about deliberately giving smallpox to the Ohio Indians in 1763. It concerns marching the Choctaws into a cholera plague zone during their already genocidal Removal in 1832. It looks at the irresponsible and even criminal acts that sent hemorrhagic smallpox abroad to the High Plains peoples in 1837. It takes the Cayuses seriously when they claim to have been poisoned in 1847. It all rests on frightening primary source documents.

At this point in my summation, I am supposed to pretend that not all the facts are in or pettifog around just who was culpable, ultimately pretending that everyone was at fault or, alternatively, assigning guilt to the least elite individual on the scene, but I cannot. The past cannot be changed, but it can be owned up to.

One of the problems with owning up is simply getting up much of the information contained in the following pages. Even when the dire facts are pretty hard to evade, as with the 1763 smallpox distribution at Fort Pitt, the records lie scattered and uncollated, gathering dust in unlikely places that challenge the researcher to crawl through cobwebs just to turn up documents that ought, in this digital age, to be readily accessible.

Such records as are on the Web, like the 4,271 printed pages of all five volumes of the official Removal Document 512, lack interactivity. In the instance of Document 512, the researcher must know going in precisely which page of which volume she wants, even though the letters, receipts, notes, rolls, and regulations that comprise Document 512 are tossed in just any old how, in no order of chronology or topic. There are 1,179 pages in the first volume, 972 pages in the second, 846 in the third, 771 in the fourth, and 503 in the fifth, so that the only alternative to ESP is to do what I did: read every last, cramped, demented page, only to discover that thousands of vitally important documents were never typeset for publication. Hand-scrawled pages of considerable significance remain squirreled away in microfilm archives, sometimes illegible, often illiterate, not necessarily in English, and once more, in but the crudest of orders.

The suspicious among Natives American scholars speculate that the undulating swamp that is the archives of *Letters Received* and *Letters Sent* by the U.S. Office of Indian Affairs, from 1824 on, provides a nifty cover. It allows the record to *look* completely available while effectively making thorough research a daunting and time-consuming task. A scholar has to be profoundly motivated, a little obsessive, or both, to drain the swamp sufficiently to expose the lurking alligators.

Given modern technology, there is really no reason that pulling up, say, the important Pratte-Chouteau Company papers surrounding the fur trade on the upper Missouri basin, should have required a Sherpa guide through various paper archives, just to locate. I do understand how the subsequent agony of trekking through the trackless wilderness of the Office of Indian Affairs' microforms might choke ambition, but once more, why is this information not digitized? The upshot of its remaining in microformat—the original often in French script with hacked English typescript—is that modern histories of, say, the 1837 smallpox epidemic, just tend to ignore them. Instead, scholars essentially retell the same story that Clyde Dollar told in 1977, using only the sources that he pulled up. This secondary-source approach to history seems like wasted motion, especially when important documents that shed a vital new light on the matter sit untapped in hard-to-access archives.

Tackling the Whitman saga presented a different kind of mess, this one fully interactive, but only around the most ill-conceived of its murky edges. The webbed information in this instance almost entirely derived from an antique conspiracy theory featuring evil "Papists" manipulating bloodthirsty "heathens," with long discredited documents being circulated anew as pristine. Book- and Web-published material abounded, but it all came with an agenda and a skew. Some of the most primary of the information was hidden behind a mountain of fraud.

Native American scholars have long cast a gimlet eye on this very juxtaposition: the nearly insurmountable difficulties, on the one hand, of just getting at the raw information, especially that in the possession of the government; and, on the other hand, the regularity with which western historians churn out "new" presentations that do nothing but rehash the same old tidbits, interpreted in the same old way, so that the only thing new about the most recent offering is the name of its author. At least in private conversation, Native scholars speculate that this is because old ground is safe ground; its well known contours do not challenge conscience. Much of the reticence on the part of settler historians stems from squeamishness at the prospect of looking in the face the bloody, violent, diseased, and sometimes criminal history of this country.

The pain of seeing American history without her make-up and adoring entourage has not been noticed just recently. From the beginning, honest settler historians have grimaced at what they uncovered, from Francis Parkman's first dismay in *The Conspiracy of Pontiac* (1851) at finding the Amherst letters on the 1763 smallpox distribution, to Angie Debo's shock a century later in *And Still the Waters Run* (1940) at uncovering the fate of the Indians under the 1887 Dawes Act. Recording the facts as found is the mark of a great historian, but all too many are mediocre historians who replace their initial gasp of horror with mealy-mouthed dissimulation. They rationalize the crime, minimize the injury, and even deny that the event occurred at all, using arguments that may work in their day, but that fall flat on their ugly faces in a new milieu.

Take, for instance, an extended apologia I found by Hiram Chittenden, who uncovered some very unsavory facts while researching his *American Fur Trade of the Far West*. He began with rationalization:

> It would be alike idle and unjust at this period of our national history [1902] to arraign the methods of the government in its dealings with the Indians—idle because the past is behind us; unjust because, whatever its failures, the purposes of the government towards the native races within its domain have ever been those of paternal benevolence.

In addition to skullduggering via the popular it-happened-so-get-over-it argument, he moved to minimize the damage:

> The policy of government, so far as it has been able to control this course of unavoidable change, has always been the highest good of the Indian. While it was powerless to save the Indian's lands, or to preserve his customs from extinction, it has ever sought to ameliorate an unhappy situation and to secure the most ample reparation for an irremediable loss. The failures of the government have never been those of purpose, but rather those of lack of ability to carry its purpose into effect.

Ah, yes, this was all unavoidable. The government chose to set up the reservation system and to run it through military force, but what happened there was unavoidable. Forced sterilization, forced assimilation, and cultural genocide were all governmental programs, but, heck, they were too unwieldy for the government to manage. Gosh gee whillickers, it was an accident that two-thirds of the land mass of North America was illegally seized, and the other third "bought," under questionable circumstances. Things just got out of hand. Besides, it's the thought that counts, and all this was kindly meant, so let's all let bygones be bygones.

For his grand finale, Chittenden denied any wrongdoing at all:

> A fundamental misconception of the nature of the Indian problem underlies the common assumption that a very different result might and ought to have ensued, and that the policy of our government in its treatment of the Indian has been actuated by motives unworthy of an enlightened people. It ignores the operation of that evolutionary process by which a weaker race disappears before a superior in spite of all that laws or military force can do to prevent [it]. That aboriginal tribes were doomed to complete displacement on the soil of their nativity after once the European races had discovered this continent is a proposition that few will care to deny.

Nope, the settlers did not do it, after all. They are innocent. It was, instead, the natural, impersonal process of biological evolution that eugenically decreed death to the Indians, a development "as inevitable as the progress of the stars."[1]

Today, with paternalism in disrepute, with it obvious just how much the government can and does control, and with death-dealing eugenics proclaimed criminal, Chittenden's squirming around the truth is obvious. Any squirming that works today will be just as obvious in another century, but we will all be dead by then. I say that there is no value in putting off until tomorrow what can be done today, so let us try truth in our time.

"White guilt" is no substitute for truth telling. First, sloshing around in guilt does not expiate the evil done. Worse, having once sloshed, sloshers just grow angry or compassion-fatigued should the topic recur, even though the damage remains unaddressed. Second, "white guilt" is modeled on Christian forgiveness, which paralyzes its prey before consuming it. Wallowing helps no one. Worse, people stuck in guilt mode have been taught that the harm done can be expunged by praying fervently enough to their God. For the record, it was the worshippers of the Christian God who did the damage in the first place, and purportedly for Him, no less. Thus, He is in no position to grant absolution for deeds in which He had a vested interest.

Finally, "white guilt" suggests that one, lone Indian, say someone innocently showing up to speak at a conference, is in a position to forgive things that happened to a nation of which she is neither an elder nor even a member. Whoa, doggies. Only the people who were injured can grant forgiveness, and they can only grant it to those who injured them. People who did not commit an injury cannot apologize to people who were not injured.

To begin with, the lines of accountability have to be clear. Next, to the extent possible, descendants of the offenders must make restitution to the descendants of the injured. If the children of offenders "own" a Shawnee burial mound, they should legally deed it back to the Shawnee descendants living in the area. If a light-fingered anthropologist lifted a medicine bag, his descendants should give it back to the descendants of the anthropologist's "informant." Museum collections of sacred objects should be returned to the people from whom they were taken.

Elie Wiesel once stated that the children of murderers are children. I say that the descendants of killers do not own the crimes of their ancestors, unless they willingly shield those crimes today. I have noticed that some modern Euro-Americans feel backed into a corner, as though by mere virtue of being Euro-descended they must defend the mythology of conquest over its very brutal reality; as if they would be race traitors should they concede the depths of it. This is recidivist racism, but the backsliding is emotional, and emotion cannot be reasoned away.

I have found out the hard way the visceral nature of this emotional resistance, so to forestall it, I now prepare my Euro-American students to hear difficult information. Here is what I tell them: "You are about to learn some very unsettling facts, mournful things that may even contradict what you heard in the fifth grade. You will want to turn away from these awful facts, but do not turn away from them. Instead, remember: You did not do this."

Then, I repeat, "*You* did not do this."

After that sinks in, I continue, "There is no reason for you to assume that you must defend misdeeds, simply because Europeans once committed them. You are not responsible for what happened."

I conclude with: "All that you are responsible for is what you do, once you walk out the door, knowing that these things did happen."

The stories that follow reflect no glory on the European invaders of North America. However, I am told that racism is happily passé, so let me say to my Euro-American readers: You do not have to feel like a race traitor should you pause to wipe your eyes or shake your head over what was done. You did not do this. You are not responsible. The only thing that you are responsible for is what you do after you close this book, knowing that these things were done to Native America.

CHAPTER 1

~

"Out of Our Special Regard for Them": The 1763 Gift of Smallpox

Between 1754 and 1763, the major colonial rivals of France and Britain waged an all-out war of domination against one another, with each seeking to involve Native Americans as its proxy fighters. Well before the February, 1763, peace was signed with France, Britain had tacitly claimed victory, which somehow in the British mind included the "right" to North America. A frenzy of settler-on-Native crime followed, triggering a follow-up war between the Crown and the Natives of, primarily, western Pennsylvania, Ohio, and Michigan. Often erroneously dubbed "Pontiac's Revolt," this coordinated action reclaimed Native land rights, especially to Ohio, and forced gifting economics and trade regulations on the Crown and its unruly settlers.

The road to Native success was strewn, however, with smallpox blankets. As Native coalitions demolished British forts one by one, sending settlers scurrying east, the Crown's armies fell precipitously to disease. In a last-ditch effort to prevail over Native forces, British military and militia leaders at Fort Pitt took it upon themselves to "inoculate the bastards with some blankets" taken from the fort's smallpox hospital, touching off a massive and lethal epidemic that, over the subsequent year, ballooned north, south, and east of Ohio.[1] When Colonel Henry Bouquet, the crown's lead field officer, and Lord Jeffrey Amherst, its General of the American colonies, heard of Fort Pitt's nifty gift, they heartily approved and urged that the tactic be used again. The bald intentionality behind this sorry set of events is so hard to deny, that it is typically ignored by mainstream historians. Nevertheless, as evidence that disease was deliberately spread as a tool of conquest, it must be pulled into the light for unflinching examination.

Contrary to lingering racial stereotypes of "Indian allies" as bit players doing the bidding of this or that European overlord, between 1754 and 1763, none of the Native nations favored either European power. Instead, all of them had their own goals, analyses, and strategies. Native counselors knew all too well that their people's survival depended upon playing the Europeans off against each other. The majority of chiefs and clan mothers had concluded that restraining the tsunami of English squatters was the primary goal, and this required a French presence, at least for a time. They realized that the English plan for Native America was genocide. As four messengers of the Catawbas—enemies of the French—put it in 1759, the British "sought only to pit them one against the other in order to destroy them one after the other as soon as the French had been eliminated from the land."[2]

The Iroquois League did not quite agree on the usefulness of the French, but neither did League nations actively align themselves with Britain, as is often asserted. Instead, they sat neutral, simply agreeing not to aid the French. This was because the Six Nations had concluded—in a council kept secret from the British—to chase out *both* the French and British interlopers, but in succession, to allow the full force of the Iroquois to concentrate on each singly.[3] They targeted the French first. When Sir William Johnson, the Crown's Indian Agent in North America, looked as if he might beguile too many Iroquois away from this scheme in 1758, a narrowly avoided plot was raised by the Onondagas, Firekeepers of the League, to assassinate him.[4] (Under the Great Law, or Iroquois Constitution, the "Firekeepers" were the executive administrators of the men's grand council of the League.)

Despite the League's strategy, or possibly because of Johnson's effective interference, in 1758, the disgusted Ohio Senecas and some Cayugas broke ranks to take up the hatchet against the British.[5] It was, after all, their land that was primarily targeted by incessant invasion. Also angered by the League's tactics, more westerly nations menaced it in 1758 and 1759; with the aid of the French, they had themselves learned of a French contrivance for "cutting off and utterly exterminating" them.[6] To their credit, however, the western nations did not attack the League as the French had hoped.

In the end, the French collapsed, and the British bankrupted themselves. These results would have been of little moment to the Natives, had the British not regarded Native North America as an "All They Could Eat" buffet for their delectation. For all its imperial posturing, England was driven by a rough-and-tumble, muddy-and-bloody capitalism that included price-gouging and land-grabbing. A greedy Crown wasted no time in making itself roundly hated by the Natives through robber-baron "trade," on the one hand, and stepped-up land seizure, on the other.

The pig-headed British Governor, Sir Jeffrey Amherst, was instrumental in provoking the War of 1763, through two obtuse refusals: the first, to accommodate woodland economics, and the second, to repatriate stolen Native lands.

Despising the gift economies of Native North America as a kind of extortion "purchasing the good behavior" of Indian allies, Amherst attempted to cut off presents to the Natives.[7] On January 31, 1763, he arrogantly sniffed that, postwar, the Natives could "have Nothing to Mind but their Hunting, so that they may very well provide for themselves, as the Trade will, I doubt not, Continue to be Free."[8] The airy oblivion thus expressed of not only Native economics, but also of English cupidity, is staggering and, as events happened, it proved very costly to England almost immediately.

First, woodlanders were large-scale farmers, not "hunters." Under normal conditions, agriculture supplied two-thirds of their food. The crops and planting methods developed by the female woodlands farmers currently sustain the modern world.[9] They did not do less for North America in the 18th century. Natives were entirely aware of the value of their farming, even if Europeans were not, except on such occasions as the Denonville attack of 1687 or the Sullivan attack of 1779.[10] Thus, if their delegations brought in pelts to the factories (trading posts), it was only because that was what their somewhat silly Younger Brothers, the Europeans, demanded.

Second, woodland economies operated on gift-giving. To this day, western scholars stumble around the edges of gifting, trying to explain it as either protocapitalism or a failed exchange economy. It is neither. Gift economics cannot be grasped until it is understood that they are based on binary mathematical progressions. The unit *Two* equals normalcy.[11] With *Two* as the base number, viewed as irreducible, ONE is dangerous, a destructive, rogue isotope. In a system that has to work to create odd numbers, it is not accidental that a detached ONE is viewed as fragmented and deranged, or that the traditional number of danger, warning, and alarm is three.[12] Gifting is the socioeconomic expression of this cosmology, and it aims at communal, not individual, goals. Thus, the one-counting, linear math of European exchange looked (and still looks) demented to woodlanders.

In European exchange economies, the purpose is to maximize personal gain. The basis of gifting is, by contrast, to satisfy communal human needs (both material and spiritual), thus creating an ongoing, or at least a renewable, relationship among the parties involved.[13] Gifting not only cemented relations among clans, but also among foreign nations. The stronger the gifting alliance, the mightier the confederacy it created. Since gifting partners were prohibited from making war on one another, gift-giving was a necessary prelude to any peace. The European War on Beaver was seen as strange, but if his pelts were what it took to establish a gifted peace with the Europeans, then that was what the Young Men brought into the circle. Especially once the English had announced a new peace in February of 1763, their pelt demands had to have been met.

When speakers came, as they frequently did, to forts and settlements asking for gifts, it was as the ritual precondition for setting up a gifting relationship. This required them, as the approaching party, to express needs that they expected the greeting side to fill, even if filling them strained the greeting side's own resources. The greeting group then expressed its needs, meeting with the same generosity. This second round of requests and gifts completed the ritual, making it the perfect TWO, thus creating the gifting alliance.

Over their tenure in North America, beginning with the 1608 founding of Quebec and ranging through to their withdrawal in 1763, the French had come to something like a grasp of gift economics. The British were another story, however.

By refusing to gift, they were effectively declaring war. In early June 1763, at Niagara, Jean Baptiste de Couagne relayed ominous warnings on this score to the British. "We should soon hear bad News," he said, as a result of the British allowing their traders to "go so far into the Indian Country, as they gave them no presents."[14] Although Johnson did grasp some of this, he was unable to impress the importance of gifting alliances on his smug and stubborn superiors. Only after the loss of nearly all their western forts, most of their traders, and many of their border settlements were British officials dragged, kicking and screaming, into a semblance of gifting.

It was not as though the woodlanders had not tried to educate the British on the operation of gifting. When, in the spring of 1760, the Six Nations pressed the Crown to make up for crop failures that had left them "in a famishing condition," they were attempting to open a gifting circle with the apparent victors in the French-British struggle.[15] It was in just such another attempt that the Six Nations dispatched speakers to Johnson Hall on April 2, 1763, immediately before the outbreak of the new war, in a renewed attempt to short circuit hostilities by creating a gifting circle. Pro forma, they asked the British "to take pity of us, and afford us Some Assistance, such as a little Cloathing to cover our nakedness," along with ammunition, hoes, and axes.[16]

In woodlands culture, this plea would have been immediately recognized as a last-ditch attempt to create a "common bowl" for shared dining, the standing woodlands analogy for peaceful relations.[17] Moreover, in addition to its obvious literal meaning, the injunction to "tie up the clothes of the orphan" was the standing metaphor regarding the proper interface of people in plenty with people in need.[18] Poverty was seen as a crime perpetrated, not by the poor, but by those who had enough yet refused to share it with those who had too little.[19] A flat demand that the British *tie up the clothes of the naked* was as open a call for acquiescence to gifting as woodlanders knew how to give.

These were not extravagant requests, yet, speaking for the Crown, Sir William Johnson derisively answered with the party line that the Natives' "poverty," which they "so complain of, must I imagine be owing to Indolence."[20] Personally, Johnson understood the political ends of gifting sufficiently to shell out a little ammunition and other small presents immediately following this cold slap. In a quiet aside to Amherst, he suggested a strategy of bestowing "some presents as formerly, gradually lessening the Value thereof," the better to wean the Natives from gifting, as an alternative to forcing market exchange on them all at once. However, the schoolmarms in charge of British policy refused to relent.[21]

Far from showing a willingness to learn the woodlands system, Amherst was personally livid over gifting expectations. On April 24, 1763, before the attacks began—that is, while he still had a chance to maintain peace through gifts—he snidely remonstrated with Johnson for having found it "absolutely Necessary to Supply the Indians who Visit you, with Provisions," although he did grudgingly order Johnson's gifts to be covered.[22] On September 30, 1763, after nearly all the intruding

British forts had been uprooted by ungifted Natives, Amherst fulminated against them for their "Ingratitude." Looking on the bright side, however, he informed Johnson that the "Late Defection of so many Tribes, in my opinion, ought to Lessen the Expences in your Department," for "as to *presents* it would certainly be the highest Presumption in them to Expect any."[23]

This failure to grasp the purpose or forms of the gift economy was dangerous enough, but the niggardly avarice of the traders tipped the balance. The savvy French had provided high quality goods in a trade system heavily regulated to disallow price-gouging, fraud, and general piracy, thus earning the contempt of the British for being soft on the savages. Once the French wilted in 1761, however, British traders licked their lips over their new prospects. As "villains of the vilest sort," they perpetrated every imaginable crime against the Native populations.[24]

Natives arrived at English forts and factories looking to gift, only to be cheated, kicked, spat upon, and not infrequently, *fired* upon, while any Native women who happened by were liable to be raped. On January 13, 1758, a Mohawk delegation bitterly denounced one such set of incidents that had occurred the day before, in which a young man was attacked by fort soldiers for no reason other than his Native identity. When his sister attempted to shelter him, she was "cut in two places under her arm," and only "an officer a sargeant" rushing out of the fort prevented the soldiers from "doing more mischief" to her. That same day, two Mohawk women were yanked out of their canoe "by the hair of their head." Just a short time before these events, the elderly wife of a Mohawk chief had been "attacked by the soldiers, who wanted to ravish her," an attack the plucky grandmother had thwarted by "defending herself with her axe."[25]

Fort officers were no better, using their military positions to enrich themselves by selling, and at outrageous prices, the paltry items that the Crown had sent as gifts.[26] Worse, as Johnson complained to Amherst on July 1, 1763, British military leaders' "Ignorance" of "Indian customs" had set up common soldiers "to consider every Indian" in sight "as an Enemy."[27] This boded ill for those Natives still attempting to set up gifting circles with the British. Knowing full well of these abuses, the Crown blithely failed to regulate trade until the War of 1763 forced the British Board of Trade to end the criminal mayhem.[28]

In addition to their failure to gift, or even to regulate trade, the British Crown, its colonial officials, and individual settlers grabbed land in some breathtaking ways. The British had a habit of unilaterally making "exorbitant grants" of Native lands, such as that to the Ohio Company in 1749,[29] but the flagrant maneuvers to acquire land also included attempts to hold on to supposedly temporary inroads made during their conflict with the French. The Six-Nation Iroquois League, for example, had grudgingly allowed the British to construct certain forts on their western lands during the French and Indian War. However, the grants had been made with the emphatic caveat that those same forts were to be demolished at the end of the war, with the land instantly repatriated to its donor nation. Britain had agreed to this.[30] Then, at the war's conclusion, the British simply refused to dismantle the forts. In

September 1763, Amherst even went so far as to use the new war to rationalize keeping the forts, whose existence had inspired the attacks on his forces in the first place.[31]

Despite having had long experience of European double crosses, the Six Nations were aghast at what they viewed as a total betrayal of the Crown's solemn pledge to demolish all forts at the close of the French and Indian War. League counselors believed that the failure to dismantle the bastions presaged a British plan, "by degrees," to "Surround them on every side, & at length Extirpate them."[32] Seeing disaster looming, the Christianized, British-disposed Lenapes pleaded with Johnson to rectify the oversight, warning him that the forts would "disturb our peace," by inciting certain among the so-called Foolish Young Men to hostilities. Consequently, the Lenapes asked that the "forts may be pulled down and *kicked out of the way*" (italics in the original).[33] "Foolish Young Men" purportedly acting beyond the control of the Chiefs was a woodlands convention of speech meaning that a declaration of war was being contemplated in the Clan Mothers' councils. (Clan Mothers declared war, handing its black wampum directly to the Young Men. The Grandfathers had no control over this decision.[34]) Forts were thus seen as death knells of Native land ownership and, incidentally, as a prelude to the enslavement of local Natives, so that their construction and maintenance were resisted at all costs.[35]

Settler governments also promoted land seizure. On September 10, 1762, the Six Nations complained to Johnson that "in every Assembly, and Company of Governors, and Great Men," nothing was "scarce spoke, or talk'd of, but claiming, and wanting, large Possessions in our Country."[36] Individual settlers perpetrated astounding frauds, which colonial and royal authorities permitted to continue. A standard tactic of one of the worst offenders, George Klock, was to invite Natives of no official standing in their nation to a drinking party and, once they were falling-down drunk, to induce them to sign away the national land-base. When the actual, elected officials of a defrauded nation protested one such "land deal," colonial officials upheld the supposed sale.[37] This is tantamount to a youth gang in New York selling the Brooklyn Bridge to the City of Toledo, and the U.S. Supreme Court declaring the sale Constitutional.

With the spring of 1763, British avarice had reached a fever pitch, resulting in the Pontiac Revolt, but "revolt" is an insulting term that denigrates what happened, for it indicates one, disgruntled chief leading an ad hoc and lawless movement against a legitimate power. On the contrary, Pontiac was but one of the war's many chiefs leading attacks officially sanctioned by their Clan Mothers, while nothing about the British occupation of Native land was legitimate. In 1763, the British had usurped "French" territory under their cherished legal fiction of "right by conquest," yet the French had, themselves, been usurpers.[38] What happened in 1763 was that the legitimate proprietors of the woodlands pulled together to put a stop to land seizure while defending themselves against forced assimilation into a hostile, alien economy.

The federation attacking the British, only some of whose forces were led by the Ottawa war chief Pontiac, included Pontiac's own Three Fires Confederacy composed of the Ottawas of Ohio, the Pottawattomis of Indiana, and the Anishinabes ("Chippewas") of Michigan. In addition, Ohio defenders included the Lenapes, Shawnees, Wyandots, and Senecas, along with some Miamis.[39] In fact, Johnson saw the Senecas, Lenapes, and Shawnees as "the principal authors of the Hostilities," while Amherst fingered the Senecas alone.[40] Beyond these, the Kickapoos and Foxes from points farther west were somewhat involved. The War of 1763–1764 consisted of a massively orchestrated Native push back against European invasion, led off by a brilliantly managed set of simultaneous attacks.

The British were not unaware of this, especially after all their western forts were kicked away in one heavily coordinated set of strikes in June 1763, leaving only those at Detroit, Niagara, Bedford, Ligonier, and Pittsburgh just barely surviving their sieges.[41] The forts of Le Boeuf, Venango, Presque Isle, La Bay, St. Joseph, Miamis, Ouachtanon, Sandusky, and Michilimackinac were leveled, basically wiping out British power west of its seaboard settlements.[42] The Natives made special targets of the deeply hated traders, killing them in droves. Of the 120 known to have been scattered among the nations in the spring of 1763, only two survived, and they were financially ruined.[43]

At first, Amherst was in denial. In May, he waved off the rumblings of war, refusing to believe that "the Indians have it in their Power to Execute any thing Serious against Us."[44] British officials were typically this dismissive of Native moves, cheerily attributing any and every burp to vile French machinations.[45] It is true that the French seldom missed an opportunity to assure Native nations that the British intended to kill them all to steal their land, but the fact that *the British were doing exactly that* should not be ignored today. The Natives were working from experience in forming their opinions. The portrait of Natives as the grinning dupes of the French is a racist insult, not a historical analysis.

By July, having received sure news of the Native attacks, Amherst's tone lurched from snide to bellicose. He swore the "Certain Ruin" of the Iroquois League should it join the Senecas on the Ohio front. Acknowledging that, although the war might "be attended with the Loss of our Inferior Posts, and a few of Our People at *first*," he proclaimed that it would ultimately excite "Such measures" as ultimately to "Bring about the Total Extirpation of those Indian Nations" (italics in the original).[46]

Amherst's field commander, Colonel Henry Bouquet, a French-speaking, Swiss mercenary, shared Amherst's racial hatred of Natives. Indeed, Bouquet favored what was termed the Spanish method of dealing with them, which meant loosing armored dogs of war upon civilians. These dogs were trained to tear at and then eat human flesh, in a tactic that the conquistadores had shamefully perfected in Central and South America.[47]

Dogging Natives was openly bandied about by the British and their colonial officials as a terrific idea. In a letter of July 11, 1763 to Bouquet, for instance, Pennsylvania Assemblyman John Hughes urged dogging, gruesomely detailing how just 300 dogs would "be of Great Use in the pursuit & Enable yᵉ Soldiers to kill the Indians at pleasure." In the interests of terrorism, Hughes suggested that Bouquet take "one or two Indians kill^d & the Dogs put at them to tear them to pieces," predicting "You wou^d Soon See the Good Effects of it."[48] Bouquet shared this thrilling suggestion with Amherst, who, on July 16, 1763, commended Bouquet's "Scheme for Hunting them down by Dogs."[49] Peace did not quell the blood-thirsty plans. Writing up the recommendation section of his official history of Bouquet's 1764 counteroffensive, Crown historian William Smith posited that "Every light horse man ought to be provided with a Blood-hound."[50]

Taking the cue from their leaders, lower-level British officers shared in the blood lust. In one typical event during the taking of the French Fort Levi in 1760, Six Nations members overheard a British officer offhandedly remark to his comrades that they might as well "exterminate the Indian race" on their way back from that sortie.[51] Near Pennsylvania's western border, the settlers likewise nursed a homicidal fury toward Natives. From the post of Bedford, for instance, Captain Lewis Simon Ourry wrote Bouquet on June 20, 1763 that it was with "difficulty" that he had been able to "restrain" the locals "from murdering Indian Prisoners," whom he had kept alive to pump for intelligence.[52] Hatred bubbled up in all the European settlements, with racially motivated serial murder justified by what, on June 26, 1763, Amherst termed the "Perfidies and cruelties" of the Natives.[53] No retaliation seemed over the top to British officers or settlers.

These genocidal intentions found another outlet, which left its inventors chuckling at their own cleverness. It was nothing other than to mock gift-giving by handing out "presents" of smallpox to the Natives surrounding Fort Pitt. This occurred early in the siege of Fort Pitt, during conversations between fort officials and the speakers of the neutral Lenapes, who were trying to negotiate a peace settlement with the British.

Settler histories looking at this smallpox distribution typically start with Francis Parkman's 1851 *Pontiac Conspiracy,* go on to Bernhard Knollenberg's 1954 "General Amherst and Germ Warfare," and end around 2002 with articles like Francis Flavin's "A Pox on Amherst." They assume that:

- the event revolved around Amherst
- the smallpox articles in question were "dried," that is, long removed from any actual smallpox patients[54]

Both assumptions work to undermine the facts by seeking, on the one hand, to excuse Amherst while arguing, on the other hand, that no real damage could have ensued, in any case.

Both assumptions are demonstrably false.

First, the principal agents involved were Simeon Ecuyer, William Trent, and Alexander McKee, with Bouquet and Amherst commenting on the smallpox distribution only after the event. Second, the blankets, handkerchief, and liquor distributed came directly from the smallpox hospital at Fort Pitt. Their smallpox bacilli were active.

It is perhaps understandable that Francis Parkman should have focused on his hero, Amherst, whose portrait hung in his private study over his caribou rug and

beaver sofa throws.[55] Unfortunately, Parkman's truncated account has long mis-
led researchers into the false impression that the Bouquet-Amherst exchange was
the "smoking gun" of the event, when it was nothing more than second-hand gloat-
ing. It is McKee's euphemistic report to Johnson, in combination with the very ex-
plicit journal entries of Simeon Ecuyer and William Trent, that nail what occurred.
The subsequent correspondence among Ecuyer, Johnson, Bouquet, and Amherst
mostly serves to show that a person or persons unknown later sanitized the paper
trail, but missed the Trent and Ecuyer journals.

During the French and Indian War, disease followed the British. Smallpox popped
up in New York, the British troop collection point, in October 1759, and by the
spring of 1760, sickness at Quebec had pared down the original 10,000 British
troops dispatched there to "little more than three thousand effective men."[56] The
500 British Highlanders of the 42nd and 77th regiments, whom Amherst forced
into the fray in 1763, staggered west to Fort Pitt, almost too sick to deploy from
the disease that they had picked up on their ship *The Havana* while returning from
their recent posting in the West Indians.[57] The men at Fort Pitt were already sick,
however, two months before Bouquet marched his regiments in. Notably, only the
Natives around Fort Pitt were in health.

A tiny spit of land riding the confluence of the Allegheny and Monongahela Rivers hosted Fort Pitt, the fourth post to have been cobbled together where Pittsburgh now sits, almost on the western border of Pennsylvania. The first fort there
was British, built in 1754 by Virginians under their militia captain, William Trent.
It was seized in 1755 by the French, who retooled it as Fort Du Quesne, only to see
it fall again to the British in 1758. Raised on a slightly different spot not far away
was a third, temporary militia post, "Mercer's Fort," built just at the turn of 1759.
The final and permanent Fort Pitt (named for the elder William Pitt) was con-
structed later in 1759.[58] This last stronghold swiftly became a lynchpin of British—
and, in the Revolution, American—military prowess in "the West."

When the War of 1763 broke out, the British commander at Fort Pitt was another French-speaking mercenary, Captain Simeon Ecuyer. Early in June, Ecuyer
counted up 250 men, including Captain William Trent, primarily there as a trader
but also as a militia commander. The crowded fort yielded less than desirable sanitation. On June 16, 1763, Ecuyer wrote Bouquet that, despite his best efforts to keep
the fort as tidy ("*Nette*") as he would have liked, "*la petite vérole est parmi nous*"
("smallpox is among us"). Consequently, Ecuyer had set up "*un Hopital sous le
point a lépreuve du Mousquet*" ("a hospital under the bridge, out of musket-range")
of the fort, or 100 yards away.[59] The already bad conditions only worsened as time
passed. By June 27, Ecuyer had amassed 330 men, as the fort geared up for an
outright attack that did not materialize until August 28.[60] Bouquet quickly passed
along the news of Fort Pitt's epidemic to Amherst, in a letter of June 23, 1763.[61]

Europeans of the day might not have known how to cure smallpox, but they certainly understood that contact with the sick would pass the disease to the well. This
was, for instance, the entire basis of the old European measure of quarantine, which
isolated the sick from the healthy for 40 days. Accordingly, Fort Pitt's orderly

book entry of August 30, 1763 commanded that "nobody" was to go "near any person that ha[d] smallpox, except the doctor and the people attending them," who were "themselves to be very careful not to go near any person that ha[d] not had them," that is, smallpox.[62] In another instance, knowing that Bouquet had never had smallpox, a surgeon friend of the colonel considered Bouquet's lack of immunity so dangerous that he failed to visit him. The surgeon excused his breach of etiquette by explaining that his presence might well have made Bouquet "uneasy," given the doctor's medical attendance on "soldiers sick of that disease."[63] Obviously, settlers of the time understood the transmission, if not the chemistry, of smallpox.

Natives in the borderlands also understood enough about smallpox to avoid it whenever they saw it. In 1778, in what is now West Virginia, for instance, one Bernard Sims was shot during a Native attempt to push the Sims family off Indian land. Approaching Sims, intending to take his scalp, the Natives nearest to him saw that he was "affected with a disease, of all others the most terrifying to them." Instead of scalping Sims, they fell back, "exclaiming as they ran 'small pox, small pox.'"[64] Clearly, 18th-century Natives would not knowingly have accepted smallpox-infected gifts.

Neither was smallpox Ecuyer's only worry. By mid-June, the situation was looking quite desperate for Fort Pitt. The six nations of Ohio front, the Ottawas, Miamis, Shawnees, Wyandots, Senecas, and Lenapes—not to be confused with the Six-Nation Iroquois League—were closing in on Fort Pitt. Their Young Men were reconnoitering the area and shooting stray settlers, as well as any soldiers out cutting horse fodder.[65] They even had the cheek to burn down "Croghan Hall," the plantation house of George Croghan, Johnson's Deputy Indian Agent at Fort Pitt.[66] Croghan's mansion had been located immediately across the river from the fort, so that burning it was a piece of Native street theater, for the edification of those quivering behind Pitt's walls.

Needing all the help he could get, on June 2, 1763 Ecuyer wrote Bouquet that he had appointed Trent the Major-Commandant of the militia. He soon undercut Trent's real power, however, by scattering the militiamen among his British regulars, placing the best of the militia with his grenadiers.[67] Ecuyer's demotion of Trent might have been explained by a June 13 entry in his Orderly Book, expressing surprise and displeasure "at the exorbitant price" that "some persons have charged the poor and unfortunate people in the garrison for Indian corn."[68] On June 20, Ecuyer threatened to punish any traders caught gouging the people.[69] It seems fairly obvious that, failing any Natives to cheat, Trent was extorting the Pittsburghians now captive in the fort, engendering hostility between himself and the fort's commander, who did not need to cope with internal strife in time spared from mounting a defense of 330 men, 104 women, and 106 children.[70]

The night of June 23, 1763 seemed particularly dangerous to Ecuyer, as speakers of the Lenapes came to the fort at midnight, asking Alexander McKee to come out for a parley.[71] Son of a Shawnee mother and a British father, McKee was a man of standing in Native circles, trusted to carry truthful messages.[72] Inside the fort, Ecuyer was hesitant about sending out McKee, probably having heard from Croghan that on June 5, 1763, to take Fort Miamis, a woman warrior had lured its commander, Ensign Robert Holmes, out of the fort "by Pretending another Woman was very sick" and begging him "to Come to her Cabin, and bleed her." Once the gullible Holmes had "gone a little Distance from the Fort," he was shot dead, and Fort Miamis was taken.[73]

Just past midnight on June 24, 1763, however, McKee did go out to speak with Turtle's Heart, a local Lenape war chief, and a civil chief, Mamaltee. At this point, the Lenapes included as many neutrals as participants in the war, and these two claimed to have come from the neutral camp. The fact that McKee came back to the fort alive argues that they were telling the truth. The message that Turtle's Heart and Mamaltee brought was that all of the British forts (they inaccurately included Ligonier in the count) were destroyed and that "great numbers of Indians were advancing"—Johnson put the number at 200[74]—to take Fort Pitt, as well. However, "out of regard" for the 540 people in the fort, the neutral Lenapes had prevailed upon the approaching armies not to attack, should the settlers agree to leave Native territory immediately.[75] By way of reply, Ecuyer fell to dissimulation, lying through McKee to say that three large British armies were descending even then to wipe out the Natives, who had better have done the fleeing.[76]

The Lenapes' phrase, "out of regard to you" was a convention of woodlands rhetoric used by peacemakers, which the Lenapes were, par excellence. Revered as the "Grandfather Nation" (because they were the first Natives to settle the eastern seacoast), they had been inducted into the Iroquois League in 1664 as "women."[77] It was a position of high honor. In woodlands cultures, jobs are gendered. Warfare is gendered male, for instance. This does not mean that women cannot sign up to fight, for they can and do. It just means that, for the duration of the hostilities, such women are honorary "men." Similarly, the positions of judge and negotiator are gendered female. This does not mean that men may not become judges or negotiators, but just that, for their tenure in such jobs, they are honorary women. When the Lenapes came into the League, it was on the understanding that their appointed function was to act as judges and negotiators, that is, as official women. Their high position as the Grandfather Nation was expected to ensure that all comers would listen to their words with respect, and all woodlanders did.

Unable to grasp the distinction between woodlands job-gendering and European sex-role stereotyping, the British were beside themselves over the supposed perversion of Lenape men's dressing, acting, and speaking as women.[78] Not only did these speakers look like cross-dressers to the British, but the fact of their official position as women prevented them from taking up arms in war, thus paring down the number of allied Lenapes the British could call up as reinforcements. Especially with the inception of the French and Indian War, the British needed cannon fodder. To render the Christianized Lenape men able to fight, Johnson ended a 1756 council by "taking off from the Delawares the petticoat," that is, remaking them men eligible to fight.[79] The British thereafter crowed that the Lenapes were again "MEN," but this alien interpolation was humored by the Native nations rather than taken seriously.[80] Among the woodlanders, the Grandfather Nation was still expected to act the part of peacemaker.

Thus, when five Lenapes, including the important personages of Shingask, "King Beaver," and Wingenum, came to Fort Pitt on May 27, 1763, just before the coordinated Native offensive, it was genuinely as they claimed, "Out of regard to you and the friendship that formerly subsisted between (our) grandfathers and the English."[81] Similarly, in their urgent warning of June 24, 1763, the Lenape counselors Turtle's Heart and Mamaltee spoke again "out of regard to" the settlers.[82]

All backwoods Europeans knew enough of Native rhetoric to recognize and understand the Lenapes' "regard" convention of speech. It is all the more important, then, to note just how both Ecuyer and Trent recorded their response to Turtle's Heart and Mamaltee. They knew it was customary to give gifts of goodwill at such meetings, and gifting was only the more necessary in this instance, for after the two speakers had conferred with their councils, they returned at 4:00 P.M. on June 24, 1763 to announce that the combatant Lenapes had agreed to "hold fast the chain of friendship," that is, *not* to enter into the impending hostilities against Fort Pitt. The only correct response from the British was to give gifts in return for this great Lenape gift of peace.

"Out of our regard to them," Ecuyer sneered in his journal entry of June 24, 1763, "we gave them two blankets and an handkerchief out of the Small Pox Hospital. I hope it will have the desired effect."[83]

Also present at the event was William Trent, who was already fuming over his trade losses, so much so that he had recently written Amherst, demanding restitution. (On June 25, 1763, the day after the smallpox distribution, Amherst forwarded Bouquet a copy of his reply to Trent.[84]) We can only speculate what else Trent might have mentioned in this missing letter to Amherst, but on June 24, 1763, he recorded the smallpox distribution in his journal, in a mocking tone identical to that of Ecuyer: "Out of our regard to them we gave them two Blankets and an Handkerchief out of the Small Pox Hospital. I hope it will have the desired effect."[85]

In the past, I have encountered colonial military men making identically worded entries in their individual camp journals. In these instances, they were recording a sentiment given official color.[86] The snickering use of woodlands "regard" rhetoric shows that Ecuyer, Trent, and, most likely, the other top officers under their respective commands, had agreed upon the brilliance of their smallpox distribution.

These were no desiccated articles, either. The smallpox hospital that Ecuyer had established on June 16, 1763 was still a going concern, at least through August 30.[87] It was clearly in use on June 26, 1763, two days after the smallpox distribution, as shown by Ecuyer's returns (progress report) of that date, submitted to Bouquet. Ecuyer listed four men of the first battalion of the Royal Army and six men of the militia as sick on that day.[88] Thus, the two blankets and a handkerchief distributed to the neutral Lenapes were taken directly from the persons of those 10 sick men, lying 100 yards from the fort.

Unfortunately, the journal of George Croghan, Johnson's Deputy Agent at Fort Pitt at the time, was lost in a fire,[89] but an account by Wampomshawuh, The White Elk—Alexander McKee, Johnson's Assistant Deputy Agency at Fort Pitt[90]—does exist. He was present, negotiating and translating at this meeting, although his report was less clear than Ecuyer's or Trent's as to *what* exactly had been distributed. In his June 24, 1763, "Report of Speeches of the Delaware Indians," McKee stated that, in closing the conference, the Lenape counselors had asked for "a little Provisions and Liquor, to carry [them] home." McKee noted that the "Above provisions was granted to them & they set off Home about 2 oClock that Night."[91]

It is possible that McKee was vague about the exact nature of the "Provisions" for not having been clued into the plan. Given his conflicted loyalties, he might well have balked at indirectly handing smallpox to his mother's people. Alternatively, as the exceptionally astute politico he soon showed himself to be, he might simply have waxed more coy than either Ecuyer or Trent about admitting to such a reprehensible crime in writing.

It is interesting that McKee recorded liquor as part of the present, for strong oral traditions of the Wyandots of Ohio corroborate that smallpox was deliberately spread by the settlers through a gift of liquor. These traditions are not just in modern oral circulation, either. Versions of them were taken down almost a century ago—long before any debate on deliberate disease distribution erupted. Consider this tradition by the Wyandot keeper (historian), John Kayrahoo, taken down by C. M. Barbeau in 1912:

> So a terrible war followed. The white man, as a last resort, used a disease germ against [his enemy]. When he saw the wind blowing towards the Indian, he uncorked the bottle in which the smallpox germs were kept and he let them run out.[92] (Brackets in the original)

Catherine Johnson, another respected Wyandot keeper, independently confirmed Kayrahoo's account in another version, this one originally taken down in Wyandot in 1912:

> Long ago an Indian went to visit the white men's settlements. These people being gathered together hired him to introduce smallpox into his country. [They told him] "Uncork this bottle in your country, and let its contents run out!" So he uncorked the bottle in the midst of a large crowd [of his people, whom he had] convoked. When it was done, they went back to their homes, and all them were attacked by smallpox, a kind of disease unknown among them. So many Indians died that the few that were left ran off to the woods and gathered there.[93] (Brackets in the original)

The smallpox distribution certainly was a "last resort," and not only for the people trapped at Fort Pitt but also for the entire British war effort. Everyone involved, from McKee to Ecuyer and Trent, knew that, under woodlands legal structures, the Lenapes would immediately have met with the Wyandots, Shawnees, Senecas, and anyone else nearby, to share the peace gifts with them as part of Ecuyer's message. Moreover, McKee had definitely been "hired" by the British to spread their messages to the Ohio Indians, who were also his people. Uncorking the liquor to pass it around would have been a ceremonial aspect of the gifting. Ultimately, as we shall see, all the previously healthy Ohio Indians were, indeed, "attacked" by smallpox.

Unfortunately, the documents directly informing Amherst and Bouquet on the matter, as well as their mutual conversation on it, have all mysteriously disappeared. What remain in the record at the top level are references to the existence and contents of those missing documents, making it fairly clear that Amherst and Bouquet knew exactly what had transpired, and, indeed, that they approved of what had transpired. In addition to these extant documents, there are two damning "memos" inscribed on the envelope flaps of two crucial yet missing Amherst letters. It was customary at the time for military clerks to write an informative summary of the letter inside the overleaf of its envelope.

On June 23, 1763, the very day that the Lenapes began their talks with McKee, Bouquet noted in a postscript to Captain Ourry that he had just received "with the greatest Satisfaction the favourable Account of the good State of Defense of Fort Pitt," adding that Ecuyer was "a good Officer" who would keep the men's "Spirits up."[94] June 23 was also the day that Bouquet informed Amherst that smallpox had broken out at Fort Pitt, causing Ecuyer to build a hospital "under the Draw Bridge to prevent the Spreading of that distemper."[95]

On June 25, 1763 Bouquet wrote Amherst (in specific reference to negotiations with the Cherokees and Catawbas) that, "I would rather chuse the liberty to kill any Savage that may come in our Way, than to be perpetualy [sic] doubtful whether they are Friends or Foes," a sideswipe at the Lenapes.[96] On June 29, 1763, Amherst replied that "the Contents" of the letter of June 25 had "please[d him] very much," with Bouquet's "Sentiments agreeing Exactly with my own, regarding the Treatment the Savages Deserve from Us."[97]

Ecuyer's report to Bouquet from June 26, 1763 officially detailed the events at Fort Pitt on June 23 and 24. What remains of it stated that:

> *La nuit du 23ᵉ au 24 . . . apres minuit, les Delawares ont demandé a parler avec Mʳ McKee dont voux trouveres cy joint, nos diferentes conversations; Les Returns dont mois.* (The night of the 23rd to the 24th . . . after midnight, the Delawares asked to speak with Mr. McKee; you will find enclosed our different conversations; [and] the month's returns.) [98]

Ecuyer's enclosure on the talks with the Lenapes is, today, among the strangely missing, but his status report ("returns"), originally enclosed with the cover letter, is still extant. It was in that monthly report that Ecuyer listed the numbers of his men down with smallpox.[99] Bouquet clearly received the entire packet, which he mentioned on July 26, 1763 as having been the last communication that he had received from Fort Pitt.[100]

It is evident that Ecuyer's report of June 26 had also been sent to Amherst, for in a properly endorsed letter to Johnson dated August 27, 1763, Amherst enclosed a copy of "what passed between Captain Ecuyer and the very villains who were afterwards engaged in the action against Colonel Bouquet's Detachment," a reference to the Bushy Run Battle of August 5, 1763, which occurred outside of Fort Pitt.[101] Amherst went on to:

> approve most fully of Captain Ecuyer's answer to them; but I should have been better pleased had he not treated with them when they came to the Fort soon after the first mischief happened, by giving them *not only provisions but other tokens of friendship,* which entitled them to come again to the fort. (Italics added)

Amherst closed the letter by conceding that he "should not have blamed" Ecuyer had he "put everyone of those who were in his power to death."[102] To these gentle sentiments, Johnson tersely replied on September 14, 1763, that he had received "a Copy of the proceedings between Captain Ecuyer and the Indians."[103] The winking and nodding going on here were palpable. With at least two copies of Ecuyer's official report on the talks in official circulation in August 1763, it is a mite suspicious that not a trace of it exists today.

On July 7, 1763, this memo from Amherst to Bouquet appeared on the inside of the envelope leaf of a letter that has since gone missing:

> Could it not be contrived to Send the *Small Pox* among those Disaffected Tribes of Indians? We must, on this occasion, Use Every Stratagem in our power to Reduce them.[104] (Underline in the original)

Amherst apologists have made much of the script in which the initials "J. A." were inscribed under this memo, attributing them to Amherst's "usual copy clerk," as though a copy clerk's having physically written out his superior's words were an unusual procedure.[105] It was not. Any researcher of antique military records becomes familiar with the handwriting of the officers' different copy clerks. There is no justification whatsoever for insinuating that this memo was inscribed on the sly by a copy clerk gone berserk. At that time, penalties for impersonating an officer or misrepresenting a general's wartime orders included death. There is no report of a trial or execution of any copy clerk in Amherst's employ. Moreover, the copy clerk in question continued in his capacity, and the envelope-leaf memo was retained, so the logical inference is that, in posting this memo, he was simply doing his job. Later sanitation removed the letter but missed the memo on the overleaf.

On July 13, 1763, Bouquet responded to Amherst's missive: "I will try to inoculate the bastards with some blankets that may fall into their hands, and"—ever mindful of never having had smallpox—"take care not to get the disease myself."[106] In researching his *Conspiracy of Pontiac,* either Parkman or his research assistant copied this Bouquet letter, which Parkman cited as "among the manuscripts of the British Museum, *Bouquet and Haldimand Papers,* No. 21,634."[107] Too squeamish to spell out "bastards," Parkman (or his editor) dashed out the word, but in 1933, Amherst's biographer, John Cuthbert Long, daringly printed it. Louis Waddell inexplicably omitted this letter from his compilation of the Bouquet papers. This was the same letter that conveyed the dogging plan to Amherst, a plan to which Amherst alluded in the second of his famous memorandums.[108]

July 16, 1763, was a busy day for Amherst. He wrote Henry Hamilton that he wanted Bouquet free to "take Revenge of the Savages who have Committed the Depradations."[109] In addition, there is no question that Amherst also sent Bouquet three letters on that day, of which but two remain in existence.[110] Once more, what is missing is a fairly strategic communication, with all that remains being the second Amherst memo, dated July 16, 1763:

> You will Do well to try to Innoculate the *Indians,* by means of Blankets, as well as to Try Every other Method, that can Serve to Extirpate this Execrable Race.— I should be very glad your Scheme for Hunting them down by Dogs could take Effect; but *England* is at too great a Distance to think of that at present. (Underlines in the original)[111]

Here again, a supposed dispute arises over Just Who Wrote the Memo, Amherst or his copy clerk, but the suggestion that the same clerk had gone postal twice in one week with no repercussions is even shakier as a proposition than that the clerk had run amok six days before without rebuke. Perhaps the initials on this memo were "intended to look like Amherst's writing" because they *were* Amherst's writing.[112]

Bouquet certainly believed that the message was legitimately from Amherst, for he replied on July 26, 1763 that he had received the "letters of 16th with their Inclosures," adding that the "signal for Indian Messengers, and all your directions will be observed."[113] (Since the soldiers were shooting at everything Native that moved, the British moccasins, or Native couriers, had to give a particular high-sign to authenticate themselves.) Bouquet had received a second instructional letter with enclosures from Amherst that same day, but his mention of "letters" with "their Inclosures" makes it clear that he was responding to *both* missives in this one reply.

Whatever the antique circumlocutions passing among Ecuyer, Amherst, Bouquet, and Johnson, there is no question of the praise lavished on both Ecuyer and Trent for their actions at Fort Pitt. On July 9, 1763—a month before Bouquet squared off against the Ohio Natives and a month-and-a-half before their outright attack on Fort Pitt on August 28—Amherst wrote Bouquet that:

> Captain Ecuyer Seems to Act with great Prudence, & I Approve of Everything he mentions to have Done: A Fixed Resolution should be taken by Every Com-

manding Officer, whose Post is Attacked by Savages, Never to Trust to their Promises, but to Defend his Post to the Last Extremity; and to take Every Occasion he can of Putting them to Death while they are Attempting to Take Every Life away that they can.[114]

In his Orderly Book entry of August 11, 1763, Ecuyer recorded Bouquet's personal praise of Trent for his "firm and prudent conduct" towards the Natives. Bouquet announced his:

particular pleasure in expressing to Major Trent how agreeable his services and those performed by the brave militia under his command are to him, and returns him his sincere thanks for the ready assistance he has constantly given to the commanding officer.[115]

On August 31, 1763, Amherst assured Bouquet that "Captain Ecuyer's Behavior" during the siege of Fort Pitt "Deserves my Approbation."[116]

Absent Amherst's and Bouquet's knowledge of the smallpox distribution, this praise is hard to explain, especially given Trent's temper tantrums over trade losses and his price gouging of captive settler families, not to mention Ecuyer's rather poor performance in other regards. Yes, Ecuyer did repair flood damage to Fort Pitt before the war began, but, as mercurial as Amherst, once it broke out, he also recklessly wasted *cannon* shot by firing the big guns at mobile snipers; feuded publicly with Trent, while both were commanders in a tense situation; played the invalid to avoid active duty; and ultimately *deserted* his command at Fort Pitt by fleeing to Philadelphia in February 1764, to the flabbergasted ire of Bouquet.[117] Amherst and Bouquet could not have been commending such deeds. Neither could they have been applauding any military action against the Natives, since it was Bouquet, not Ecuyer or Trent, who led the actual fighting in August. The British top brass could only have been slyly sanctioning the gift of smallpox.

Finally, it is important to note that the smallpox distribution worked. Some have claimed that the epidemic was already abroad *before* the smallpox distribution, but the "Sickness" that had "afflicted" the "whole Nation" of Pottawattomis in the summer of 1762 occurred the summer before the siege and hundreds of miles west of Fort Pitt, as did the unnamed "Severe Sickness" that "Seized almost all" of the Miamis and Kickapoos in 1762.[118] Moreover, commentators knew and named smallpox when they saw it.

By contrast, smallpox broke out among the southeastern Ohio peoples suddenly at the end of June 1763, within the smallpox incubation period, and ravaged Ohio for the next year. On January 20, 1764, Johnson mentioned a Mohawk messenger from Niagara and Detroit returning home "afflicted with a severe *Bloody flux*" (italics in the original), although he might have meant syphilis rather than smallpox.[119] On April 14, 1764, Gershom Hicks, a servant of one of the attacked traders who had purportedly just escaped from the Ohio Natives holding him, reported in a sworn deposition that:

> the Small pox has been very general & raging amongst the Indians since last spring and that 30 or 40 Mingoes, and as many Delawares and some Shawneese Died all of the Small pox since that time, that it still continues amongst them.[120]

"Mingo" was a derogatory term for the Ohio Iroquois, including Senecas and Wyandots. Hicks went to the Natives even as the war erupted in 1763, and late June qualifies as "spring" to a man who lacks a calendar. On April 19, 1764 having found that Hicks had actively fought *alongside* the Natives, instead of just having been an innocent captive, officials threatened to hang him. In a hostile cross-examination, Hicks primarily detailed Native plans and troop movements, all that the prosecutor was interested in. Nevertheless, without naming smallpox this time, Hicks volunteered that he had left his Lenape family because "he saw they would this Year be vastly Distressed."[121]

Hicks aside, the fact of a smallpox epidemic was certain. Over the summer of 1764, the contagion spread like wildfire among the Iroquois and Shawnees, also moving south to the Choctaws, Chickasaws, and Muskogees.[122] On September 10, 1764, Colonel Andrew Lewis of Virginia gave Bouquet "certain Intiligance" that those "poor Rascals"—the Shawnees and Lenapes—were "dieing very fast with the small pox."[123] On January 25, 1765, a New York report documented smallpox among the Shawnees, whose clans lived not only in Ohio, but also in nearby Tennessee and Pennsylvania, as well as in South Carolina and Missouri, which helps to explain the southern spread of this induced epidemic.[124]

All too often, western histories focus so heavily on Bouquet's successful 1764 military expedition that they gloss over the fact that the Natives effectively *won* the War of 1763. The British might have boasted a few military triumphs, but, in the end, they were forced to:

- reintroduce gifting, which continued through the American Revolution, to Britain's Native allies
- regulate trade, which the British Board of Trade was forced to do in 1763[125]
- leave their ruined forts leveled, leading into the Revolution
- sign treaties keeping settler hands off Ohio, a move set forth strongly in the 1768 Treaty of Fort Stanwix and reiterated in the 1775 Treaty of Pittsburgh[126]

Were it not for the heavy Native losses resulting from the induced smallpox epidemic of 1763–1764, the Native victory would have been complete.

CHAPTER 2

∼

"The Land of Death": The Choctaw Removal into Cholera, 1832

Two mighty engines of death were converging on the Choctaw nation in the year 1832: pandemic cholera and Jacksonian Removal. All ethnic groups knew cholera, but it was the dispossessed poor—especially Native Americans—who stuffed its gaping maw. Removal was even more inequitable in its effects. In creating an economic boom for Euro-American settlers, Removal visited physical, cultural, and documentary genocide on Native America, with the Choctaws cast as the government's experimental population, the one on which U.S. officials perfected their death marches.

Regarding the first engine of death, there was no possible excuse of medical ignorance or political necessity in the 1832 exposure of the Choctaws to cholera. U.S. officials were entirely apprised that cholera was coming a good year before it hit, and they knew, moreover, that it especially propagated on steamboats. Once cholera arrived, they knew exactly in which locales it was centered before they marched the freezing, starving, barefoot, and often nearly naked Choctaws directly onto sick boats at plague towns. In one instance, officials even reversed the march of a group being guided away from the epidemic, dragging everyone *back* into the epidemic and then firing in disgrace the humane army officer who had tried to save his party.

Regarding the second engine of death, Removal, Hannah Arendt's reflections on the "banality of evil" apply. In the context of her work on *Eichmann in Jerusalem* (1963), Arendt was struck by the ordinary way that a nondescript man could calmly view the transportation of all those living, feeling, desperate human beings to their deaths as a career-advancement ploy. The same might be said of the U.S. governmental officials who cooked up and then pulled off Removal. In reading their dull correspondence, as it plods bureaucratically through price lists for corn, head counts of deportees, or frustrations with suppliers, I found "banal" to be the perfect adjective to describe their actions. However, honest discussions must not deflect attention away from the murderous actions undertaken to favor safe, dry recitals of enabling statutes, governmental regulations, or treaty stipulations.

Too much obviated—or, worse, left uncontemplated—by scholars following the stumbling lead of the innocuously titled Document 512 is that Removal was no more inevitable than was the Jewish Holocaust. It was an event *entirely chosen* by U.S. officialdom and willfully imposed on subject, powerless groups. Everyone settler from the elite to the yahoo was encouraged to take part in its ravages, and almost everyone did. The few missionaries and ethicists who objected were shunted aside, their reputations carefully broken. The notion that, just because the word "genocide" was not coined until 1944, no genocide could have taken place before 1944, is so much dissimulation.[1] People on the ground in 1832 knew exactly the level of destruction that they were visiting on the Choctaws, yet they consciously chose not to stop.

Genocide does not just pop up one day as a solution to social ills. It prepares its perpetrators over decades. Prior to killing people, it needs a fine-sounding rationale to divert attention from its criminality onto its supposed necessity. In the instance of Removal, hifalutin "science" circulating in elite circles justified Europeans in taking everything in sight.[2] As Ben Kiernan ably documents in *Blood and Soil* (2007), "cults of cultivation," or agriculture as practiced by Europeans, provided a major rallying cry for genocide in North America from colonial times through the 19th century.[3]

The argued necessity of an Indian-*rein* America was predicated on *lebensraum* needs, articulated since the Revolutionary War attacks on upstate New York and Ohio ordered by General George Washington.[4] After the Revolution, the United States had to honor the Revolutionary War land certificates that had constituted Revolutionary soldiers' pay.[5] Then, in a sort of dry run for Jacksonian Removal, relocations of Indians began in the 1790s, especially to Ohio, the first "Indian Territory." In 1801, Thomas Jefferson floated the notion of pushing all woodlands Indians directly into the "Stony" (Rocky) Mountains as the only alternative to physical genocide.[6] The idea of Indians remaining in and retaining their own homelands was never posited as an option.

Theory was complicated by an orgy of wasteful farming practices that tore through fertile ground, sucking it dry of nutrients. The settlers assumed that obtaining fresh land to replace whatever they had exhausted was as simple as seizing new territory in the west.[7] Such environmental depletion was decried as a problem at the time by early conservationists, including James Fenimore Cooper.[8] However, no one official made the slightest attempt to curtail the "wasty ways" of the settlers, for whom inconvenient Indians in the way of "progress" were as expendable as the unwanted flora and fauna.[9] The invention of the cotton gin in 1793 only added to land pressures in the south by encouraging slaveholders to expand, working the pitiless plantations of King Cotton. That President Andrew Jackson was a large land- and slave-owner was not incidental to Removal.[10]

If private land waste and greed drove Removal, so did the public economy. Jackson's reputation as a financial wizard, for having paid off the national debt as it existed in his time, typically ignores the fact that he did it largely by transferring wholesale *all* the assets of eastern Indians to the settlers' balance sheet, from fine land and solid homes to livestock, furniture, and even clothing.[11] The cost of seizing these assets was mostly borne by the army, whose Commissary General contracted for minimal supplies of food and inadequate, dangerous transportation. Since the military overseerers, or conductors, involved in the forced marches would have been paid by the army for their services in any case, the cost of asset seizure constituted a small fraction of the value of those lands, houses, goods, and livestock. Simultaneously as the seized land was "opened" to settlers, lucrative governmental supply contracts pumped money into the domestic economy. Together, these factors comprised Jackson's supposed miracle.

Discussions of Removal should also never gloss over its impact on the Indians, but they almost always do. I read through literally thousands of pages of primary as well as secondary source documents on Choctaw Removal to compose this chapter. Of those sources, I counted exactly two that considered the meaning of Removal to the Choctaws, both stemming from the pen of one historian, Donna L. Akers.[12] Scholarly oblivion of such an important aspect of Removal should not be acceptable. All Americans, not just the Indian ones, need to grasp what Removal meant to the Removed.

Identity of place might have been left out of Abraham Maslow's famed hierarchy of (European) needs, but it tops the list for Indians.[13] Connection to geographical place is a basic Indian requirement for survival, one that was not unknown in 1832. Land-based identity was why Andrew Jackson took it upon himself to ridicule this Indian need in his December 6, 1830, Second Annual Address to Congress. "Doubtless" it would "be painful" for the Indians "to leave the graves of their fathers," he conceded, "but what do they more than our ancestors did or than our children are now doing?"[14] In other words, peasants were fleeing Europe for America in the millions, without the slightest glance backwards, so what was wrong with the Indians, that they could not do the same? Ralph Waldo Emerson soon made such contempt for historical roots a positive requirement of self-reliant Americans, cementing the call for a roving lifestyle as All-American.[15]

However, Indians across the country regard the soil of Mother Earth as the actual essence of their physical ancestors. For at least the first five feet down, the dirt is the "blood, the flesh and the bones" of their forebearers.[16] For the Choctaws, the sacred burial mound called both *Nanih Waiya* (Leaning Hill) and *Ishki Chito* (The Great Mother), located in Winston County, Mississippi, encapsulates this idea.[17] The bones of the ancestors are protected and honored in the womb of Mother Earth; the bodies of the rising generations are composed of them. To take Indians from their homeland is to sever their ties to the cosmos, leaving them to wander as helpless, and often destructive, ghosts.

Moreover, for all North American Indians of whom I know, west is the direction of death for the blood (earth) spirit, called *shilup* by the Choctaws.[18] Breath (sky) spirits usually travel north to embark on the Milky Way Trail home to the stars, unless they are Lenape, in which case, they travel south.[19] Thus, in forcing the Mississippi Choctaws north and west to Arkansas, the government was effectively announcing its intention to kill them all. This is one reason that large percentages of the Choctaws (and all Removed peoples) endured brutal penalties for remaining east. Among the Choctaws, "mothers and grandmothers adamantly refused to abandon the bones of their dead children" by leaving on governmental cue, with at least 4,000 ultimately remaining in Mississippi.[20] Thereafter pushed to the fringes of various eastern settlements, they wandered homeless, destitute, and despised.[21]

Removal's acknowledged result was a 30 percent death rate among the Choctaws, but that standard guess just looks at the better-fed, better-clothed cadres recorded in government documents.[22] The true percentage of dead was higher, much higher, but that total is strategically missing from the official record, to be extrapolated only from the numbers of those who starved in situ, refusing to leave; of those omitted from the official rolls who died along the way; and of those who died trying to transport themselves as "commuters."[23] It certainly does not include the fatalities from the "lamented" situation in 1833, *after* Removal sustenance was withdrawn, when officials (gleefully, to my ear) "re-brined" putrid pork to hand out to starving Choctaws when they pleaded for help.[24] Neither does it include the 1,000 who died of smallpox during the epidemic of 1836–1840 in Arkansas, which they came to call "The Land of Death."[25]

The peaceful Choctaws were chosen as the model Removal nation, to be transported first, not the least because they had long been faithful allies of the United States, generally, and of Andrew Jackson, specifically.[26] Moreover, the Choctaws were seen as pushovers due to their recent history of ceding massive tracts of land to the United States, almost for the asking. In less than half a century, from 1786 to 1825, they had handed over 25,385,238 acres in Mississippi, with 14,962,108 of those in the 1820 Treaty of Doak's Stand, negotiated by Jackson himself.[27] When the Choctaws resisted more concessions in 1830, the government bullied, threatened, and ultimately swindled them.

Fraudulent treaties as the legal justification for land seizure were as old as the United States, whose original "pen-and-ink witchcraft" of the 1795 Greenville Treaty set the standard for coercion, deception, and interlineation in all subsequent U.S.–Indian treaties.[28] The 1830 Treaty of Dancing Rabbit Creek was no exception. Commissioner John H. Eaton threatened the Choctaws that President Jackson would march in an army to destroy them if they dissented, causing two-thirds of the Choctaw delegation to stalk angrily off the field, proudly refusing to be hectored.[29] Undaunted by their vociferous and massive opposition, the United States met secretly with its own yes-men chiefs and, pretending that they spoke for the Choctaws, bribed their cooperation.[30] Although the Choctaw people immediately threw all of the signatory chiefs out of office, Congress ratified the Treaty of Dancing Rabbit as legitimate.[31] The few missionaries who sought to prevent and then expose the fraud of the treaty talks were first advised to shut up and then unceremoniously booted out of the council by the local Indian agent and the U.S. treaty commissioners. The missionaries bitterly grieved these moves, but to no avail.[32]

Like the treaty fix, the Removal con was on from the start, as shown in a letter of December 27, 1830, from General George Gibson, of the U.S. Commissary General Subsistence, charged with supplying Removal contracts. Gibson ordered Lt. J. R. Stephenson of the 7th Infantry to take "special pains" to treat the first Choctaws removed to Arkansas "with all the kindness and civility" he could muster, so that "no unfavorable impressions may be carried back to their nation that will have the slightest tendency to discourage the emigration of the main body."[33]

Euphemizing Removal as voluntary "emigration" allowed the government to perpetrate "documentary genocide" against the holdouts. Documentary genocide consists of the government's killing people on paper when they are not, in fact, dead on the ground.[34] The U.S. government flatly denied Indian identity to any Natives (not just Choctaws) who remained east after Removal by forcibly declaring all holdouts to be citizens of the state in which they resided, while unilaterally cancelling their membership in their nations.[35] For Indians, the threat of state citizenship was acute, since the affected states made no noticeable effort to protect their new Indian citizens from their old settler citizens. Instead, the states eased the way for the seizure of formerly Indian assets, while the U.S. government lay supinely by.[36]

Also typically, the Dancing Rabbit Treaty rewarded the U.S.–collaborating Choctaws with sumptuous tracts of personal land under Article 19 and with miscellaneous goods under Article 20.[37] As a sop, hopefully pulling in the approval of the dissenting two-thirds, Article 14 was also inserted. Under its stipulations, any Choctaw who so wished could apply for and receive land in the State of Mississippi, on the understanding that he/she willingly gave up his/her Indian identity to become a second-class citizen of Mississippi, legally barred from voting, suing, performing jury duty, or testifying in court.[38]

Only agreed to by Congress because the U.S. treaty commissioners wrongly supposed that no one would activate it, the government simply disregarded Article 14 thereafter. Any petition under it was summarily declared void for, basically, whatever reason tickled the addled fancy of William Ward, the frequently drunk and completely corrupt U.S. Indian Agent of the Choctaws.[39] Although Ward's deliberate nonregistration of Choctaws was repeatedly documented, along with his general habits of deception and graft, no pressure was ever put on him to clean up his act.[40] In full knowledge of what Ward's services had been from 1830 to 1831, Secretary of War Lewis Cass retained them until December 31, 1832, when Ward was released. Purportedly, this was because there were no Choctaws left in Mississippi, but actually it was because of the pounding legal headaches that his revealed schemes, from cattle and annuity kickbacks to land fraud, had caused federal officials.[41]

After the honeymoon trip to inspect Arkansas in 1830 by the collaborating chiefs, Removal operations hobbled into broken gear in 1831.[42] Very ill-prepared to cope with large parties moving west, governmental agents routed groups on the wing, as the first waves of Choctaws were pushed through the cold hardship of a freezing winter, with few to no amenities afforded them. Many arrived in Arkansas very sick, the wild lack of official preparations for their arrival there only adding to their desperation.[43] The government was entirely aware that its 1831 Removal operation was a chaotic mess but hoped, "the first difficulties in the way of emigration being now overcome," that the quasi-system since emplaced would streamline later efforts.[44] In this, governmental officials were primarily speaking of maintaining regular financial accounts, not of making Removal a survivable experience for the Indians. Despite government muzzling, the "suffering lesson" of the 1831 Choctaws' misery returned east with certain chiefs, reinforcing the resistance of the remaining Choctaws to moving west.[45]

One enticement to leaving for those still back east was the option called "commutation," under which the government promised to reimburse the expenses of people moving on their own, once they arrived out west. Consequently, "self-guided" Choctaws in the hundreds, if not thousands, moved west independently, on the promise of a $10 per head "commutation" fee, payable upon their arrival at Fort Smith, Arkansas.[46] Ongoing land invasions by Mississippi settlers, so intent on grabbing land that they did not even wait for the Choctaws to quit it, coupled with rumors that the 1832 commutation fee was rising from $10 to $13 a head, to spur 10,000 Choctaws to consider leaving Mississippi in 1832.[47] The rumor having succeeded in convincing many reluctant Choctaws to go, Removal guidelines promptly pegged the commutation fee downward again, to $10 per person.[48] This May 1832 fee schedule, reiterated in October, was promulgated partly to thwart the Cherokee demand, formally made in August but percolating through the ranks before, that commutation fees be set at *the actual cost* of each person's removal, placed by Andrew Jackson himself at $20 per person.[49] In other words, at $10 a head, every Choctaw commuter who made it to Arkansas alive had effectively borne half of the cost of Removal him- or herself.

Even as the commutation fee was fixed at $10 per person, deposits as high as $60,000 each were being made into Removal bank accounts for Indian agents to draw upon.[50] Meantime, army officers called conductors were paid rather handsomely for leading the Choctaws to Arkansas. Colonel George S. Gaines, one conductor of Choctaw parties, was paid $4 per day for his efforts, an allowance he complained was inadequate to support his needs.[51] A removal agent's monthly emoluments were:[52]

Item Allowance	Amount per Month
Monthly pay	$20.00
Quarters, two rooms, $10 each room	$20.00
Forage, two horses, at $8 each	$16.00
Fuel, 24 cords per annum, at $2.50 a cord	$5.00

This schedule totaled $61.00 per month per agent, or $732 per annum. Thus, over the course of a six-month trek, a commuting Choctaw pocketed all of $10, whereas a conductor received $366.

Moreover, simply arriving in Arkansas in one, ambulatory piece did not guarantee that the commutation fee would be paid. Upon arrival at Fort Smith or Fort

Towson in Arkansas Territory, each Choctaw first had to produce a government certificate, theoretically handed out by Ward in Mississippi, to prove that his or her journey had been officially sanctioned.[53] A few of those in the 1831 group who had lost their certificates were allowed their commutation fee, anyway, as the government was still trying to sweet-talk those back east into leaving, but that liberal sentiment shifted abruptly in 1832.[54]

By November 1832, when the second body of Choctaws started arriving in Arkansas, governmental officials were investigating, not paying, claimants on the suspicion that those pesky Choctaw commuters were double-dipping or otherwise "speculating" in—that is, selling—their certificates.[55] By April 1833, when survivors of the 1832 Removal were still trying to cash in their certificates, officials were either prorating the amount due any who had failed to "remove themselves all the way," having required governmental assistance at some point, or simply refusing payment altogether due to alleged bad "conduct" back east that had "caused the expenditure of money uselessly by the disbursing agents of the Government."[56]

This "bad conduct" two-step alluded to the 10,000 Choctaws who had tentatively indicated that they intended to remove in 1831 but who then reneged.[57] For the second round in August 1832, the government anticipated 14,000 Choctaws in Arkansas, again to be disappointed once the eastern Choctaws learned that no one could possibly commute for a mere $10.[58] Around 5,000 were recorded turning out to march in 1832, so that, once more, the government was left holding the bag for thousands of no-shows.[59] To top off this bait-and-switch, the Choctaw rolls, registers, and ledgers had been so very badly drawn up and then physically mangled by Ward—probably on purpose to facilitate his frauds—that still others who did go were denied their commutations for lack of records.[60] One can only assume that Ward pocketed (or speculated in) their commutations.[61]

While the commutation frenzy gathered steam, on May 5, 1832, Congress passed the Indian Vaccination Act, CH. 75, 4 STAT. 514 (1832). This seemingly benign Act was used, on the one hand, to embed U.S. Army personnel in certain targeted nations and, on the other hand, to punish uncooperative nations by withholding vaccinations.[62] It was also very definitely conceived of as part of Removal. Although packaged as beneficence towards the Indians, one consistent concern was that soldiers, suppliers, and settlers not pick up smallpox from infected Indians being shoved west through their towns.

From 1831 to 1832, Elbert Herring of the Commissary General was in charge of Indian Affairs, which were managed out of the Department of War. Due to his sterling services in the 1831 Removal, Herring next sat from 1832 to 1836 as the first Commissioner of Indian Affairs. In his November 22, 1832 "Report on Indian Affairs," Herring very specifically linked the Vaccination Act to Removal, although he voiced "serious doubt whether, even with the fostering care and assured protection of the United States, the preservation and perpetuity of the Indian race are at all attainable," given the savagery of Indians.[63] Leaving aside the truly frightening thought that a man espousing such sentiments was in charge of Removal, Herring listed, as having been spent on vaccinations so far, $1,786.17 (or $9.33 less than he had requisitioned) of the $12,000 initially appropriated by Congress.[64] His requested funds amounted to less than 15 percent of the total available.

The twisted use of the Act was apparent in its application to the Choctaws being massed for Removal in 1832. In January 1832, smallpox "of a most virulent character, attacking the vaccinated as well as those who have not had that advantage," had popped up in Vicksburg, one of the steamboat embarkation points for Removal.[65] Not wishing smallpox to threaten Removal, the head Removal Indian Agent for the east, William Armstrong, reported on August 21, 1832 that he planned to vaccinate the Choctaws when they massed at the Agency East for that year's annuities, just before they left for Arkansas.[66]

By September 28, Armstrong had changed his tune. Now, he stressed "the impracticability of vaccinating the Choctaws" in the east, arguing that they should be vaccinated, instead, during their 1833 annuity distribution in Arkansas, because they were "anxious to have it done" in that way. Armstrong argued that their necessary proximity to the western fort for the distribution meant that cheap army doctors could easily "perform the operation" at that time.[67] This anti-vaccination attitude continued, despite the serious illness of one of the Choctaws' conductors, Wharton Rector, and the death of Doctor McCurry, the expensive civilian physician William Armstrong hired to administer the vaccines at Choctaw East.[68]

Historians have simply taken Armstrong at his word that the Choctaws themselves wanted to delay their vaccination, but this was patently false, in light of other letters not included in the main Removal Document 512. On May 28, 1832, shortly after the Vaccination Act had passed, early bills began piling up from private physicians.[69] The sudden interest in army doctors' administering the vaccine surfaced only after private physicians' rates became known. William Armstrong simply did not wish to pay them, as the ensuing quibble over accounts payable showed. Dr. William M. Gwin's cost justification documents of July 27, 1832 make it likely that expensive duplication, rather than Choctaw choice, had decided Armstrong against vaccinating the Choctaws.[70] Moreover, since Dr. Gwin was "an old comrade" of Andrew Jackson, while other physicians involved, such as Dr. James Smith, were prominent members of society, the whole Vaccination Act begins to stink of pork-barrel.[71]

Claims by the private physicians were still being investigated, not paid, the next spring, when Major Francis W. Armstrong, big brother of William and the head Indian Agent west of the Mississippi River, wrote a formal statement dated April 6, 1833, to defend his brother's 1832 failure to vaccinate.[72] In it, the story about why the Choctaws were not vaccinated changed dramatically, and the source of the testimony was clearly William. The "humane object" of vaccination was called off in 1832, F. W. said,

> because the Physician failed to attend after having been notified, as I under-
> stood from the Superintendent East of the Mississippi; and if he had made his

appearance at the time, I doubt whether they would have availed themselves of his services, when on the eve of setting out on their march. I confess that, for one, I was fearful of commencing it at that time, and under the existing circumstances, for many of them would have been unable, for at least some days, to travel.

The price allowed the Physician has been a barrier against effecting the object East.[73]

This letter makes it clear that it was William, not the Choctaws, who had stymied pre-Removal vaccination in 1832, and that he was massaging the details for all he was worth during the investigation of 1833. First, William knew full well that Dr. McCurry had not shown up because he was dead. Second, the doubt about vaccination was now the Armstrongs', not the Choctaws'. Third, the known withholding of the vaccine to punish uncooperative Indians later on should not be overlooked as a motive in view of the "bad behavior" of the Choctaws that had already led to the withholding of their commutation fees. In the final analysis, it is apparent that the Choctaws had left Mississippi unvaccinated due to high physician fees, governmental ire over resistance to Removal, and the worry that side effects of vaccination might delay their 1832 march. The results of William's unilateral decision were devastating. The smallpox epidemic from 1836 to 1840 claimed more than 1,000 of the Removed Choctaws in Arkansas.[74]

It was very sick out in 1832, with smallpox at the Mississippi steamboat landing of Vicksburg, yellow fever at another main steamboat landing, New Orleans, and cholera everywhere. Of the three fatal diseases, cholera was the most dreaded. A brand new plague, the likes of which the world had never seen before, cholera hit the United States like an atomic bomb. Called "The Blue Death" for the utter dehydration and low blood circulation that turned patients blue in their death throes, cholera was a swift and terrifying killer.[75]

A water- and food-borne bacterial disease that wreaks havoc in the intestine, cholera apparently began in India, from whence it followed worldwide trade routes west in 1831. Cholera's northern route forked through Russia and Afghanistan into Germany.[76] The southern route hopped along shipping lanes to Great Britain, before it headed across the Atlantic to the Canadian and U.S. seaboard, from whence it went continental via steamboat travel along the Mississippi River and its tributaries.[77]

Not deserving the name of science at the time, western medicine killed as many patients as the disease itself, heightening the public's panic at its approach.[78] Physicians knew shockingly little in 1832, with their cockamamie treatments, which primarily included letting blood while deliberately inducing vomiting and diarrhea in the same, poor patient—the three worst things anyone could possibly have done to a cholera victim.[79] However, physicians *did* know that isolating patients could contain an epidemic. Thus, among the useful tactics at their disposal was the *cordon sanitaire,* or quarantine, from the Latin *quadraginta,* or "forty," for the biblically 40 days and 40 nights during which the ill were sealed into a restricted area, either to die or, less frequently, to heal.[80]

Disease theory left as much to be desired as remedies in 1832, but here again, silly "miasmic" prattle aside, physicians certainly did understand that the cleaner the environment, the healthier the public. Sanitarians might have waged war against the contagionists, but both medical schools realized that they saw fewer patients in clean than in dirty homes.[81] Ideologically, ruling elites promptly turned this into the brief against the poor, while public officials spent their time railing at the indigent, as though they could scold them into health. Nevertheless, the commonplace was sound that patients with clean homes, food, and water were more likely to survive than filthy patients in mucky homes consuming contaminated food and drink.[82]

Thus, it is simply not true that no one knew what to do about cholera in 1832. Although the realization that cholera was waterborne had to wait until John Snow's 1848–1849 research, public health officials in 1832 knew perfectly well:

1. to quarantine active cases
2. to refuse port to sick ships and steamboats coming in from plague areas
3. to keep food, water, quarters, and patients clean

Hence, a bevy of broadsides and advice pamphlets were distributed, especially by the sanitarians. At the very least, everyone knew that crowding people into squalid areas in company with cholera-infected others sharing food and drink increased the incidence of disease. Officials might not have known how to cure cholera, but they did know how to contain it.

Thus, when cholera surfaced in England in 1831, a physician freshly returned from India knew exactly what he was looking at and imposed an immediate quarantine.[83] The disease spread, not because containment was an ineffective measure, but because the local captains of industry resisted shutting down commerce for the requisite period of time due to the economic losses that they stood to incur. They pressured the prestigious in the local medical community to downplay the "Indian cholera" (fatal, true cholera) by putting out the word that it was just the "English cholera" (nonfatal, gastrointestinal flu).[84] This pronouncement lifted the quarantine, so that tradesmen could resume buying and selling.[85] It was not, therefore, a failure to recognize and isolate cholera that spread it abroad from England, but the spin-meistering of the business community that decided a 40–50 percent death-rate was acceptable, if it maintained commerce.[86]

The same, selfish reasoning that allowed cholera to spread to North America spread it across North America once it arrived. Canadian medical officials learned in the fall of 1831 that cholera was on its way and officially alerted their U.S. counterparts in New York City on June 16, 1832.[87] The rumor of its impending arrival had preceded them. Once more, however, economic losses attendant upon ship quarantines, border closings, and total embargos encouraged

American doctors to refrain from diagnosing Asiatic cholera.[88] It was common in this period for public health officials to yield to the dictates of the chamber of commerce.[89]

From the eastern port cities of, especially, New York and Philadelphia, cholera traveled west with the settlers on the squalid steamboats (and their lesser jitney cousins, the snags) used to ferry settlers along the massive river systems of North America, connected by the public-works canals. The continental progress of the disease has literally been traced moving through Great Lakes shipping, as well as into the interior following the Erie Canal into Ohio and down the Ohio River to Memphis, from there to the Mississippi River, and finally down to New Orleans.[90]

Privately operated, steamboats were sinkholes of human waste, never cleaned between passenger runs. Their passengers were, primarily, lower-class workers and immigrants, in an age when not even one in five settlers bathed more than once a year.[91] On the steamboats, crowding and a complete lack of sanitary washing or restroom facilities contributed heavily to the advancing disease. People simply relieved themselves where they stood, on deck or below. However, the largest contributing factor was that clean, potable water was not supplied by the steamboat companies. Like food, water was to have been carried on and shared by the passengers themselves, some of whom were ill, even as they clambered aboard.[92]

Well known for spreading disease, steamboats had long been actively avoided by anyone who had a choice, both well before and well after the 1832 cholera pandemic. For instance, James Fenimore Cooper, the father of American Literature, went to considerable trouble to avoid standard steamboat accommodations in April 1823. Finding that the general fare available for purchase was disgusting while, in the absence of passenger cabins, he and his friends were expected to sleep, well, *anywhere*, including the grubby floor, Cooper used his wealth and fame to bribe his party's way into the captain's clean cabin, as well as to arrange to dine from the captain's private mess.[93] When Prince Alexander Philip Maximilian of Wied-Neuwied (in Germany) traveled down the Missouri River in the spring of 1834, to his grave dismay, his cholera-free steamboat was forced to take on passengers jumping their cholera-ridden ship.[94] The Prince understood that such fraternizing courted death.

This recognition among settlers that disease was the main property of steamboats continued for the next quarter century, at least. The settlement of Washington and Oregon territories was not a little stimulated by the ironic search for health via steamboat escape. Speaking nostalgically to the Oregon Pioneer Society in 1884, F. O. M'Cown recalled that his father, "suffering with fever and ague" in 1851, moved his family west the second he heard of "Oregon as a country where a graveyard could not be started, because so healthful," that is, free of settlers.[95] Alas, Oregon's disease-free reputation jammed "the steamers on the Missouri river [sic]" with "immigrants," all headed west, bringing cholera along with them. In 1851, families thus "broken up by death would burn all the outfit of clothing to destroy the cholera germs," a panic step, for by then, cholera had been shown to have been transmitted in drinking water.[96]

The panic that the 1832 cholera epidemic wrought in the populace cannot be overstated. One eyewitness to the frenzy in New York City recounted in a letter to his sister that, at the first "rumors" of cholera there, the poorhouse was emptied, dumping around 1,200 sick indigents "into the streets . . . under the pretence [sic] of danger from contagion, crowded rooms, etc. They all died, to a pauper." In just one week of July, he tallied up 882 burials, of which "638 were in the Potter's field."[97] So great was the public hysteria over such reports as these, that public health broadsides took to condemning "terror" as an "exciting" cause of the disease and recommending calm.[98]

No one listened. Throughout the summer, people fled their homes in waves of refugees from cholera. In the spring of 1832, as New York City dwellers saw it coming, 70,000 of the city's total population of 220,000 fled inland, carrying the disease with them.[99] Hard hit was New Orleans, simultaneously battling yellow fever and cholera, and losing 10,000 people between the two, roughly 5,000 to each disease.[100]

The only thing that could possibly have been worse for disease containment than the steamboats and the waves of cosmopolitan refugees was a war, calling up lower-class men as soldiers to spread disease through the ranks and then carry it back home—yet war is exactly what transpired. In 1832, the Sauk leader Makataimeshekiakiak ("Black Hawk") pushed back against invading settlers, returning to Illinois from Iowa with his people. Since Indians moving east directly controverted the U.S. policy of Indian Removal west, Governor John Reynolds called up the Illinois militia, while the U.S. government sent in troops to put down the Sauk push-back against invasion.[101]

Up to 2,000 U.S. reinforcements traveled exclusively by water aboard the steamboats *Sheldon Thompson* and *Henry Clay* across the Great Lakes to Fort Dearborn (Chicago), Illinois. Despite a desperate and utterly ineffectual boat cleaning with chloride of lime on July 4, 1832, once the first case of cholera was detected among the recruits on the *Henry Clay*, both steamboats did their wonted work of ferrying cholera into the Old Northwest. Meantime, the 370 soldiers encamped at Fort Gratiot (Detroit) fell profoundly ill, with all but 68 of them dying. Even had the steamboats been shut down, cholera would have spread courtesy of the many U.S. deserters from the Black Hawk War roaming the territory.[102]

Ominously, in August 1832, as all this transpired, the Choctaws were being massed for their march to the Mississippi River, for transport west via steamboat, particularly at the riverboat landings of Vicksburg, Mississippi, and Memphis, Tennessee. There is not the slightest doubt that the U.S. government officials, the Indians, and the population at large knew that cholera was awaiting the Choctaws at the Mississippi River. Aside from the broadsides and bulletins of the east coast newspapers, picked up for reprinting by lesser journals, the *Arkansas Gazette,* the primary outlet in the territory to which the Choctaws were pushed, kept careful track of the approaching debacle.

In mid-August, the *Gazette* devoted an entire column to reprinting the report of the Medical Commission of New York City on the progress of the disease, replete with detailed descriptions of its symptoms.[103] This was followed up on August 29 and again on September 5, with two more articles tracking the disease's progress.[104] On September 12, another long column enumerated death tolls.[105] On October 2 came the frightening news that cholera was at St. Louis, not so far away from Arkansas as New York or Philadelphia.[106] Then, on October 31, came the news that cholera "was prevailing at Vicksburg, and on many of the boats passing down."[107] In the same issue, a column alarmingly announced "CHOLERA!!!— *at last!*" The first case in Arkansas had been diagnosed in an attorney just returned from Philadelphia.[108] There followed on November 7 a lengthy medical discussion by "Dr. Drake, an eminent physician of Cincinnati," who recommended a long list of preventatives to *Gazette* readers, along with scary stories about the speed with which cholera took its victims.[109]

Given the close monitoring of the situation in Little Rock, where the head Removal Agent West, Major Francis W. Armstrong, was stationed, and the accompanying news that cholera was abating in the east by November even as it picked up steam along the Mississippi, there is no question that government conductors knew that they were dragging the Choctaws directly into the heart of the epidemic.[110] On September 10, 1832, William Armstrong, at Choctaw East, recorded the conscious effort of the conductors to beat cholera to the Mississippi River, musing that, should cholera "reach the western country, doubtless it will be at Memphis and Vicksburg."[111]

Despite this mortal certainty, government officials made two reckless decisions to:

1. go ahead with the 1832 march to the Mississippi River landings at Memphis and Vicksburg, the very sites of contagion;
2. herd the hungry and exhausted and Choctaws onto steamboats there.

The use steamboats for mass evacuation had been decided upon at the inception of the 1831 trek.[112] Even in that cholera-free trek, they were dangerous enough, as was reported by Lt. William S. Colquhoun on December 10, 1831. He described his revulsion having had to use the expensive *Walter Scott*:

> The disgusting sight of a vessel loaded with human beings under no control or regularity, leaving their evacuations in every direction through the whole range of the cabins and decks, would create in the mind of any one an additional allowance for the transportation.[113]

Unfortunately, Colquhoun's further description of the sick Choctaws boarding this mess as "generally very naked," having just "marched the last twenty-four hours through sleet and snow, barefooted," did not result in a higher allowance of steamboat fees, so that the people could travel in less packed conditions.[114]

Instead, it just decided officials to use the cheaper, governmentally owned steamboats as much as possible.[115]

For the purposes of Removal, the steamboats were stuffed to standing-room-only capacity, threatening to sink the conveyances. The U.S. government had decided that steamboats should load 400 to 500 people aboard on any given trip, which allowed "seven superficial square feet" to each person, but this square footage was theoretical, in practice being frequently given over to tonnage shipped, with passengers standing any way they could among the crates.[116] It was not until 1847 that Congress passed the Act to Regulate the Carriage of Passengers in Merchant Vessels, CH. 34, 9 STAT. 127 (1847), which prescribed sufficient space per passenger, partly in response to the 1832 cholera pandemic.[117]

Throughout Removal, accommodations on board steamboats remained simply deplorable, with *600* or more Indians packed on each like sardines. The "crammed condition of the decks and cabins" were "offensive to every sense and feeling," keeping the Indian (in this case, Muskogee) passengers "in a state unfit for human beings." In the instance of the Muskogees just cited, a steamboat that should not have carried more than 300 passengers was packed with 600 Indians, thus sinking easily in a collision, killing the extra 300. As noted at the time, the steamboats employed for Removal were generally "rotten, old, and unseaworthy," put into service just "to increase the profits on the speculation" in government contracts, without "the slightest regard" for "their safety, comfort, or even decency." This last circulocution meant, as Colquhoun had remarked more directly in his report, that there was nowhere but the floor for passengers to relieve themselves, privately or otherwise.[118]

All these well known facts notwithstanding, at the express desire of Andrew Jackson, acted upon by his subordinates in full knowledge of the cholera epidemic that took root in the United States in June, steamboats were ordered to be used again in July, 1832.[119] This decision was heatedly resisted by all Removing Indians, not just the Choctaws, but the government refused to budge from its steamboat position, even as cholera raged.[120] The Secretary of War, Lewis Cass—to this day, known in Ohio Iroquoian oral tradition as "The Butcher"—reaffirmed the steamboat order when James B. Gardiner, the U.S. Special Commissioner comanaging Ohio Removal, apparently questioned it on June 2 and 3, 1832, indicating the intense repudiation of steamboat travel by the Ohio clan mothers. He had also had the bad form to challenge Removal's insufficient rations while asking to add people to the Ohio Removal rolls, a move that would have forced the government to pay for *all* the people actually traveling west.[121]

As codified in the "Regulations concerning the Removal of Indians," Indians were allowed but one pound (down from the original one-and-a-quarter pounds) of fresh meat, or three-quarters of a pound of salt pork; three-fourths of a quart of corn or corn meal, or one pound of wheat flour per person per day. In addition, four quarts of salt per 100 people was allowed.[122] These provisions were far below the amount of food reasonably required by anyone, let alone freezing, starving, naked, unsheltered, diseased beings force-marched barefoot through all weather. Worse, family members who had been barred from enrolling were thus barred from receiving rations, too, meaning that the measly rations were perforce shared with unrecorded travelers. As shown by F. W. Armstrong's letter dated March 1, 1832, to Captain Jacob Brown, then the army head of Removal, officials were well aware of the "insufficiency" of rations and that "the allowance of corn ought to be doubled."[123] It was not.

Instead, Gardiner received a stern reply on all counts, transmitted from the lips of Jackson and Cass, through the pen of General George Gibson, the Commissary General of Subsistence, on June 28, 1832:

> The Secretary of War has answered your communications to him on the following points: In relation to the aversion of the Indians to traveling in steamboats; as to the insufficiency of the ration; and as to enlarging the muster-roll. With regard to the first, he had informed you of the President's determination that the Indians shall move by steamboats; on the second point, he has told you of the sufficiency of the ration provided by the regulations, in the aggregate issue to men, women, and children; and on the third, that the idea of enlarging the muster-roll cannot, for a moment, be entertained.

The clan mothers' very sane resistance to the filthy, disease-laden steamboats was brushed aside as superstition, while Gardiner was ordered "to correct their impressions" by telling them "of the rapidity and certainty with which they will travel; of the distress to which the Senecas who removed last year were subjected in their land route; and use any other arguments which may occur to your mind; but, above all, say that the plan of removal by steamboat is unalterable."[124]

The sternness of Gibson's earlier reply notwithstanding, Gardiner attempted again on September 17,1832 to elucidate more clearly the nature of the Indians' resistance to steamboat travel. Just "risen from a sick bed" himself, and still "very feeble," he wrote that, that very morning, the wife of his party's military "conductor" had "died suddenly, in an apoplectic fit" (of cholera). Her demise made forward progress even harder, as she "was beloved by the Indians, having been raised among them." Meantime, some "heartless villains" among the settlers, wishing "the Indians to remain longer, for the sake of filching the few dollars" that they had "just received," were "trying to make them believe we 'brought the cholera here and killed her,'" and that the agents would also "kill them if they go" (italics in the original). As "strange and ridiculous" as the situation might appear to Gibson, then, Gardiner assured him that this was a "difficulty of a serious nature."[125]

What happened to Gardiner, personally, for having questioned the more genocidal aspects of Removal is instructive, and not isolated. His reputation was trashed at the highest levels of government, and he was removed from his lofty position.[126] Colonel John J. Abert was dispatched by War Department to "investigate the conduct of J. B. Gardiner," and "to hasten" Ohio Removal.[127] Abert returned an extremely negative report of Gardiner as a "very weak man: swelled like a toad with his appointment." Abert accused Gardiner of falling into "all kind of follies," while forestalling and annoying his co-agent and making himself "obnoxious to the Indians."[128] By November 2, 1832, Gardiner was on administrative leave, demoted and left with little authority.[129] Gardiner was no flaming liberal. He was as smugly racist as the rest, but the officials clearly did not like the line he drew in the sand at outright genocide.

Because of the utter chaos that prevails in extant governmental archives on Removal, many ominous documents, taken singly, can sound banal for lack of context. For instance, on October 13, 1832, William Armstrong admitted to General Gibson that he had not yet employed a physician for the Choctaws, although he felt that "medical aid" was a necessity "where there are two thousand Indians" as well as Removal camp followers like teamsters.[130] Absent a reader's prior knowledge that both a cholera and a smallpox epidemic were abroad, side-by-side with knowledge of William Armstrong's failure to vaccinate the Choctaws against smallpox, this letter could easily be bypassed as innocuous. So could Armstrong's offhand news in the same missive that conductor Wharton Rector had been so ill that Armstrong had had to take over his party.[131]

In light of what the Choctaws were marched directly into, however, Removal letters take on an impending sense of doom. On October 21, 1832, F. W. Armstrong precongratulated Removal officials should the Choctaws evade the cholera epidemic. "I confess I fear that we are to encounter the cholera with our Indians," he wrote, dreading "what course such a people will take under such circumstances."[132] He had clearly tracked the disease as spread by Mississippi steamboats, naming specific boats, including the fatalities on each, to calculate whether it were possible to drive the Choctaws to Memphis by November 5 or 10, which he supposed would be ahead of the cholera epidemic. However, if the Choctaws did not arrive in time, neither did the government steamboats engaged to transport them from Memphis into Arkansas.[133]

Two days later, William Armstrong, with 900 Choctaws in the most forward of the parties, reported being 70 miles from Memphis, while the second party, numbering 1,702 under the ill Wharton Rector, was 12 miles behind. Armstrong anticipated "the other parties," that is, the Choctaws taking the southern route, making it to Vicksburg by October 31.[134] The Choctaws had "understood the cholera [wa]s in Memphis" and were "much alarmed." Armstrong hoped that the report was false, for fear that "it would nearly disperse the Indians."[135] By October 28, all 2,700 Choctaws he was in charge of were within 25 miles of Memphis, the northern steamboat embarkation point. He downplayed the cholera there as "very much exaggerated" although still leaving "the Indians much alarmed."[136]

Despite his pooh-poohing of cholera, his own life was at stake, so William Armstrong was clearly worried. Plans to put all the Choctaws on steamboats at the White River Landing, "near where the Memphis road to Little Rock" crossed, were abandoned in favor of pushing overland, through a swamp, "leaving the baggage, and as many of the old men and women and children to go on the boats as we can get to do so, and join us at the landing."[137] In other words, the stronger adults were crossing by swamp, leaving the weaker elders, women, and children to die by cholera transport. His bravado spent, Armstrong closed on the hope that, if he could "only pass the river," he yet hoped "to avoid the cholera," although he could not predict what would happen "should it . . . appear amongst us." Taking the safer, overland route, he planned to stay on duty himself, were his life "spared."[138]

By November 3, 1832, William Armstrong was flummoxed. "The Indians are greatly alarmed about the cholera," he informed Gibson, "and I find much difficulty in getting even the women and children, with the old and infirm, to take the steamboat. This party are more averse to it than the one just crossed." Consequently, he was dividing up the parties, sending the enfeebled Rector with the water group on a four-day steamboat ride.[139] Since cholera was even extant that very day "in boats that have been lying at the town wharf," two miles from his position, he was trying to isolate the Choctaws at his landing.[140]

On November 10, 1832, William Armstrong's overland party was 42 miles from Memphis, although "the late incessant rains had made the swamp almost impassable." For over 30 of the miles they had traveled, the water "was from knee to waist deep."[141] William had tried to convince the women, children, and those with no horses, "to take passage in the boats," to meet back up with the rest at the White River Landing in Arkansas, where all parties were to rendezvous. However, they "were averse to going on board the steamboats," and "in these *cholera times*" William "felt unwilling to coerce them, but left it to their own choice." He persuaded only "about one thousand to go by water" (italics in the original).[142] Those who continued through the swamps suffered, having been "sorely handled with sickness, and very many deaths."[143]

Meantime, his brother F. W. Armstrong was expecting the parties coming from Vicksburg to Memphis, places where he clearly knew disease was.[144] On October 28, 1832, he admitted to Gibson, "To be plain, our prospects are gloomy, owing to the breaking out of the cholera: *otherwise, every thing goes on well and rapidly,* and with all the economy that could be expected" (italics mine).[145] In the very next sentence, Armstrong announced that a case of cholera was "on one of our boats," which he "discharged," reiterating his brother's plan of pushing ambulatory "Indians from this point through the swamp," with the rest put "on boats for White river."[146]

By October 31, F. W. Armstrong had written Gibson from Memphis that cholera was "actually in our camp, and all through the country, at all the landings and towns even in the rear of this. Therefore you see we must go ahead, for in this matter we cannot stop to *look around*" (italics in the original).[147] Nevertheless, because of the rampant cholera, F. W. was finding it hard to hire steamboats.[148] He comforted himself with the thought that at least the government would not be price-gouged too badly, since "five thousand, or a little upwards, appears actually to be all that will go this fall." Instead of concerning himself with the death rate from the cholera epidemic, F. W. slid off into railing against those Choctaws who had refused to go, snarling that officials knew "the fellows who worked against us" and feeling "vexed" that government officials had reckoned on "two thousand more" who had decided "to bolt" at the last minute.[149] Since the 5,000 whom the Armstrongs were "conducting" west were already marching headlong into cholera, F. W. was effectively lamenting that the number exposed was not 7,000. (In fact, by February 1833, about 7,000 were ultimately counted as having arrived in Arkansas from the 1832 march; this is 2,000 more than recorded on the rolls.[150])

On November 14, the *Arkansas Gazette* was filled with news of Choctaws and cholera. One story recounted the "considerable excitement" wrought in Little Rock by "reports brought by several teamsters and others from Rock Roe," a steamboat landing outside of Little Rock, "that the Cholera had broken out and was raging with great violence" among the Choctaws there. Conductor Dr. John T. Fulton reported to the Little Rock Board of Health that "the disease" had been "violent," resulting in 16 deaths among the 1,000 Choctaws there. As usual, the Little Rock Board of Heath tried to downplay the situation by seeding confusion about whether the diagnosis should have been English ("Spasmodic") or Asiatic ("Morbus") cholera, but the dead Choctaws and hysterical teamsters spoke for themselves.[151]

This incident had occurred on November 5, 1832, as reported by Major A. S. Langham, in charge at Rock Roe until William Armstrong arrived. Under his pen, the situation on the White River was one of total panic. The steamboat *Reindeer* had arrived with 455 Choctaws, having been in transit since November 3. In the course of its two-day trip, 10 or 11 of the Choctaws had contracted cholera, with 2 of them dying *en route*. Once landed, 53 came down ill, with 12 of them having died by November 8.

Notwithstanding these grim statistics, the doctors, Fulton and Rayburn, both governmental physicians, disagreed about the cause, with Fulton recklessly siding with the Little Rock Board of Health to claim that cholera was *not* responsible for the epidemic. This lofty pronouncement hardly persuaded the locals, however, let alone the teamsters hired for the Arkansas leg of the journey. Seventeen teamsters departed Rock Roe immediately, with three wagons and teams accompanying them. In addition, hired teamsters then on their way to Rock Roe turned tail and ran for their lives upon learning of the situation.[152] Langham anticipated the worst, including no forward movement failing the wagoneers, and worse, that local civil authorities might "prohibit their passing through" Arkansas, with local settlers withholding or destroying supplies.[153]

When William Armstrong finally arrived to report the event officially on November 10, it was already old news. William stated that, at the White Landing, where he had hoped to have met up with his brother F. W. and the Vicksburg party, 30 teamsters had deserted the Choctaws and their conductors, making sure to take their wagons and teams along with them. The nearest landing was White's, just then in full cholera mode, leaving William to fear that he was "to have a serious time in getting on," since, if walking failed, the only recourse left to the party was steamboat transport.[154] William planned to keep the Vicksburg party clear of his own, since it had had "seven deaths since leaving Memphis, laid to cholera." Even at this late date, he downplayed the epidemic in his own ranks, claiming that those of his party who had "died so suddenly" had been victims *not* of cholera, but of "severe exposure" induced by wading through the swamps.[155]

On November 21, 1832, two main parties of 1,799 people arrived at Rock Roe, which was six days' march from Fort Smith. F. W. Armstrong reported that these two groups had "suffered from the cholera," although their "mortality" had "not been great," so that he now considered them "healthy."[156] What troubled him was that the expenses for the Vicksburg party had "been considerably increased, owing to the influence of cholera upon the minds of every one we had to do with." Some settlers had "refused to come near us, or to sell us any thing we wanted. In ascending the river the wood-yards were abandoned; and they had cause of alarm, for scarce a boat landed without burying some person."[157] So much for healthy Choctaws. Throughout November, the graves piled up, as the Choctaws "suffered dreadfully" with cholera, which "now raged with increased violence."[158]

On December 2, 1832, F. W. Armstrong reported that Rector and Fulton were still in the swamps around the White River, working at "getting out the last of their party" of around 400 people, "a number of them sick." Instead of trying to make for their new territory before the snows, "some large parties of them" had "actually taken up camp for a winter's hunt." As soon as he heard this, F. W. sent couriers to force the starving Choctaws to break camp and move along.[159]

The Armstrongs' reports on all of these disasters were late in being composed and dispatched to Washington, D.C., probably in part because their news chagrinned the brothers in light of their earlier, happy-faced predictions of being able to evade cholera if the Choctaws' pace were just lickety-split. Having discovered that the elderly and the toddler—not to mention the pregnant, the disabled, and the simply starving—could not match the quick-march pace of a fed, clothed, and healthy army, the Armstrongs were chewing the cud of their own embarrassment.

In his formal report, however, F. W. excused their joint tardiness on the plea of unique positioning, claiming that "no man but one who was present can form any idea of the difficulties that we have encountered owing to the cholera." Concerning his and his brother William's determined silence on the epidemic, F. W. presented them both as stoics:

> It is true, we have been obliged to keep every thing to ourselves, and to browbeat the idea of the disease, although death was hourly among us, and the road lined with the sick. The extra wagons hired to haul the sick are about five to the 1,000; fortunately they are a people that will walk to the last, or I do not know how we could get on.[160]

How, indeed? The "articles, arms, blankets, & c." did not catch up to the moving Choctaws until after the people, themselves, had passed Little Rock, that is, until they were fewer than 10 miles from Fort Smith.[161] Despite being ill himself, F. W. hoped to hand out the goods at Fort Smith.[162]

However much they might have dissembled, governmental officials demonstrated consciousness of wrongdoing in the ferocious way that they silenced dissenters in their midst. Harder than they had Gardiner, top officials slapped down Lt. William S. Colquhoun, a minor conductor whose trifling position in the scheme of Removal hardly justified all the big guns they trained on him. Appointed by Cass as a Choctaw conductor in a letter of July 9, 1831, the lieutenant, previously familiar with Arkansas, immediately acquainted himself with Choctaw lore, as noised about by Removal officials.[163] As of mid-August 1831, Colquhoun had already requested "one hundred common tents" to meet the Choctaws at Vicksburg "for the use of the women, children, sick, and decrepid [sic]" among them.[164] By September 2, 1831, as the Choctaws were on the march, Colquhoun was in Vicksburg, the southern steamboat landing for Choctaw Removal, arranging logistics.[165] He was building a reputation for energy.

On August 31, 1831, Colquhoun was described by General Gibson to Colonel George S. Gaines, Colquhoun's new boss, as "very capable," an officer upon whom Gaines could place "the utmost reliance" as a "faithful, active, and intelligent assistant."[166] Meantime, Gibson was writing to Colquhoun, describing Gaines as "a gentleman in whom the Choctaws have great confidence" and, therefore, asked to have serve as a conductor.[167]

On September 21, 1831, once Colquhoun had gotten a good look at Removal in action, as opposed to in theory, he made his first misstep. He filed complaints. Gibson replied curtly, but still with an element of patience, that the Choctaws' starving horses, which could not be accommodated on the steamers, were not eligible to receive the corn rations given the army horses. Moreover, Colquhoun's complaint to the Commissary General about the inadequacy of a pint a day of corn as human rations was brushed aside, with the brusque quip that no such complaint had been lodged by the Choctaws in Arkansas under Colquhoun's counterpart, Lieutenant J. R. Stephenson. Finally, Colquhoun was strictly told that the blankets promised the moving Choctaws were not to be distributed until after their arrival in Arkansas, despite their having been required by the Treaty to have been handed out in the fall.[168] Nevertheless, the War Department was still pleased enough with Colquhoun in December 1831 to appoint him acting eastern superintendent in the absence of his boss, Gaines.[169]

With the 1832 round of Removal in swing by the next May, the head office was asking Colquhoun to double-check the math on his accounts before he submitted reports.[170] This sounds routine enough, but it fed into later aspersions, once the War Department wanted rid of him, that covertly cast Colquhoun as a schemer and grafter, in frauds actually mounted by Gaines and a land speculator, Colonel Daniel L. Wright, the latter of whom conspired with William Ward.[171] Pressed by Cass on the Wright matter in 1833, the by-then beleaguered Colquhoun confessed to having been hoodwinked by Wright, "a man of fascinating manners," whose "flattery and friendship" Colquhoun had found it "impossible to avoid" in his working relationship with Wright's partner-in-crime, Ward. Colquhoun had been "used" by Wright, but had not been his accomplice.[172] Since no charges were filed against Colquhoun on this score, it is clear that the War Department found no evidence of misappropriation by Colquhoun, or Cass would certainly have used it to obliterate the lieutenant who was now stuck in his craw.

Instead, Colquhoun was fired for his humanity towards the Choctaws. Gibson sent him various angry letters over the summer of 1832, for a variety of offenses, primarily involving arrangements that, while kind to the Choctaws, were costing the government more than what Cass and Gibson wanted to pay.[173] In July, Colquhoun was effectively demoted, being placed under the supervision of William Armstrong, and by December 1832, Francis W. Armstrong had fired him from the Removal enterprise.[174]

Colquhoun's high crime had been trying to steer his party, 1,098 strong, away from the cholera raging in Vicksburg.[175] On October 25, 1832, when he docked at the Pearl River, Colquhoun learned of the cholera outbreak there.[176] Gaines had been in charge, but, in Vicksburg awaiting the Choctaws, he had taken ill with "the prevailing influenza," military code for cholera.[177] This left Colquhoun in charge. Although Colquhoun became "seriously indisposed," as well, he remained in Vicksburg to coordinate efforts.[178] Meanwhile, Colquhoun's cohort conductor, Lt. S. T. Cross, also fell ill, repairing to the relative safety of Madison, Indiana, in "delicate health."[179] Only Lt. J. P. Simonton remained, and he was no friend to Colquhoun.[180] On October 28, 1832, F. W. Armstrong sent his brother, William to Vicksburg to meet the parties now under Colquhoun.[181]

About the same time as William was coming to meet his party, Colquhoun was deciding to evade the cholera by routing his party away from Vicksburg, via Alston's Bluffs on the Yazoo River, to Santatia, a place rumored to have had ample supplies. Instead of finding "any resources whatever," all Colquhoun found was an unnavigable river. He decided to return to Alston Bluffs to rethink a route still clear of Vicksburg.[182]

F. W. Armstrong had scant patience with such coddling of the Choctaws. For instance, on September 17, 1832, after Choctaw chiefs had lodged formal complaints about F. W.'s Removal cruelties, far from denying the allegations, F. W. presented his harshness as justified. In earlier years, Armstrong fumed in his formal statement to Cass, the Choctaws had been "indulged beyond anything you can imagine," a situation making life tough for Removal officers in 1832. The Choctaws not only expected but even demanded consideration equal to what they had received earlier, ensuring that Removal officials under F. W. would "become unpopular *for a time*" (italics in the original).[183] Consequently, the moment that F. W. learned from his brother, William, that Colquhoun had embarked on an unapproved route, he dispatched an irate order to the lieutenant to return forthwith, dragging the Choctaws back into the maelstrom at Vicksburg.[184]

Colquhoun felt he had to obey this direct order from his superior, but realizing that he was "approaching the country in which the cholera existed," he deemed it "an act of humanity, which the department would sanction, to employ a physician to accompany the party."[185] Accordingly, Colquhoun engaged Dr. Silas Brown of Jackson, Mississippi, a civilian physician, at the high rate of $6/day.[186] (Being "seriously indisposed," himself, around this time might have fed into this decision.) Colquhoun also immediately and expensively acquired tent materials to shelter the shivering and exhausted Choctaws, most of whom were already sick.[187] Neither of these expenditures was sanctioned by the War Department. Once in Vicksburg, in desperate need of supplies, Colquhoun was forced to pay the "exorbitant" prices demanded by those locals who had not fled the epidemic.[188] By November 21, 1832, F. W. Armstrong was relieved to report to Gibson that he had just seen the tardy Choctaws off on the approved routes on November 12 and 13, and had thus been able to discharge the government steamboats.[189] Had Colquhoun let the cause of his mini-mutiny rest here, the matter would probably have been closed at this juncture.

Colquhoun was, however, unwilling to let the issue of Armstrong's mistreatment of the Choctaws rest. He openly condemned F. W.'s cruelties, especially when Armstrong refused blankets to the sick, wet, and dying Choctaws he had ordered back to disease in Vicksburg for steamboat transportation to the Land of Death. According to John Samuel, the captain of the government steamboat *Heliopolis,* in his statement of November 24, 1832, Colquhoun went ballistic at this final, callous affront. First, he attempted to drink himself into quiescence, but his strategy backfired. Instead of reconciling him to the abuse, on the one hand, liquor gave him the faux courage to confront Armstrong directly, and on the other hand, it muddled his judgment as to the best way to do it. Arming himself with a pistol, he "came in and cussed Armstrong" in his cabin before firing two shots, hitting the wall instead of F. W. For his grand finale, Colquhoun attacked F. W. bodily, smashing at his head with the pistol. In self-defense, Armstrong disarmed his lieutenant, and then, in his own frenzy, beat Colquhoun before tossing him off the steamboat.[190]

This incident gave Armstrong the ammunition he needed to have Colquhoun fired. Not content at having charged him with assaulting a superior officer, Armstrong also began circulating rumors, at the highest levels of government, that Colquhoun was a habitual drunkard. In his own sad and deflated statement of events, penned on August 15, 1833, Colquhoun accused Armstrong of retaliating against him for having "infringed on his prerogatives as Indian agent," that is, in altering routes, hiring the doctor, and supplying the Choctaws with expensive food and shelter.[191] Colquhoun resented the "indignities" that Armstrong had "heaped on" him from their first acquaintance, only to have been "driven from the service at a single breath, and accused falsely of drunkenness." After having been "treated as a slave set on shore in disgrace"—that is, beaten and thrown off the steamboat—Colquhoun argued that he had had sufficient reason for having attacked Armstrong.[192] In that day, when allegations of drunkenness could sink someone's prospects for life, whereas dueling for honor was not unusual among military officers, this defense flew more plausibly than it would today.

Admittedly, taking inebriated potshots at one's commanding officer is not the way to advance in the army, but what happened to Colquhoun, as well as to Gaines and Gardiner before him, smacks of more than personnel issues. Consistency of motive arises. Price-gouging and fraud in government Removal contracts were everywhere winked at—unless charges of fraud could be used to derail Removal critics like Gaines. Rations were known to have been inadequate, just as steamboats were known to have been disease factories, but questioning their use in Removal was used as cause for demotion, as with Gardiner. Officers were frequently drunk on duty, but the moral disrepair imputed to alcoholics in that day was charged only to Removal dissenters like Colquhoun. By contrast, drunken, amoral, walking frauds like Ward were never checked. There is a pattern here. It is obvious that retaliation against dissenters was the tacit order of the day, one issued by both the President and the Secretary of War, and followed, right down the line.

The desire to make Indians disappear was not just a side-effect, but a clear if denied motive of Removal. In the case of the Choctaws, they were deliberately marched into cholera, the worst plague of the 19th century, and even rerouted to ensure that they would be dragged through the heart of the epidemic. They were deliberately overloaded onto disease-ridden steamboats, in full, prior knowledge that steamboat travel would sicken them. Tents, blankets, and food were denied to unsheltered, starving people forced to march, often nearly naked, into winter. No one of any reasonable experience or intelligence could possibly have expected anything but a high mortality rate to have ensued. That at least one-third of the Choctaws would die from Removal was entirely predictable. Removal thus "deliberately inflicted" on the Choctaws "conditions of life calculated to bring about [their] physical destruction in whole or in part," which is the definition of genocide under Article II (c) of the Geneva Convention on Genocide.

CANADA

△ Assiniboine

Fort Union

Knife River

Fort Clark

NORTH DAKOTA

Hidatsa △

Mandan △

Arikara △

Yanktonai ▲

▲ Teton

SOUTH DAKOTA

Fort Pierre

Sioux Agency

Missouri River

▲ Yankton

Omaha ▲

NEBRASKA

Pawnee ▲

Platte River

Otoe ▲

COLO.

KANSAS

Fort Leavenworth

MONT.

Yellowstone River

WYO.

MINNESOTA

Lake Superior

MICH.

WISCONSIN

Mississippi River

▲ Santee

IOWA

▲ Iowa

Council Bluffs Agency

MISSOURI

ILL.

St. Louis ●

● trading post / annuity house
▲ vaccinated tribe
△ nonvaccinated tribe

N

0   100
MILES

CHAPTER 3

❧

"Death Put into Her Arm": Smallpox on the Upper Missouri, 1837

*I*n the spring of 1837, the American Fur Company's swift steamboat, the *St. Peter's,* sped away from St. Louis carrying more than just annuity goods and trading fort supplies. Smallpox was on board. How it got on board and, thereafter, how it spread virulently to the Upper Missouri nations of the Pawnees, Otos, Hidatsas, Assiniboins, Arikaras, Blackfeet, Mandans, Crows, Cheyennes, Piegans, Lakotas, Nakotas, and Dakotas (to name just the best known nations) is a sorry and deeply conflicted tale. Official documents are scanty, vague, or cryptic, while secondary accounts are demonstrably falsified, and eyewitness accounts are fragmented, confusing, and often deceitful. Accidental tourists loom large.

The official story is that, in April 1837, the American Fur Company's steamboat, the *St. Peter's,* pulled out of St. Louis on its way to its various trading and military posts along the Missouri River, as high as the confluence of the Yellowstone and Missouri Rivers. A known but mild case of smallpox broke out during the journey, but that passenger was isolated from the rest and recovered. Nevertheless, "a mulatto deckhand" came down with smallpox but remained on board, also recovering.

In the meantime, three Arikara women were granted passage, starting at Council Bluffs, and continuing on to the Mandan village at Fort Clark, where their Arikara cohorts were living. During their voyage, the three Arikara women came down violently ill with the smallpox, but were in the scabby stage of recovery when they disembarked at the American Fur Company's Fort Clark. It is probable that, during a "frolic" or drunken party that occurred there, including not only the Mandans and Arikaras but also steamboat and fort hands, these women, still infectious, spread the disease to the Mandan and Arikara villagers. Disgusted that neither trade goods nor governmental annuities were being offered, the Indians at Fort Clark demanded the treaty goods owed to them. Instead, the Indian agent attempted to pacify them with a few presents, but an Indian chief stole a blanket, taking the disease away with him, thus contributing to the infection among his people.

In addition, smallpox broke out at the American Fur Company's Fort Union, the last stop of the *St. Peter's,* where it turned around to head back to St. Louis. Thirty Indian women at Fort Union were promptly vaccinated, and the personnel at the infected fort shooed away the Indians who came to trade by holding a small boy with a very scabby face visible over the fort walls. Despite precautions, smallpox also, although inadvertently, leaked out of the fort. The epidemic spread from these sources.[1]

Aside from neatly laying the blame for the epidemic on the Native victims, this story sets events in sharp and isolated relief, as exploits belonging solely to the American Fur Company. In the process, this telling simplifies or omits crucial economic and governmental contexts around westward expansion, the exhaustion of the fur trade, and the politics of smallpox vaccination. In addition, shockingly racist stereotypes of the Upper Missouri Indians, as well as of African-European mixed-bloods, remain unchallenged in the record, for, central to the official story are drunken Indian women behaving loosely, light-fingered Indian men stealing blankets, and lying "mulattos," all of them segregated from governmental and company "gentlemen," whose pronouncements are taken at face value.

By 1837, Manifest Destiny was a hoary, if as yet unmonikered, operating premise of the U.S. government.[2] Using the expansionist Greenville Treaty of 1795 as the standing model, one questionable treaty after another was imposed on Native America.[3] It was commonplace for U.S. commissioners to defraud, bully, impose upon, and dicker with any Natives who could be coaxed into talking, without regard for whether said Natives enjoyed any official standing in their nation or authority to commit to anything for their groups. Thus were four primary treaties, collectively termed the "Prairie du Chien Treaty," secured to authorize settler presence in the Upper Missouri region.[4] Based on the Prairie du Chien concession treaties, American traders felt empowered to invade the Upper Missouri, there to compete ferociously with each other as well as with the British Hudson Bay Company, fomenting in the process the two standard prongs of invasion: One tong consisted of fur company invasion, which systematically looted the fauna of the area, driving Indians into the arms of the traders for sheer physical survival. The other tong consisted of missionary invasion, which disintegrated standing cultural systems, thereby demoralizing the people and dissolving traditional social bonds, preparatory to imposing western "civilization." Once the game animals were almost gone, with the local Indians left high and dry by the fur companies, the United States established military posts in the place of the vanguard missions and trading forts. At this point, a lively rivalry erupted amongst the players, not all of them aware of the process at hand. Now, Indian agents scorned missionaries as ineffectual, and fur companies as overly cozy with the "heathen Redskins." As the U.S. military moved in, beckoning masses of settlers, the traders and missionaries moved farther west to repeat the process, until the United States spanned the continent.

The U.S. government was deeply invested in both prongs. Dragoons were posted specifically to protect the interests and outposts of Christian missions and fur company forts, both entities in competition with their British counterparts for control of populations and land. In grand disregard of the First Amendment's separation of church and state, the federal government financed the operations of pet missionary organizations, backing them up through force of arms, treaty-assured annual funding (creamed off the top of the *Indians'* money), and other governmental aid.[5] Missionaries reciprocated with not only Indian crowd control but also a regular census of local Indian populations, including head counts of the number of "warriors" that each group could field at any one time. Their ratio of one in four persons as "warriors" always generously overstated the actual number by assuming that any able-bodied male between the ages of 16 and 60 was necessarily a soldier. This assumption was no truer of Indian populations then than it would be of the U.S. population today, but it certainly helped justify military expenditures while shoring up racist cant about "savage" peoples in need of missionary uplift.

At the same time, various fur traders attached to the United States began moving heavily into the high plains with (militia) General William H. Ashley's fur company in 1822–1823. Although Ashley's men remained crucial players, recycled into the employ of other fur companies, the main actor became John Jacob Astor, whose American Fur Company's numerous if crude posts, termed "forts," dotted the Missouri River.[6] Aside from the controlling post, Fort Pierre, located at the mouth of the Bad River on the Missouri, the company's two primary forts were Fort Clark, situated near where the Big Knife River dumped into the Missouri, and Fort Union, located at the mouth of the Yellowstone on the Missouri River. Lesser forts included Fort Laramie on the Laramie River, near the North Platte River, and Fort McKenzie, the most westerly American Fur Company post of the Upper Plains, located on the Missouri between the Marias and the Teton Rivers.[7]

Stories justifying governmental backing of both Christian missions and private businesses rested on carefully articulated concepts of western law and pseudo-science. At the elite level, vigorously promoted, violently negative propaganda against Indians was labeled science and used to predict that the "Red Man" was destined for extinction in competition with the supposedly superior European race.[8] Clerics were as implicated in the rhetoric of genocide as anyone else, probably because the original basis of western land-seizure law was Church law.[9] Individual missionaries were often ferocious racists, some of whom called for genocide. For instance, in 1835, Samuel Allis, a missionary to the Pawnees, illiterately characterized the Arikaras as "a very bad Indian, hostile to whites, are a verry [sic] treacherous, will be friendly where there cannot injure a person, & as soon as they have opportunity will kill; him; . . . I know of no other way to stop them than to kil them off."[10]

Fur traders were even more volatile in their Indian hating, exercising quasi-police powers to "punish" this or that Native group for exaggerated or imaginary crimes against their forts and steamboats (all as defined by the trappers). Old

trapper memoirs are brimful of "how we whupped the Injuns" lore, all quite popular into the third quarter of the 20th century, while their company forts were well
armed, even to possessing cannons.[11]

The Upper Missouri was actually invaded toward the end of the fur trade, which
had been moving steadily west since the early 16th century, devastating the fauna
of North America. It was standard European practice to move into a new area like
a plague of locusts, with company trappers consuming everything in their path.
The only business plan was continual westward movement. Conservation of assets was eschewed as profit-unfriendly. Extinction hunting resulted. Thus, the fur
industry lived off the crudest plunder of the environment. Worst of all, no dire
need was involved in the fur trade. The American ecosystem was catastrophically
assaulted simply to sate the vagaries of European fashion, on the purchasing end,
and European greed, on the supply end.

The big losers were the Indians. Although the fur trade used local Indians to
secure its hides, the "raw slaughter" of their natural resources left Native nations
destitute, their people not infrequently starving in the traders' wake, unable to
recover their former lifeways because all the materials necessary to sustain them
were gone.[12] In the early 1830s, one eyewitness to the resultant devastation, the
gentle-hearted artist, George Catlin, roundly denounced "the unlicensed trespass
committed through [Indian] country from one end to the other, by mercenary
white men, who are destroying their game, and catching all the beaver and other
rich and valuable furs out of their country, without paying them an equivalent,
or, in fact, anything at all, for it." In Catlin's view, the rapacious settlers, not the
Indians, merited the reputation of thieves for "this never-ending and boundless
system of theft and plunder, and debauchery" perpetrated against the "rightful
owners of the soil."[13]

By the spring of 1837, it was clear to one and all that the fur companies' future
lay in the Rockies and on the Pacific Northwest coast, not on the Upper Missouri
plains. John Jacob Astor, renowned in 1837 as "the richest man in America," had
recognized the fur industry's impending collapse as early as 1832, when a business excursion to London left him "very much" fearing that "beaver will not sell
very soon unless very fine" because English hatters had started to "make hats of
silk in place of beaver."[14] Positioning himself to withdraw from the trade in 1827,
he made a deal with the Pratte-Chouteau Company, allowing it "control of the
fur trade from the Arkansas to the Northwest boundary" of the U.S. territories.[15]
By 1834, he had completely sold out his interests in the Upper Missouri, although
he allowed his successors to continue using the name that he had made famous,
the American Fur Company.[16] The name did not help the company to survive the
changing market, however.

Records of the American Fur Company track a serious decline of the fur business heading into 1837. Ramsay Crooks, the president of the new American Fur
Company found by 1836 what the astute Astor had discovered in 1832, that silk
was displacing beaver as the hatter's main material.[17] By March 1837, the company had a "large quantity of muskrats on hand" as their price declined, a trend

that only worsened.[18] All in all, despite a "large" shipment from the Upper Missouri in 1837, sales were very discouraging.[19] In 1837, the American Fur Company had supported around 375 trappers in the Upper Missouri, but by 1838, it barely retained 125. By 1839, it "held its last mountain rendezvous."[20] The beaver and muskrat trade was screeching to a halt.

Not only was the return on beaver and muskrat furs slipping badly, but months before the smallpox epidemic hit, the disappearing game had left the Upper Missouri Indian nations starving, fruitlessly seeking buffalo, and struggling to turn in pelts. In the early spring of 1837, an *engagé,* or employee, at the American Fur Company's Fort Clark, Francis Chardon, recorded the famine in ongoing journal entries. By January 31, 1837, the trappers had "not tasted a Morsel of fresh Meat since fifteen days" and "the Mandans Much longer," with his hunters reporting that the more northerly Natives were "in a fair way to starve." Matters had not improved by February 14, 1837, when Chardon noted, "Mandans all starveing [sic]." Ten days later, he scribbled, "Fort full of Women and Children, begging Meat."[21]

Fur trading accounted for only part of the animal extinction going on. As many memoirs and journals of the day show, the invading trappers regularly helped themselves to the Indians' dwindling food supply, sometimes killing animals just for fun.[22] Neither were Native farmlands safe from plunder. (Yes, some Plains Indians farmed.) A former fur trader turned government Indian agent, Joshua Pilcher recalled a supposedly funny tale of traders stealing from Pawnee corn fields, with "great pains being taken" in the process to scatter the thefts among various cornfields, so as to disguise the crime, at least until the traders were clear of Pawnee land.[23] Without batting an eyelash, the fur–trader freeman and sometimes Crow adoptee, James Beckwourth, announced that "within half a century the race of buffaloes will be extinguished on this continent. Then farewell to the Red Man! for he must also become extinct, unless he applies himself to the cultivation of the soil, which is beyond the bound of probability."[24] Such cheerful predictions, laced with racist stereotype, were a commonplace of the time, and as freely uttered by African-European mixed-bloods like Beckwourth as by European settlers.

In 1837, the Upper Missouri was at the breaking point, with traders and missionaries fixing to move west and the U.S. Army ready to set up military posts. The 1837–1838 *Annual Report of the Commissioner of Indian Affairs* to Congress officially reported that the game was almost gone, code talk announcing that enfeebled Indian resistance now made the area ripe for land seizure.[25] U.S. governmental officials were, therefore, not at all unaware of the impending collapse of the fur trade. The government had watched with interest for the best time to move on the Upper Missouri, passing legislation and fixing its posts strategically against the right moment to act decisively.

The political infrastructure had been set to spring since 1818, when William Clark, then the governor of the Missouri Territory, began agitating for U.S. trade control in the face of British and Spanish incursions on what was seen as rightfully U.S. land.[26] (Indian claims never counted.) Council Bluffs, on the eastern edge of Pawnee country as well as the site of the U.S. Fort Kearney, was specifically chosen to host the Indian agency created, not the least in an effort to quell the Pawnees, then described as "especially troublesome."[27] In 1827, the government moved its main military fort from Council Bluffs to Cantonment Leavenworth, creating a new military presence on the Missouri River, confirmed by more activity in 1829.[28]

Importantly, just as the fur trade weakened and the politically connected Astor sold out, Congress passed the new Intercourse Act of 1834. Intercourse acts had been passed regularly since Washington's presidency, but the 1834 Act set new ground rules under a special section that redesigned Indian Affairs and ordered military forts to be placed along, essentially, the old fur trade fort routes.[29] President Jackson's new regulations defined the territory as land "west of the State of Missouri and north of the Northern Territory," the latter also vaguely defined and including lands of the Otos, Pawnees, Omahas, and Poncas.[30]

Then, in 1836, Congress passed a law to create a "military road from a point on the upper Mississippi (between the mouths of the St. Peters' and Des Moines rivers [sic]) to Red river [sic] in the south;" to be located west of Missouri and Arkansas. It also authorized the physical establishment of military forts by the U.S. Army, appropriating $100,000 for the project. The act authorized the use of military force.[31] Since, by the time the act was signed into law, it was too late in 1836 to begin, work was scheduled to start in the spring of 1837.[32] In March 1837, two dragoon units were sent to fix the locations, and in August 1837, the surveying began.[33] On July 9, 1837, Major-General Edmund Pendleton Gaines arrived at Fort Leavenworth on an inspection trip.[34]

Despite the army's low troop strength in 1837, it declared its need for 15,000 men in the west—twice as many as it had at all—stimulating a report to the Secretary of War on plans for a western defense, including population statistics on the Indians of the area and the progress of the road project.[35] In October 1838, the government contracted for construction, again despite its low personnel count out west.[36] The payoff to the positioning came in April 1837, as the new Upper Missouri Agency basically claimed rights over the Siouan peoples, Cheyennes, Assiniboins, Blackfeet, Crows, Arikaras, and Minnetaree Hidatsas (called "Gros Ventres" in documents of the time).[37] In 1837, the new Department of Indian Affairs ordered the Superintendent of Surveys to find the best place for a centralized government of the plains on land along the Osage River, in hopes of organizing the Native nations to federal taste. In other words, by the spring of 1837, the U.S. Army sat poised to enter the Upper Missouri to co-opt Indian land from both the Native nations inhabiting it and from the fur companies that had "opened" it. Not only fueled by ongoing expansionism, these moves were also preparatory to facing off with Great Britain in the race to grab the Pacific Northwest. All that stood in the way by the spring of 1837 were those pesky "Redskins" of the Upper Missouri.[38]

This problem was tackled in advance, too. A politically powerful anchor of the impending land seizure was the Vaccination Act of 1832. Not only was it a humane-sounding way to assert the settler right to meddle internally with Native nations, but it also afforded the government a way to snub or favor targeted nations. I have already shown in chapter 2 how the Removing Choctaws were penalized by the Indian Agent, William Armstrong, for their reluctance to line up for death marches by being left unvaccinated. As J. Diane Pearson has shown more generally, the U.S. government's "imperial medicine" routinely rewarded "good" Indians by vaccinating them or punished "bad" Indians by withholding vaccination.[39] Bad Indians were, of course, those who stood in the way of Removal and/ or westward U.S. expansion.

Unlike modern Americans, 19th-century settlers were hardly unaware that, in the past, smallpox had been deliberately spread, as in the 1763 Fort Pitt incident recounted in chapter 1. Similar events were such common knowledge among settlers that, in calling for the Vaccination Act of 1832, then-Commissioner of Indian Affairs Elbert Herring mentioned them and then casually recounted an example of one. In 1768, the Chippewas resisted traders' intrusions onto their Leech Lake lands by confiscating their trade goods, only to be threatened with violence by the same traders should they not "make reparations." As an act of goodwill to quell brewing retaliation, the Chippewas came to Mackinaw in 1770 with furs. There, the traders presented them with a tightly rolled flag and a liquor cask, one or both poisoned with smallpox.[40]

In a later instance, Isaac McCoy, a leading missionary, sent U.S. governmental officials his evidence that the 1831 smallpox epidemic had been instigated by Rocky Mountain traders who had "brought with them from the settlements the virus of small pox," which they "designed to communicate" to the "troublesome" nations of "Pawnees, Camanches [*sic*], and other remote tribes" through gifts of tobacco, clothing, or whatever was handy. The traders "did fall in with Indians," and an epidemic broke out, wreaking "dreadful havoc" among the Pawnees, as well as the Omahas, Otos, and Poncas, with McCoy believing that "the Sioux and other northern Indians" would "contract the disease" as well, were they not vaccinated immediately.[41] It was this epidemic that triggered the 1832 Vaccination Act.

Contrary to much contemporary media puff, the High Plains Indians were not only entirely familiar with smallpox from previous bouts of it, starting in 1780, but some had also been vaccinated against it prior to 1832.[42] Around 1815, the Omaha nation was vaccinated, helping it to survive the 1837 epidemic.[43] Similarly, 200 Assiniboins were vaccinated "in former years," that is, pre–1837, "by the Hudson Bay Company."[44] Isaac McCoy claimed that the 1831 smallpox epidemic among the Pawnees had been "arrested" due to the vaccinations performed by the Hudson's Bay Company.[45] Interestingly, the agency doing most of the Upper Missouri vaccinating was the British Hudson's Bay Company. Left conspicuously unvaccinated by the U.S. government, with vaccine matter not even offered to them, were the Mandans, Arikaras, Hidatsas, Blackfeet, Crees, and Assiniboins.[46]

To counter such reports as McCoy's, propaganda relentlessly presented Upper Missouri Indians as balking at western medicine in general and at vaccination in particular, due to their profound "superstition."[47] In fact, Natives *were* wary of

European medical cures, preferring their own remedies such as aspirin rendered from willow bark to treat chills, fevers, and pain, or plants of the Penstemon digitalis genus to alleviate pain and heart attacks. Such botanical treatments, based on observed reactions in the human body, were a far and welcome cry from the standard bleedings, blisterings, emetics, expectorants, and "elemental" medicines of Europe.

The superstition really belonged to the Europeans who indulged in such dangerous "cures," but this did not stop the settlers from waving off the Indians as "ignorant of any true knowledge of diseases or medicines" because they lacked "mineral medicines" and "the theory of diseases."[48] The theory of disease here was the miasma, or bad-air, theory, largely fingering stenches as the cause of disease, while European "mineral medicines" consisted of such dainties as calomel (powdered mercury), sugar of lead (lead acetate), strychnine, and even *gunpowder* or its elements (sulfur, charcoal, and potassium nitrate) in isolation.[49] If these treatments failed to kill a patient, "copious" bleedings were tried.[50] Well might any sane Indian have shrunk from such cockamamie cures. What the Europeans had in 1837, and all they had, was smallpox vaccination.

It was, however, politically expedient to present the Indians as too ignorant to allow themselves to be vaccinated, thus explaining why, notwithstanding the Vaccination Act of 1832, Indians were not vaccinated. In fact, a sloppy misuse of terms disguised the source of resistance. "Vaccination," a relatively safe procedure of infection with cowpox, was not resisted by the Indians. Rather, Natives shied away from the far more dangerous "variolation" or "inoculation" (the deliberate infection with live smallpox). Just to keep life exciting, the early term "variolation" was haphazardly conflated with the later term, "inoculation," with both rather sloppily applied. This imprecision carried over to the newest term, "vaccination," which the settlers used indiscriminately, sometimes to mean inoculation.

As much as the terms can be separated, variolation was the act of inserting scabs or pus from smallpox patients into small incisions on the bodies of the healthy to confer immunity on them. Variolation was practiced in India as early as 1000 B.C.E., from whence it was picked up by Tibetan Buddhist nuns and, most likely through the Buddhists, transported into China, where it was being practiced at a Buddhist monastery in Sichuan Province around 1000 C.E.[51] European peasants were also recorded as variolating each other in 1675, and when English physicians investigated, they found that peasants had been practicing variolation for centuries.[52] Inoculation was much the same thing as variolation, but western physicians added protocols, dosing their patients with their mineral medicines, primarily mercury, but also including emetics and purgatives, opium, and "effervescing saline," as well as applying leeches.[53] Both variolation and inoculation saw high and unpredictable death rates in those so treated.

Vaccination was a vast improvement on variolation and inoculation, stemming from the long-standing European observation that milkmaids did not contract smallpox, although, to be sure, they contracted cowpox, a mild disease. In 1796, it dawned on the English physician Edward Jenner that cowpox might inure milkmaids to smallpox, so he experimented by inoculating patients with the non-lethal cowpox and then exposing them to deadly smallpox, which most withstood. By 1799, his findings that cowpox did, indeed, immunize people against small-pox spread like wildfire across Europe, and then to North America. "Vaccina-tion"—from the Latin, *vacca* for cow—was all the rage, with Congress legislating for vaccination in 1813, and vaccination for all troops mandated by the U.S. Army by 1818.[54]

Vaccination had its drawbacks, however, in both preparation and storage. Trans-parent fluid was gathered from a cowpox pustule on the eighth or ninth day of infection, to be used before it desiccated. If dried, the fluid lost its potency.[55] Obviously, the vaccinee had to have been located near the fresh pustule for this to work. As a method of preserving and transporting the fluid, *kinepock* was created. A cotton thread was repeatedly drawn through the liquid pox until thoroughly saturated by it. This thread was then packed and shipped, but uncontrolled dosages might leave the thread ineffective. Moreover, improper handling and transportation often left it either contaminated or too dried to be useful upon arrival.[56] An alternative method that was more effective suspended the cowpox fluid in diluted glycerin and carbolic acid, but this process was not required until 1902.[57] Most of the *kinepock* shipped to the American west in the 1830s was dried and thus useless when it arrived, leaving inoculation from live smallpox as the alternative.

Despite the settlers' use of the term "vaccination" when they meant inocula-tion or variolation, the Indians knew and observed the difference among the types, balking at the last two but almost always allowing vaccination.[58] Thus, in 1854, when Edwin Thompson Denig clucked over the Native resistance to vaccination with kinepock (cowpox), he was really describing the *inoculation* of Assiniboins at Fort Union in 1837 with live *smallpox*.[59] The cover story of Indian resistance was exposed in 1838, when Sioux Indian Agent, Major Joshua Pilcher, went on a vaccination jaunt (a year too late to forestall the smallpox epidemic of 1837). The venture met with absolutely no resistance at all from the Siouan peoples ap-proached, so that Pilcher expressed official surprise.[60]

From 1832 on, at precisely the same time that the fur trade was failing in the Upper Missouri, the U.S.-mandated vaccination of the Indians was supposedly going on—except that it was not. The vaccination of Upper Missouri nations was actually stopped by order of the Secretary of War, Lewis Cass, an official who de-serves more scrutiny than he ever receives. An Indian-hater of the first mag-nitude who became the logistical architect of Jacksonian Removal, he aimed to capture the presidency. His protégé, the make-it-up-as-you-go-along ethnogra-pher Henry Rowe Schoolcraft, turned his writing talents and public visibility to account for his old mentor by preparing a swaggering political biography of Cass, one noisy enough to kick off Cass's 1848 presidential bid. (Cass ran again, still unsuccessfully, in 1852.)

Hawk credentials as an Indian fighter provided the fastest route to high po-litical office at the time, so in *Outlines of the Life and Character of Gen. Lewis Cass,*

Schoolcraft sensationalized *General* Cass's rock-'em, sock-'em qualifications by drawing heavily on Cass's Indian-bashing credentials, presenting him as among the "hardy pioneers of the west" who "put no faith in the sincerity of the Indians." Instead, Cass was "one of the earliest" stalwarts "to fly to the rescue of the frontiers." He was depicted as personally rescuing his mother-in-law from tomahawking in 1827: "Her shrieks instantly hurried him, together with his attendants, to the spot." Although such constant vigilance might be personally inconvenient, the General was always "sinking every consideration of rank and place," being "*intent alone* on the honor and safety of his country" (italics in the original). Meanwhile, because Indians "manifested a hostile disposition," Cass drafted the Indian code "enacted by Congress"— that is, the Jacksonian Removal code. As it turned out (according to Schoolcraft's revisionist history), Removal was entirely the fault of *Native Americans*, who were bullheadedly out to "avenge themselves for wrongs, which were to be found, in truth, in the effects of their own weak institutions, and discordant and misguided counsels."[61]

A man willing to offer himself to the public in such lurid terms was not one to cavil at obviating the federal Indian Vaccination Act of 1832, by seeing to it that "bad" Indians remained unprotected. In May 1832, Cass notified Indian Agent, Major John Dougherty, that although a couple of physicians had been appointed to vaccinate Indians under the new law, "no effort would be made . . . under any circumstances . . . to send a surgeon higher up the Missouri than the Mandans, and I think not higher than the Arikarees."[62] Even though in 1832, vaccine and instructions on how it was used were sent to Fort Pierre, the American Fur Company's principal distribution point on the Upper Missouri, complaints were lodged that same summer against fur trader Frederick Chouteau for actively "persuading the Kaws not to submit to vaccination."[63] There is no evidence that the vaccinations were ever offered to non-treaty peoples of the high plains, that is, those unwilling to cede land to the United States, including the Mandans, Arikaras, Hidatsas, Blackfeet, Crees, and Assiniboins, none of whom "signed" any treaties until 1851.[64]

Given these facts, the politics of who in the Upper Missouri region was vaccinated—and who was not—becomes quite instructive. The major trading partners were the various Siouan peoples, who had access to the best furs and thus were not characterized as "a menace to advancing white civilization" until the 1850s.[65] Meanwhile, the Arikaras and Blackfeet, having been more resistant to invasion in the 1830s, were presented as unremittingly hostile and savage.[66] Partly because of their "traditional" enmity with the useful Siouan groups, but also because they had been quite reduced by smallpox since their manifold kindnesses to Meriwether Lewis and William Clark in 1803 and 1804, the Mandans were regarded as friendly but negligible.[67]

Personally, I have often wondered how much of the passive hostility toward the Mandans owed to the fact that their very existence forcibly exposed the racist lie, still shamefully current, of Europeans as the world's only "white-skinned" people. Like the Iroquois and the Cherokees, the Mandans were famously light-skinned

Indians, whose members sported brown or even blue eyes and light-colored hair, sometimes described as "gray."[68] When a country's expansionist propaganda paints Indians as half-baked hunters, farmers like the Mandans reality-check the fantasy. Worse, when a country's genocidal rationale is based on a racist assertion of "white" skin privilege, Indians who can "pass for white" are a decided obstacle.

Be that as it may, it was not until 1838—one year too late—that the government got around to sending Dr. Joseph R. De Prefontaine to vaccinate remaining high plains Indians with "vaccine scabs 'all carefully put up.'" Even then, only some of the peoples were vaccinated, enumerated as the Yankton and Santee Sioux, the Otos, and the Omahas.[69] In his postmortem on the 1837 epidemic, written in 1838, Isaac McCoy doubted the usefulness of even the delayed vaccinations, noting that previous "attempts to vaccinate under instructions from Government" were not only slapdash, but that the "virus" used was often "not good." Governmental vaccination failed, he claimed, due to these, or "some other cause," which he left unnamed, although lack of will obviously fills in the blank. Vaccinated Indians "afterward contract the small pox," he noted, "leading to the supposition" that the vaccine matter itself was "useless, or worse than useless."[70] An employee at Fort Union, Charles Larpenteur, also claimed that the pre–1837 vaccine was no good.[71]

Thus, heading into the fatal year 1837:

- Native cultures had been disrupted by fur traders and missionaries
- the fur trade was failing in the Upper Missouri
- the U.S. government had strategically positioned itself to assume control of the high plains militarily
- the Vaccination Act had been deliberately sidestepped

All that stood in the way of land seizure were the unvaccinated Indian inhabitants of the area, now all primed by starvation to fall before *any* epidemic disease, let alone hemorrhagic smallpox.

The journey of the American Fur Company's steamboat, *St. Peter's,* began in St. Louis, transporting its forts' own annual supply requisitions, as well as the government's Indian annuities and gifts. The *St. Peter's* trailed its Mackinaws, or supply barges dragged along behind the steamboat, although these might have been attached at Fort Bellevue. The exact date of departure from St. Louis is not recorded, but it can be estimated closely from letters, accounts, and company documents:

- In a letter dated April 16, 1837, from Pierre Chouteau at St. Louis to Pierre D. Papin at Fort Pierre, Chouteau stated that "the boat is leaving three weeks later than I would have wished" due to "hindrances" that had "piled up."[72]
- In early May, the steamboat *St. Peter's* out of St. Louis dropped off American Fur Company employees and equipment for their overland trek.[73]

- On May 24, 1837, having received their annuities, the Pawnees set out for home from Bellevue, meaning that the *St. Peter's* had arrived on or before May 24.[74]

- In a letter of May 30, 1837, to Jacob Halsey written from the *St. Peter's* stop at "Ceder Island," or Fort Recovery, Joshua Pilcher wrote that "the *smallpox* has been raging on board for thirty five days" (italics in the original).[75]

- Passenger Francesco Arese stated that the steamboat arrived at Blacksnake Hills (now St. Joseph) the night after arriving in Fort Leavenworth.[76]

- Arese recorded that the *St. Peter's* pulled into Council Bluffs on the 11th day of its having been on the Missouri.[77]

- On June 5, 1837, the 1837 annuities arrived at Pilcher's Sioux Agency.[78]

- On June 19, 1837, Chardon recorded the steamboat's arrival at Fort Clark.[79]

- Charles Larpenteur stated that the *St. Peter's* arrived at Fort Union on June 20, 1837.[80]

- James Beckwourth recorded that, all told, it took him 53 days to arrive in Fort Clark from St. Louis.[81]

- Captain Bernard Pratte, commanding the *St. Peter's,* stated that the first steamboat to make the *roundtrip* St. Louis-Fort Union-St. Louis run required 52 days to complete the journey.[82]

- Pratte stated that he arrived back in St. Louis on the return trip on July 13, 1837.[83]

- Pilcher stated in a letter of June 10, 1837, that it had taken 40 days to arrive at his Sioux Agency after the *St. Peter's* left Fort Leavenworth.[84]

This gaggle of known dates allows us to calculate the *St. Peter's* departure date. I am giving preference to Pratte's 52–day roundtrip over Beckwourth's 53 days to Fort Clark. Consistent with the dates and places at which *St. Peter's* was known to have stopped, Pratte's exact count of a 52–day round-trip in 1837 and return date of July 13, the *St. Peter's* departed St. Louis on or about April 28, 1837, *not* on April 17, as Clyde Dollar and R. G. Robertson calculated.[85]

Fur company men always disembarked early, traveling overland to their Rocky Mountain round-up. In an interesting departure from this normal procedure, in 1837, the fur company's overland men disembarked at "Chouteau's Landing two miles below the Kaw's mouth," at the confluence of the Kaw and Missouri Rivers, to prepare the company's "cavalcade," that is, the wagon train, to the far west for the annual "rendezvous of Rocky mountain [sic] trappers."[86] Based on notes and the water-color painting, "Crossing the Kansas," made on-the-spot by Alfred Jacob Miller, an artist along as a tourist with the 1837 cavalcade, from Chouteau's Landing, the wagon train proceeded across the Kansas River.[87] Robert Newell, a member of the cavalcade, stated, "We left Sublette & Vasques fort on the 19th of may" (all text as in the original), which was located three miles south of present-day Platteville, Colorado.[88]

The route thus indicated was Sublette's Trace, which the American Fur Company had not used since 1834, having found, instead, a quicker and less arduous route starting from Bellevue, Nebraska.[89] Just why the company should have selected a more difficult, time-consuming, and expensive route in 1837 than it had used in 1835 and 1836 is nowhere addressed in the primary sources. It is noteworthy, however, that Sublette's Trace gave very wide berth to the company's Upper Missouri forts, keeping traders of the now more lucrative far west away from the *St. Peter's* cargo and landing points, as well as from the Indians of the Upper Missouri in the year the epidemic began.

From contemporary documents, it is also possible to identify the following people as passengers on that fateful trip of the *St. Peter's*:

- Samuel Allis, a missionary to the Pawnees[90]
- Francesco Arese, an Italian Count who was touring the American west[91]
- James Beckwourth, American Fur Company *engagé* attached to Forts Cass and Union, and the adopted War Chief of the Crows[92]
- A "young son" son of Francis Chardon, possibly Andrew Jackson Chardon, and probably an attendant, possibly Chardon's second wife, Marguerite Marie[93]
- Major John Dougherty, U.S. Indian Agent at Council Bluffs[94]
- John Dunbar and his wife, missionaries to the Pawnees[95]
- Four unidentified men, "taken with terrible colic and vomiting"[96]
- Major William Fulkerson, Indian agent at the Mandan subagency at Fort Clark[97]
- Antoine Garreau, in St. Louis in 1836, and at Fort Clark on July 13, 1837, probably having returned on the *St. Peter's*[98]
- Jacob Halsey, American Fur Company *bourgeois* (fort boss), formerly attached to Fort Pierre but going to take over at Fort Union, along with his pregnant wife and young son[99]
- A Papin son who had gone to St. Louis in 1836[100]
- Major Joshua Pilcher, U.S. Indian Agent for the Siouan peoples at Big Bend[101]
- Bernard Pratte, the American Fur Company's captain of the steamboat, *St. Peter's*[102]
- A man who boarded at Council Bluffs, to act as Arese's guide to the Vermilion River[103]
- Three Native American women of disputed nation[104]
- An unnamed Indian woman with a "little Indian boy"[105]
- The wife and children of "one of the Pincipal Cheifs [sic]" of the "Mandans & Rees" at Fort Clark[106]

I listed Major William Fulkerson as a passenger, but there is some doubt about this, since his letter of August 9, 1837 indicated that he was already at Fort Clark when the *St. Peter's* docked.[107] Apparently unaware of this letter, both Clyde Dollar and R. G. Robertson assumed that Fulkerson had been aboard the *St. Peter's* since St. Louis.[108] On the other hand, it is worth noting that Fulkerson was fired around March 1, 1838 for not having been at his post in January and February of that year.[109] Being AWOL, and then covering as much up, looked to have been a habit with Fulkerson.[110] He might well have been aboard the *St. Peter's*, after all, with the letter deliberately falsifying his whereabouts for cover. General Clark tended not to believe Fulkerson's accounts, and Clark's judgment is worth recognizing in evaluating him. Thus, I included Fulkerson as a passenger.

Just when Halsey and Pilcher boarded and left can be assumed from the May 30, 1837 letter to Halsey from Pilcher, written from aboard the *St. Peter's* at "Ceder Island," or Fort Recovery.[111] There would have been no need to write the letter had Halsey and Pilcher been aboard at the same time. Apparently, Halsey did not board until the steamboat stopped at Fort Pierre, whereas Pilcher disembarked earlier, at Council Bluffs, for his own post at Big Bend.

I have also wondered whether Major-General Edmund Pendleton Gaines, who arrived at Fort Leavenworth on July 9, 1837 for his inspection of the post, traveled aboard the *St. Peter's*.[112] He certainly made the inspection tour, and Fort Leavenworth was an early *St. Peter's* stop. If Gaines did travel aboard the steamboat, he was with it during its whole trip up, stopping at Fort Leavenworth on the return journey. In this case, he would have made his inspection and climbed back aboard, returning with it to St. Louis on July 13, 1837. Alternatively, he could have traveled by land to Fort Leavenworth, catching the *St. Peter's* back to St. Louis on its return trip. Either way, it is very interesting that he chose to make his inspection tour of the fort and its troops during the diseased trip of the *St. Peter's*.

In addition to these passengers, Count Arese gave a generalized portrait of the remaining, unenumerated passengers:

> Some of them were heads of factories [trading forts] and depots, but the largest number was made up of hunters, trappers, and voyageurs, mostly French, or to speak more precisely, of French extraction, and well assorted for giving an idea of the shades of human skin in Europeans—creoles, negroes, mulattos of different degrees, half-breeds, and who knows what not?[113]

Shortly after the *St. Peter's* steamed out of St. Louis, smallpox erupted on board. According to a letter of June 10, 1837, from Joshua Pilcher to General William Clark, then Superintendent of Indians at St. Louis, "The Small Pox broke out on board the steamboat before she passed for[t] Leavenworth," one of the earliest stops.[114] Despite the fact that passengers contracted and even died of smallpox *en route,* the *St. Peter's* steamed on. Everyone official on board, from the captain, the top local fur company officials, and missionaries, to three Indian agents and possibly a general, were entirely aware of the smallpox outbreak and the lethality of smallpox to unvaccinated Native groups. Nevertheless, only one official on board asked that the first passenger with an active case—identified by Captain Pratte as James Beckwourth—be put off the boat.[115] The suggestion was overruled.

The reasons given for refusing to put the sick passenger off the *St. Peter's* change quite a bit, depending on who recites the incident. In his 1977 discussion of the debate, Clyde Dollar implied that, along with staffing concerns, humanitarianism helped prevent Pratte from stranding the man on the riverside.[116] In 2001, R. G. Robertson proposed that putting the invalid ashore would have left him "better off," since "there were people to offer him care," and then puzzlingly cited Dollar as his source on this supposition.[117] Neither speculation squares, however, with the reported reasons given by either Pilcher or Pratte, who never mentioned humanitarian considerations.

In 1838, Pilcher wrote that Captain Pratte (who had admittedly never seen smallpox before) refused on two grounds: first, that of "doubting the reality" that smallpox was the disease at hand, and second, of needing "the man" (*not* "the deckhand," a pure license that Dollar, and Robertson following him, took with the sources).[118] In his account, Pratte did not even record the suggestion to put the man (Beckwourth) off, stating instead that, thinking the problem was a "bilious attack," he gave Beckwourth "a dose of ipecac, and he recovered."[119] (From the bark or root of the *American ipecacuanha,* ipecac induces vomiting.) Since it was rather commonplace to strand troublesome or sick passengers on shore, why the violently ill passengers, including Beckwourth, Jacob Halsey, Halsey's wife, the four vomiting men, and the Indian woman with the sick child, were kept on board requires an answer that was never given at the time.[120]

Who the recommending "gentleman" was is also a matter of speculation. Robertson concluded that it was probably Fulkerson and, by extension, that Fulkerson had examined Beckwourth; however, it is more likely that Pilcher was the gentleman in question.[121] Referring to oneself in the third person was not uncommon in the 19th century, especially in elite documents or government reports. Moreover, Pilcher had had formal medical training, especially in "smallpox prevention through inoculation."[122] I believe, therefore, that he politely meant himself when he referred to the "gentleman." It is probable that both Pilcher and his boss, General William Clark, would simply have realized to whom Pilcher alluded, so that naming himself seemed unnecessarily crude.

The records are clear that numerous people aboard the *St. Peter's* not only sickened, but also died, of smallpox during that trip. Not accidentally, the survivors were settlers. Vaccination had become routine among the general settler population in the 1830s, so that many of the Euro-Americans on board, especially any upscale, would certainly have been vaccinated.[123] Halsey had unquestionably been vaccinated.[124] So had Culbertson.[125] Pilcher and Gaines almost certainly had been, since it was required for military men; both certainly survived unscathed. Beckwourth also recovered fairly quickly, suggesting that he, too, had been vaccinated, since Pratte's ipecac could not have cured him of smallpox.

Many more were not so fortunate. Captain Pratte told the *Missouri Republican* that "eighteen men in succession were buried" during the voyage, while Francis Chardon said that the *St. Peter's* arrived at Fort Clark with "many victims on the steamboat."[126] Halsey's Indian wife died of a combination of smallpox and childbirth.[127] Arese did not mention anything further about the four men with "terrible" vomiting who had apparently boarded in St. Louis, so we do not know their ultimate fate. Arese attributed their condition to cholera, of which a few cases still lingered in St. Louis, but vomiting is also an early symptom of smallpox, and no cholera cases were ever reported in connection with the 1837 run of the

St. Peter's.[128] Similarly, we do not know the fate of the little Indian boy. All Pratte noted was that "His mother said let him go—alluding to the ipecac—better that he should die a natural death."[129]

Here, the identity of that little Indian boy should be explored, particularly in tandem with Pilcher's 1838 secondhand tale of the three Arikara women. One of Chardon's little boys was said to have been aboard the *St. Peter's*, for in 1843, Chardon recounted to Audubon having made a special, 30–mile trip downriver to take the child off the steamboat before it docked at Fort Clark.[130] That Chardon did meet the *St. Peter's* downstream somewhere and did return on board to Fort Clark is certain. In his daily fort journal, Chardon noted leaving to meet the *St. Peter's* on June 16, 1837, and then riding back on it to arrive "at the Mandans at 3 P.M" on June 19.[131] His fort journal did not mention the reason for this jaunt.

Everyone now takes it for granted that the child was the reason for Chardon's back-and-forth trip. Moreover, ever since Annie Heloise Abel, the 1932 editor of his published journal, first speculated that the child was Chardon's youngest, Andrew Jackson Chardon, historians have simply accepted her supposition as proven, as well.[132] The facts are less clear, however. Chardon merely told Audubon that he went to retrieve a "young son," of whom he had at least two. Since Andrew's slightly older brother by the same mother was in Philadelphia, Abel speculated that the child was Andrew Jackson, Chardon's son by his favorite wife, the Lakota Tchonsumonska, guessing further that Andrew had previously accompanied his deceased mother to Fort Pierre for burial among her people on April 24, 1837.[133] Chardon did not, however, confine himself to one woman, or even to his current wife, as his multiple marriages and journal-recorded escapades demonstrate.[134] He might have had many unrecorded sons.

The burial trip certainly cannot have stimulated Chardon's journey, in any case, for Chardon stated in a letter of December 24, 1836 that he planned to meet the *St. Peter's* at Fort Pierre on its 1837 run.[135] Obviously, this letter recorded his intentions four months' *before* Tchonsumonska died, so that the whole story of little Andrew Jackson starts to smell a bit fishy. Perhaps the death of Tchonsumonska and the transmission of her corpse to Fort Pierre serendipitously provided a later rationalization for Chardon's journey.

The Andrew Jackson story is, therefore, a lot of conclusion-leaping from fairly shaky grounds, but as long as everyone in sight is making assumptions, let me point out that the smallpox vaccine was at Fort Pierre, hinting at another reason for the toddler's April trip.[136] I also suggest that Captain Pratte's unnamed Indian "mother," who had refused ipecac for her sick "Indian child," might have been Chardon's second wife, the Arikara Marguerite Marie. Chardon married this woman in May 1837, almost immediately after the death of Tchonsumonska, and would have taken her with him to Fort Pierre to tend the toddler.[137] If so, it was Chardon's son who had stirred interest in a captain too socially above the Indian pair to have noticed them, absent such a connection.[138] On September 7, 1837, four months after Chardon had returned to Fort Clark on the *St. Peter's*, "afraid of the disease," he again sent "My Boy" (unnamed) to Fort Pierre. It did not help; the child died at Fort Pierre on September 22, 1837.[139]

Another potential Indian mother and son emerge from the record, a chief's wife who had traveled with her children (plural) aboard the *St. Peter's*. Chardon was unclear as to her nation, but she lived at the Mandan village near Fort Clark. However, Chardon nowhere stated that she or her children disembarked sick, just that she had arrived telling "a fine tale against the Whites."[140] I should dearly like to know what that tale was, but Chardon was silent on that score.

At this point, I put under long-deserved scrutiny the three Indian women, treated as factual by all latter-day historians. Pilcher's February 5, 1838, report to William Clark described them as Arikaras who had been living with the Pawnees but who wanted to visit relatives who had been living in the Mandan village "for some years passed [*sic*]."[141] The women "asked and received permission to go up on the boat to join their tribe," but once on board, "they all took the disease and were much afflicted with it when they passed my agency and I was informed that they had not recovered from it when they reached the Mandan villages some four hundred miles above."[142] Even though he had personally been aboard the *St. Peter's*, and, given the situation, been in medical mode, besides, Pilcher was working here from secondhand reports ("I was informed . . .") in discussing these women.

No other evidence of these Arikara women exists.

Zip. Zero. Nada.

Nothing produced at the time mentions them. They did not appear in Pilcher's letter of May 30, 1837, written *from aboard* the *St. Peter's* and discussing the small-pox then raging on the boat.[143] They were not mentioned in Pilcher's letters of June 30 or July 1, 1837, as the epidemic unfolded.[144] They were not talked of in Fulkerson's letter of September 20, 1837, announcing the epidemic to General Clark, in which he—*the Arikara and Mandan agent at Fort Clark*—merely said, "It is with regret that I have to inform you that the smallpox has broken out in this country and is sweeping all before it—unless it is checked in its mad career I would not be surprised if it wiped the Mandan and Rickaree [Arikara] Tribes of Indians clean from the face of the earth."[145] Jacob Halsey never mentioned them in his November 2, 1837, letter written from Fort Pierre to Pratte, Chouteau (d/b/a the American Fur Company) in St. Louis.[146] Missionary Samuel Allis, also aboard the *St. Peter's*, never mentioned them in his correspondence, including his letter of May 31, 1837, written from Bellevue, the Pawnee post.[147]

The Arikara women are also never mentioned in any of the other immediate, secondary material, inscribed in 1838. Although stars of his letter of February 5, 1838, to Superintendent William Clark, the women were never mentioned in Pilcher's official 1838 report over Arikara and Mandan issues sent to the Commissioner of Indian Affairs for the fatal years 1837–1838, a report the Commissioner published for Congress in November 1838.[148] Neither did Indian Agent Dougherty mention the women in his contribution to that same Commissioner's report.[149] None of the missionaries, including Dunbar, who was aboard the *St. Peter's*, mentioned the Arikara women in their 1838 reports on the epidemic.[150]

More importantly, there is absolutely no mention in Chardon's on-the-spot, day-by-day Fort Clark journal of the three Arikara women at his Arikara and

Mandan fort. The only mention Chardon makes of *any* disembarking woman, at the time or later, concerns the wife of "one of the Principal Cheifs" of the "Mandans & Rees" (as in the original). The chief's wife, traveling with her children, was not even named as Arikara. From his entry, she could just as easily have been Mandan.[151] The only other Arikara woman mentioned by Chardon was Marguerite Marie, and she survived until at least May 18, 1838, when she and Chardon parted ways, apparently with some acrimony, as can be surmised from the snide tone of his two journal entries on the split.[152] Although Chardon did record that "all hands" were "a Frolicking" on June 19, just after the steamboat arrived, nowhere did he mention three, scabby Arikara women hot-footing it straight from the *St. Peter's* to the drunken party.[153]

In fact, there is no record of *any* woman at the frolic. Chardon would hardly have let Marguerite Marie go "a Frolicking" with the "hands." It is beyond belief that the shaken chief's wife, who had just seen her children through an onboard outbreak of smallpox and who, upon leaving the boat, "told a fine tale against the Whites," would have gone "a Frolicking" with those same "Whites" that very night.[154] Nevertheless, assuming that Marguerite Marie tended young Chardon, she and the chief's wife are the closest things anywhere in the primary sources to the putative Arikara women of Pilcher's 1838 letter, and Chardon nowhere links the two real women together.

These are stunning omissions from the most on-the-spot records extant. If the three shadowy Arikara women are to receive *all* blame for instigating the epidemic among the Mandans and Arikaras around Fort Clark, as per the 20th-century stories told by Dollar, Trimble, and Robertson, one might hope that *some* direct account of their very existence appeared *somewhere* in the primary record.[155] Failing any such account, the portrait—and worse, the acceptance—of scabby-faced, a-frolicking Arikara women owes a great deal to racist minstrelsy for its power, but nothing whatsoever to the primary sources for its veracity.

The only direct record of three Indian women aboard the *St. Peter's* comes from Francesco Arese, who saw the women personally. His firsthand travelogue, taken down as events transpired, recorded matters very differently from Pilcher's secondhand account. "The evening" of the day the *St. Peter's* left Fort Leavenworth, he said, "we called at a post of the American Fur Company and landed the boss of the trading station, which is on the river bank."[156] The Indians of that fort "flooded" the boat, greeting the fort's *bourgeois,*

> affectionately, wringing his hand and calling him "Papá, papá." They played cards with great enthusiasm and even passion, and remained on board very late that night; and three young Indian women remained on board all night! . . . and with the consent of the chief of the tribe. It was the tribe of Kickapoos.[157]

Arese's horror at the women's nocturnal habits must be read in tandem with his earlier tsk-tsking over "those wretches," or Natives in contact with traders, "who had adopted no part of civilization except its liquor, its gunpowder, and its s——*." [158]

Arese's translator noted that the dash appeared in the original manuscript, a common tactic of squeamish 19th-century writers for simultaneously making yet obscuring obscene references, here, to sex. The women were on board, Arese thought, as prostitutes, although his entry makes it more likely that they were playing cards. Also, the permission granted and received was that of their *chief,* not that of Pratte, Chouteau. Finally, according to Arese, rather than being aboard for the whole trip, the women's stay on board was of one night's duration. Along with annuity distribution, this card game might help to explain the subsequent outbreak of smallpox among the Pawnees, but it does not address the situation at Fort Clark.

It is impossible that both the Pilcher and the Arese accounts are correct. Either the women were Arikaras who boarded at Fort Leavenworth to continue on, all poxy, to the Mandan village, or they were Kickapoos who came aboard to play cards for one night only, the stop after Fort Leavenworth. My money is on Arese, an eyewitness who had absolutely no motive to massage the record, whereas, by 1838, Pilcher was under considerable pressure to explain just how the epidemic had gotten so out of hand. The tale that Pilcher later pasted together was based on hearsay, most probably from the notoriously unreliable Fulkerson, who was the subagent at Fort Clark. In common with all 19th-century settler "truthiness" about the epidemic, this myth blamed the Indians for it, without offering any real evidence.

The other, major Indian-blaming story charged that some "Indian," usually given as a "chief" but never actually named and later given as belonging to various nations, stole a poxy blanket. This tale began again with Fulkerson, here in a letter he wrote on September 20, 1837 to General William Clark, in an attempt to explain the epidemic. Like the Arikara women, the stolen blanket appears in but one letter. Also, as with Pilcher's attempt, it blames the hated Arikaras.[159] Interestingly, aside from both fingering the Arikaras, the stories of how the disease spread are not otherwise in accord; indeed, they are at wide variance, with the one talking loose, poxy women and the other talking blanket-stealing chiefs.

Like Pilcher's story of the Arikara women, Fulkerson's stolen-blanket tale lacks a shred of corroborating evidence. Jacob Halsey's letter to Pratte, Chouteau, dated November 2, 1837, from Fort Pierre, mentioned no stolen blankets.[160] Pilcher's letters of May 30, 1837, June 30, 1837, and July 1, 1837 included no stolen blankets.[161] Neither Allis's letter of May 30, 1837, nor Dunbar's report of 1838 named stolen blankets.[162] Chardon's Fort Clark journal mentioned no stolen blankets. Larpenteur's Fort Union account did mention stolen *horses,* but no stolen blankets.[163] An account from George Catlin, originally published in 1841, and which he recorded based on a personal conversation he had had with "Messrs M'Kenzie, Mithchell, and others," claimed that upon arriving at Fort Clark, Mandan "chiefs and others *were allowed to come on board,* by which means the disease got ashore" (italics mine). In this version, the chiefs were knowingly allowed to have been exposed through fraternization with smallpox carriers, not through blankets, stolen or otherwise.[164]

Well after the fact, however, stolen-blanket accounts bubbled up as THE explanation of the epidemic. Audubon recorded it secondhand in 1843, supposedly quoting Chardon but wrongly giving the steamboat as the *Assiniboin*.[165] Stolen blanket accounts then continued with Thomas Farnham, also writing in 1843, misrecording the year as 1828, and blaming the *Blackfeet*, an "error" his editor corrected to the *Mandans*.[166] From there, stolen blankets turned up in Bernard Pratt in 1879; Hiram Martin Chittenden in 1902; Glendolin Wagner and William Allen in 1933; Tex Bandera in 1938; and Bernard De Voto in 1947, just to name the most high-profile sources.[167]

It is therefore noteworthy that General Clark did not believe Fulkerson's report, perhaps because, first, he had heard from Indian Agent William Hitchcock that blankets had been rejected by the plains peoples in 1837, and second, because he had Pilcher's annuity requisitions, which did not mention a stolen blanket.[168] There is literally *nothing else* in the documents inscribed on or near the spot to suggest any blanket theft. I therefore agree with Clyde Dollar that the blanket affair was cooked up after the fact and is not to be credited.[169]

The only importance of the settlers' stolen-blanket fable is that it focused upon *blankets* as the mode of smallpox transmission. Blankets and cloth meant for clothing were regular annuity items, with British and French suppliers vying heavily to corner the supply contracts. American Fur Company records frequently discussed the acquisition of blankets for trade. For instance, a December 24, 1836 letter from Chardon to Pratte, Chouteau stated that it was not in Chardon's "power to give you any idea of the quantity of Blkts" that would be "wanted" for "the next years [sic] trade," and advised that headquarters therefore supply Fort Clark through Fort Pierre, where he planned to meet the *St. Peter's*. Chardon added that blankets were "the principal article of trade" at his fort.[170] On December 13, 1836, Milton Sublette and Thomas Fitzpatrick were squabbling about blanket supplies, with Sublette turning to American Fur for help for 1837.[171] On April 16, 1837, Pierre Chouteau wrote to P. D. Papin that he was sending "French blankets."[172]

The American Fur Company definitely bought trade blankets in 1837, the majority of them from the English manufacturer, Benjamin Gott. However, rival French manufacturers were also selling blankets to the American Fur Company, and in increasing numbers. Although French manufacturers eventually squeezed Gott out entirely in 1839, over the winter of 1836–1837, they were still very much vying for American Fur Company business, and their late delivery of blankets was partly responsible for the delayed departure of the *St. Peter's*.[173] The 1837 shipment to the high plains was, then, a mixture of Gott's English and his French rivals' blankets and cloth. U.S. Indian agents also referred to blankets as annuity and gift items. For instance, a draft letter marked "Unofficial" and dated March 21, 1838, from Indian Agent William "Hitchcock" to C. A. Harris, noted that blankets were used as gifts, while Chardon's letter of December 24, 1836 mentioned blanket requisitions for the following spring.[174]

It is clear that, although not stolen by the Indians, annuity and trade blankets were implicated in the epidemic. In his 1879 interview with the *Missouri Republican*, Captain Pratte stated:

This calamity among the Indians was altogether the fault of an agent. There was a young man who had the small-pox in Hagerstown, Md. He was a trapper and had been in the employ of Pratte, Chouteau & Co. He wrote to a gentleman in St. Louis [Pratte, Chouteau headquarters] to send him money. The money was not sent, and out of revenge the young man bundled up some clothes with directions that they be put on board of a steamer, and left [at] Fort Pierre.

Jim Beckwith, the renowned desperado, went upon the boat and used the bundle which was put on board as a pillow. He contracted, in consequence, the small-pox.[175]

It is perhaps worth recalling at this point Chardon's preplanned journey to meet the boat at Fort Pierre before it docked at Fort Clark. The account that Catlin received from McKenzie in the late 1830s and published in 1841 claimed that the *St. Peter's* officials had "two of their crew sick with the disease when it approached the Upper Missouri."[176] Although they were not technically crew, Pratte's unnamed "young man" was one William P. ("Bill") May, and his desperado, "Jim Beckwith," was James P. Beckwourth. Both men were very well known characters in their time.

Pratte's placing of a smallpox epidemic in Maryland is verifiable. Despite a door-to-door "inquiry and vaccination" program among the settlers, smallpox had gotten abroad from the port of Baltimore in the spring of 1836, leaking the disease to Emmitsburg, Maryland, in the person of a slave.[177] (Emmitsburg is about 50 miles northwest of Baltimore.) A general vaccination push in Emmitsburg was stalled by an inability to secure smallpox vaccine.[178] Reported deaths in Baltimore (one of whose smallpox hospitals burned down in 1836) mounted through 1837 to 52.[179] In the meantime, smallpox had peaked in New York in 1835, and in Philadelphia, in 1834, whereas Boston remained almost entirely free of smallpox until 1839.[180] Importantly here, Hagerstown is about 100 miles northwest of Baltimore, in line with Emmitsburg, making the story that Bill May acquired the infected articles in Hagertown quite plausible. Whatever May's mood (or orders) when he did it, he seeded the smallpox articles on the *St. Peter's*.

There are several accounts of the Mackinaw boats trailing the *St. Peter's*. Fort and annuity supplies were loaded onto them for the trek up the Missouri, allowing deck space for passengers. When and where the Mackinaws were attached to the *St. Peter's* is unrecorded, but for the first run of the *Assiniboin*, Captain Pratte stated that its keel boat was attached at Pittsburgh.[181] It was clear from Chardon's journal that the two Mackinaws were in tow when the *St. Peter's* arrived at Fort Pierre on May 18, and that they were unloaded at Fort Clark on June 19, 1837.[182] It is unclear whether Beckwourth was sleeping on a Mackinaw or on board the *St. Peter's* when he used the bundle as his pillow, but it is not unlikely that, in preference to the filthy floor of the steamboat, many passengers slept on the Mackinaw boat's soft and clean loads of annuity blankets and cloth. Obviously, passengers other than Beckwourth caught smallpox, either from him or from shared sleeping arrangements.

Importantly, and completely independently of Pratte's account, John P. Cabanné and Albert Culbertson corroborated Pratte's story. An American Fur Company associate in St. Louis, Cabanné wrote to Pierre Chouteau in New York on December 22, 1837, recounting the smallpox outbreak, and commenting that the "news from the Upper Missouri is frightful. This May, the author of all its ills, is he not the most horrible and the most vile scoundrel, if, as is said, he did it on purpose"?[183] A fort director of the American Fur Company attached to Fort McKenzie and later, Fort Union, Culbertson also named Bill May as the culprit who had deliberately placed clothing infected with smallpox on the *St. Peter's* while it was at St. Louis, purportedly in a fit of pique at having been denied passage as an American Fur Company employee.[184]

In 1938, Tex Bandera claimed, with no citation, that *Pratte* had identified Bill May. Bandera might have conflated the Cabanné and Culbertson stories with Pratte's version (or known of a fourth account, since lost), but clearly, Bill May was still associated with the tale in 1938.[185] Since that time, both Cabanné's letter and Pratte's clear statement have simply been ignored, while Culbertson's account has never been discussed in conjunction with Pratte or Cabanné. Instead, Culbertson's story has been treated in grand isolation and then dismissed, either on the claim that May was not in the employ of the American Fur Company in 1837, or on the assumption that the timelines recorded in fort documents did not square with Culbertson's story.

If Bill May were truly unemployed and disgruntled, it is hard to tell from prior or subsequent events. Two Pratte, Chouteau vouchers, both dated May 16, 1836, from Kenneth McKenzie, the founder and long-time director of Fort Union, authorized payment to William P. May in the amounts of $75 and $370.94.[186] Obviously, May was on the payroll in 1836. May was also on the payroll all of 1837, as is shown by mentions of him in Chardon's Fort Clark journal:

- On April 4, 1836, May set out trapping from Fort Clark, with the intention of ending up in St. Louis.[187]
- On July 20, 1837, May is recorded, as having arrived from the "Little Missouri" River.[188]
- Chardon subsequently trusted May to go out news gathering on August 16, 1837, from which May returned on August 23.[189]
- On August 25, 1837, May again went to the Hidatsa village.[190]
- On November 26, 1837, Chardon sent May to Fort Union with letters.[191]
- On December 20, 1837, May returned from Fort Union, minus three horses that were reportedly taken by the Assiniboins.[192]

Bill May was unquestionably an employee in good standing of the American Fur Company from May 1836 through December 1837.

As part of the "disgruntled" story, Culbertson claimed that Captain Pratte of the *St. Peter's* had refused May passage for the run up the Missouri from St. Louis.[193] This hardly seems plausible. First, Pratte made no such mention in his account.

Second, while on business, employees of the American Fur Company were regularly granted passage on its steamboats. Third, and most importantly, the company had every incentive to retain its long-time employees. A letter dated April 16, 1836, from Pierre Chouteau in St. Louis to P. D. Papin at Fort Pierre, written in French with a translation accompanying it in the microform of the Chouteau Family Collection, stated that it was "impossible" for John B. Sarpy, a company agent, to hire the number of men Papin had requested due to "exorbitant" costs, which "*hommes de service*" were taking advantage of to demand high wages. (Literally translating as *servicemen*, "*hommes de service*" meant seasoned hands.) "If you have any good men," Chouteau advised, "try to keep them up there, even paying a little more than usual, because if they come down here they will ask twice as much."[194] Given this directive, it is highly doubtful that the company would have risked alienating an *homme de service* like May by denying him a steamboat ride. The "disgruntled" portion of the story thus seems a later fabrication. Certainly, the most on-the-spot source, Cabanné, mentioned nothing of the sort. Since he deplored May in his letter of December 22, 1837, had he known of any disgruntlement, he would have cited it.

Another objection to May's having had anything to do with the smallpox articles is the logistical objection, first raised by Bernard De Voto in 1947. Referring to the Chardon journal entry of July 20, 1837, mentioning that May had just arrived from the "Little Missouri" River, De Voto observed that May could "hardly have got to the Little Missouri not quite two weeks after the steamboat did."[195] De Voto's objection, credited by subsequent scholars, rested on the assumption that the name "Little Missouri" referred to the same river in 1837 as it does today. It did not. What Chardon and his traders called the "Little Missouri" is what is today called the Bad River.[196] In other words, on 20 July 1837, Bill May arrived at Fort Clark from the *Bad* River. It is entirely plausible that he could have arrived at Fort Clark via the Bad River two weeks after the steamboat, dissolving De Voto's objection to Culberton's story.[197]

The next standing objection to the Bill May story, first mouthed by George Catlin in an 1841 account citing Kenneth McKenzie as his source, has been that the American Fur Company was unlikely to have undercut its own business by destroying its Indian suppliers and customers.[198] Despite historians' assumptions that the American Fur Company's bottom line suffered from the epidemic, documentary evidence shows the opposite. The epidemic *aided* the company in what would always have been its final years on the Upper Missouri. As Bandera noted in 1938, despite the downturn in beaver and muskrat returns—ongoing since 1832—the buffalo robe trade skyrocketed for the couple years immediately following the epidemic.[199] On 12 July 1837, just as the epidemic was taking off, Pratte, Chouteau correspondence from St. Louis anticipated the collection of buffalo robes "to be greater than in 1836."[200] Although the company feared low prices for them, on 6 September 1837, the New York office informed Chouteau in St. Louis that prices on the robes were exceeding expectations, and the robes themselves were selling briskly.[201]

On 28 November 1837, four months into the epidemic, Chardon of Fort Clark notified Papin that the "whole country north and south is one sollid mass of Buffaloe [sic]" with "no Indians to kill them" but that those remaining would "make a good hunt." Indeed, in the same letter, he noted that surviving Arikaras had "a quantity of Robes."[202] The lower Indian population on the high plains meant that there were fewer Indians using the lucrative buffalo robes for themselves, allowing more to go to settlers and Europeans. Ten thousand robes were taken by the American Fur Company at Major Alexander Culbertson's Fort McKenzie immediately *following* the epidemic. In the years shortly thereafter, that total increased to 20,000 buffalo robes per season.[203] If the epidemic hurt the American Fur Company, as much cannot be discerned from its records.

Enter James Beckwourth. A strange silence also attends not only the whereabouts, but also the very existence, of this other American Fur Company employee, so central to the tale. James Beckwourth (whose name was also frequently rendered as "Jim Beckwith") is surprisingly nameless in Pilcher's 5 February 1838 letter about the outbreak of the epidemic on the *St. Peter's,* identified only as "a mulatto."[204] Why this should have been so is quite puzzling. In his time (and for some time afterwards), Beckwourth was as notorious as Daniel Boone or Davy Crockett; Pratte even termed him "the renowned desperado."[205] He was certainly known to the fur traders of all of the Upper Missouri companies, as well as to the local U.S. Indian agents, as an American Fur Company man with ties to the Crows. All the main actors in the 1837 drama would have known him by sight. His published memoirs are, moreover, still a staple among scholars.[206] Thus, *why* Beckwourth should suffer a sudden onset of anonymity, but *only* for historians of the 1837 run of *St. Peter's,* is worthy of a lingering look.

Galloping racism accounts for most of earlier historians' glowering suspicions about Beckwourth, but what are the reasons for the averted gaze from his very name today? In his revisionist take on the 1837 smallpox epidemic in 1977, Clyde Dollar (who blithely referred to "the primitive mind" of the Indians) confined himself to fingering an unnamed "mulatto" as the man who came down with smallpox while aboard the *St. Peter's,* swallowing Pilcher's highly questionable 5 February 1838 letter whole.[207] I could not find that Michael K. Trimble mentioned Beckwourth at all. In *Rotting Face,* R. G. Robertson mentioned Beckwourth exactly once, in his final chapter, where he dismissed him as a "notorious liar," calling his story a "fantasy" while citing De Voto's 1947 verdict that the Beckwourth connection was just "rumor and folklore."[208] However, De Voto based this sweeping dismissal on nothing other than a hyperbolic supposition that Beckwourth "got blamed for nearly everything that happened west of the Missouri," so that he was "blamed" for the epidemic, as well.[209]

This is hardly scholarly, yet De Voto was Robertson's only source on the matter, and, in a rather surprising lapse, Robertson did not even attribute the "notorious liar" quip to William Loren Katz's *refutation* of the aspersion in 1969.[210] Beckwourth's *Life and Adventures* are absent from Robertson's bibliography, as are Frances Victor's *River of the West,* Osborne Russell's *Journal of a Trapper,* Elinor Wilson's *Jim Beckwourth,* and Stanley Vestal's two works, *Joe Meek* and *Jim Bridger,* let alone mentions of Beckwourth in Chardon's *Journal*. (This list does not exhaust the possible sources on Beckwourth.) Such a rousing lack of curiosity here is puzzling, because, elsewhere, Robertson performed sometimes heroic research for *Rotting Face*.

As an emancipated slave, Beckwourth was certainly a "mulatto," the racist slur of the day (from "mule"), denoting the supposedly sterile African-European interspecies "hybrid." Beckwourth was one of 13 children of a Revolutionary War major and a slave woman, so he was clearly a mixed-blood.[211] That he was the "mulatto" who came down with smallpox during the trip is beyond doubt, because Bernard Pratte identified him by name.[212] In light of the Pratte, Chouteau concern, cited above, on the importance of hanging onto all seasoned employees to the exclusion of hiring new ones at high rates, Captain Pratte would certainly have refused the demand to put Beckwourth off the boat.

That Beckwourth was an American Fur Company employee is also certain. A voucher from Kenneth McKenzie, dated July 21, 1836, authorized payment to Jim Beckwourth ("Beckwith"), as being attached to the American Fur Company's primary post, Fort Union, in the amount of $341.75.[213] Like May, Beckwourth would have had to travel to the St. Louis headquarters of Pratte, Chouteau to cash in his voucher.[214] In addition, Chardon recorded giving him "letters to Mr Papin" to take along with him to St. Louis in 1836.[215]

Given this corroboration, trek to St. Louis in the fall of 1836 was certainly what Beckwourth did, although he gave the amount of his "order upon the company" as $7,800, a 23–fold increase over the amount of the voucher on record.[216] Beckwourth also claimed that, when the fur company would not, he had personally staked five traders at Fort Cass, who returned him $5,000 on his investment.[217] This money (or vouchers for it) would also have traveled with him to St. Louis.

Suddenly, unlike his tale so far, from the time Beckwourth arrived in St. Louis in 1836 through the year 1837 to 1838, his narrative becomes confusing and vague. That he went to St. Louis in 1836 and then returned to the Upper Missouri in the early summer of 1837 is clear. That he skedaddled to Florida that early fall is also known. However, just what Beckwourth was doing in between those times and his motives for hastily leaving the Crows in the summer of 1837, never to return to them again, are anything but clear.[218]

While in St. Louis, Beckwourth met with Pierre Chouteau, head of Pratte, Chouteau, and more than once. Shortly after arriving, he went to the company headquarters to deliver the Papin letters that Chardon had entrusted to him and, presumably, to cash in his voucher. While at the offices on this business, he came down too ill to walk with an unnamed malady that eventually confined him to bed. (I should like very much to know what the problem was—a reaction to smallpox vaccination, perhaps?—but all sources are silent here.) Chouteau personally drove the ailing Beckwourth home in his carriage, a signal favor from a rich tycoon to a lowly mixed-blood man.[219]

This cordial relationship continued in another meeting a few days later. "Captain [William L.] Sublet[te], [Thomas] Fitzpatrick, and myself happened to meet in the office of Mr. Chouteau" of Pratte, Chouteau, Beckwourth recorded.[220] In addition,

Beckwourth met with his first, now retired, boss, William H. Ashley, the militia general who had started the Rocky Mountain Fur Company in 1822–1823.[221]

This was heady company, with everyone mentioned having been a high-powered functionary of the fur trade, movers and shakers far above Beckwourth's pay grade. Sublette, of Sublette & Company and Sublette & Campbell, was the founder of Sublette's Trace, used by the American Fur Company's 1837 wagon train. Like Sublette, Fitzpatrick, of Fitzpatrick & Company, was actually a competitor of American Fur. How Beckwourth just "happened to meet" with a gathering that included all of the active fur company moguls of the Upper Missouri, is more than a little curious. Why these business *rivals* were meeting at Pratte, Chouteau is even more intriguing. If the F.B.I. had that much on the mob, it would move in fast.

Beckwourth explained the meeting by claiming to have learned that the traders at Fort Cass had told the Crows that he was dead, rousing them to a war of vengeance against the Upper Missouri traders. In fear that its $100,000 worth of goods at the forts were at risk, company bigwigs had begged him to return to quell the war.[222] For his trouble, Beckwourth demanded and received from Pratt, Chouteau a payment of $5,000. He then hired two men to help him save the day, for $2,500 combined pay. Beckwourth also "procured" horses for the trip.[223] They would have run him around $300. The financing here accords interestingly with his earlier-referenced $7,800 "order upon the company."[224] Although I did not see any such voucher in the archives, $5,000 + $2,500 + $300 = $7,800.

The identities of Beckwourth's hired men are vague. One, he named as "Papen."[225] Pierre Didier Papin was a premiere member of the "French Company," a one-time rival of the American Fur Company that had taken over stock in the American Fur Company in 1830.[226] Chardon had forwarded letters to P. D. Papin through Beckwourth on his 1836 trip. On 16 April 1837, a week before the *St. Peter's* left St. Louis, P. D. Papin was at Fort Pierre.[227] Given his known presence at Fort Pierre and the "Mssr." honorific of Chardon's July 18, 1837 entry, Pierre Didier Papin was almost certainly the Papin half of the "Mess[rs] Papin & Halsey on Board" the *St. Peter's* when it docked at Fort Clark.[228] Another personage well above Beckwourth's pay grade, Pierre Didier Papin would hardly have acted as the underling of a lowly American Fur employee like Beckwourth. However, there was a second Papin in the wings, "a son of Mr. Pappen," Beckwourth said, called "Joseph Pappen," who had been entrusted to Beckwourth's care during his trip to St. Louis in 1836.[229] It seems more likely to me that Beckwourth would have been able to hire the son, Joseph, than the father, Pierre Didier, and that Joseph Papin might well have been swayed by Beckwourth's offer of $1,500, a tidy sum in 1837, and $500 more than was offered to the other man.[230]

Many possibilities exist for the identity of the second, unnamed man hired for $1,000, but I have wondered whether he was Bill May, a beaver trapper, fellow "freeman" (that is, free "mulatto"), and company colleague, also just then in St. Louis and also just returned to the Upper Missouri in 1837.[231] Given the failure of the beaver trade, May might well have needed the income. However, May had disembarked at Fort Pierre, arriving individually at Fort Clark two weeks later, as recorded by Chardon.[232] Another possibility is the interpreter Antoine Garreau, whom Beckwourth mentioned as having been with him on the trip to St. Louis in 1836.[233] On July 13, 1837, Chardon at Fort Clark sent Garreau out on a "discovery" mission, so that Garreau had clearly returned to the fort from St. Louis, most probably on the 1837 run of the *St. Peter's*.[234]

Parts of Beckwourth's story are clearly questionable. First, although Beckwourth claimed credit for having founded Fort Cass in 1832 and did use the fort on company business, it was actually founded by Samuel Tulloch.[235] Often called "Tulluch's Fort," it was abandoned in 1835, so that, if Beckwourth were active there through 1836, as he claimed, he operated out of a ruin.[236] It certainly could not have been the "fort" that he positioned "within" the "grasp" of the supposedly angry Crows in the summer of 1837.[237] Second, there is no corroboration anywhere that I can find in the documents of a Crow war breaking out at this time against the traders, so that Beckwourth's purported mission to quell a nonexistent war is obviously spurious.

The story grows really dicey upon Beckwourth's 1837 trip to the Upper Missouri. Beckwourth claimed to have traveled upriver as far as "Fort Clarke" and gone overland from there into Crow country.[238] Shortly after arriving among the Crows in July 1837, Beckwourth mounted an assault on the Blackfeet, and then deserted his adoptive people, the Crows, who had made him a major war chief and among whom he had a total of three wives, one of whom bore him a child he claimed to have "loved."[239] Leaving could not have been easy. He told the disappointed Crows that he had to resume "negotiations" in St. Louis that he wanted "to complete," talks he had not "had time to finish" before leaving on the *St. Peter's*.[240] Then, he high-tailed it back to St. Louis, never again to return to the Upper Missouri.

Despite having just given the reason for his departure, Beckwourth went on to cite three more, equally squishy reasons, aimed at his "civilized" reader:

1. He had tired of "savage life."[241]
2. He was engaged to marry a "fair dulceana" in St. Louis.[242]
3. The "interests of civilization" required him elsewhere.[243]

In St. Louis again, he directly signed on for service among the Seminoles; no marriage took place, and the call of western civilization rings fairly hollow from a mixed-race African-European man, who belonged to yet a third group, the Crows. In 1837, such credentials would have made him target practice for western civilization, not one of its purveyors.

Immediately upon Beckwourth's return to St. Louis from the high plains, Sublette obligingly recommended him to General Edmund Pendleton Gaines, who had just recently returned from his inspection trip of Fort Leavenworth. General Gaines was just then "raising a company of men familiar with Indian habits" for his Seminole campaign in Florida.[244] Brother of George Strother Gaines, General Gaines was a deep celebrity in St. Louis, fêted at a gala dinner held there in his honor on 24 January 1838. Covered twice in the *Missouri Republican,* the event included toasts lauding both his service to the country and himself, personally, as "The Hero of Fort Erie" and "the Champion of the defenceless [sic] and suffering inhabitants of Florida."[245] Gaines held the highest army offices of Commander, alternately as head of the eastern and western divisions.[246] Gaines promptly signed up Beckwourth for his Florida campaign, with "the commission of captain in the service of Uncle Sam."[247] It was almost unheard-of at the time to bestow such rank, with its attendant officer's pay, on a "mulatto."

Thus, once more, Beckwourth is shown in the presence of great men, being given special treatment, this time, just after the smallpox outbreak. Why should Sublette have aided Beckwourth so mightily with one of the top men in the U.S. Army? What had Beckwourth done to garner a commission as a captain in the U.S. Army? Was this appointment, not the specious "dulceana," the conclusion of Beckwourth's incomplete "negotiations"? Taken in conjunction with later governmental and company coyness about naming Beckwourth openly, Beckwourth's convoluted, highly glossed account suggests that whatever was afoot was being deliberately obscured. Just what that might have been was fairly common knowledge in the 19th century, frequently repeated, and cited in works into the mid-20th century. By the late 20th century, however, it had dropped mysteriously from view. Perhaps the story was skirted for its racist brutality, for it does little credit to anyone involved.

A mountain man and wagon train guide also fairly famous in his day, one Jim Bridger, told a tale deemed hilariously colorful in the 19th century. Bridger claimed that Jim Beckwourth came back among the Crows just long enough to hand out smallpox blankets to the Crows' traditional enemies, the Blackfeet, before absconding from the scene of the crime. Shortly after the smallpox distribution, Bridger's wagon train was forced to fight (and whup) the Blackfeet. An 1870 source tells the rest of the story this way:

> The following day the camp [wagon train] reached the village of Little-Robe, a chief of the Peagans [Piegan], who held a talk with Bridger, complaining that his nation were all perishing from the small-pox which had been given to them by the whites. Bridger was able to explain to Little-Robe his error; inasmuch as although the disease might have originated among the whites, it was communicated to the Blackfeet by Jim Beckwith, a negro, and principal chief of their enemies the Crows. This unscrupulous wretch had caused two infected articles to be taken from a Mackinaw boat, up from St. Louis, and disposed of to the Blackfeet—whence the horrible scourage [sic] under which they were suffering.[248]

In 1946, Stanley Vestal identified the two "articles" as "two blankets" and summed the story up a little differently, closing it with: "Bridger pointed out with emphasis that Beckwourth was not only a chief of the enemy Crows, but he was a negro, and therefore *not* a white man" (italics in the original).[249] In 1952, Vestal rendered Bridger's parting rejoinder thus: "Blame the Negro, blame the

Crows, not the whites!"[250] With Bridger apparently attributing such deeds to Beckwourth on the mountain-man circuit, Beckwourth would have had every reason to have distanced himself from Bridger, were he telling lies.[251] However, Bridger and Beckwourth remained lifelong friends, with Bridger handing over to Beckwourth the power of attorney to "dispose of" some of his property in Denver in the early 1860s.[252]

Although these Beckwourth stories have been cheerfully segregated from other evidence for discarding as "folklore," the days are gone when the accounts of workers and "Negros" can simply be waved off on the grounds of the low race and class of their tellers. As firsthand accounts, their stories merit the same attention as those of the self-styled gentlemen. These stories also deserve attention for their close fit with the known facts of the case, closer than the fit of the stories of Majors Pilcher and Fulkerson. Otherwise inscrutable scraps and tidbits in the record fall into place when combined with the Beckwourth tale, especially the instructions in Pierre Chouteau's April 16, 1837 letter to P.D. Papin. Chouteau noted that he had "urged Pratte" (presumably Captain Pratte of the *St. Peter's*) to be "very particular" about the "delivery" of Papin's "Merchandise for the Petit Missouri and to the Mandannes."[253] (Again, the Petit, or Little Missouri, is now called the Bad River.) Captain Pratte had a high reputation for competence, so the special directions here indicated that something out-of-the-ordinary was in play. In combination with the coy "Merchandise" admonition, Pratte's refusal to strand Beckwourth takes on new and scary meaning, as do the Papin letters Beckwourth carried to St. Louis.

Moreover, other puzzling loose ends make sense: the pre-smallpox meeting between Beckwourth and multiple fur company heads in St. Louis; Beckwourth's hasty return to St. Louis immediately after meeting with the Blackfeet; Beckwourth's introduction to and employment by General Gaines; the Sublette-Fitzpatrick blanket squabble referred to Pratte, Chouteau; General Gaines's July 9, 1837 inspection tour of Fort Leavenworth and gala dinner in St. Louis; Chardon's preplanned visit to Fort Pierre; and, possibly, the quick dissolution of Chardon's marriage to Marguerite Marie.

In addition to the May-Beckwourth events, U.S. Indian Agents Dougherty, Fulkerson, and Pilcher distributed annuities and gifts at their various agencies in 1837. Blankets were a regular part of governmental annuities and gifts, and there is no question that blankets came up the Missouri that year, because the Hitchcock letter of March 21, 1838 clearly indicated that blankets were extended to, with some rejected by, the Upper Missouri people. Hitchcock noted that the "principal portion of the presents" for upcoming treaty talks could "readily be supplied from the goods rejected by various Missouri tribes." Fearing that, left to their own devices, the Indians would cherry-pick "blankets," leaving other goods behind, he discussed presents that "summer" for, specifically, "the Potto[ies]" or Pottawattomis.[254]

The Hitchcock letter makes it clear that these were *surplus* blankets left-over from the Upper Missouri distributions, making it curious, then, that when the *St. Peter's* first arrived at Fort Clark, Fulkerson claimed he had "nothing to give his red children."[255] Events grow more curious when, although lacking gifts on 19 June, just eight days later, on June 28, 1837, when the *St. Peter's* passed Fort Clark on its return trip to St. Louis, Major Fulkerson suddenly "distributed out a few Presents to the Rees," that is, the Arikaras, who lived near Fort Clark with the Mandans.[256]

Importantly, Fulkerson did not make the only governmental distribution of 1837. In his letter of February 5, 1838 to Superintendent William Clark, Major Pilcher stated that, at Council Bluffs, "annuities for the Ottos [Otos], Mahas [Omahas] & Pawnees were put out of the boat, and the Agent for those tribes"—Dougherty—"left her at the same time."[257] Although Pilcher does not expressly state it, on May 31, 1837, the Pawnee missionary Allis wrote that the Pawnees had received their annuities and left "(for there [sic] villages) last Wednesday."[258] Although some treaty-signing Otos, Omahas, and Pawnees had been vaccinated, the Pawnees, especially, still contracted smallpox that summer.[259] There is no reason to assume that non-treaty Otos and Omahas did not contract smallpox, as well, especially since, according to Larpenteur and McCoy, the vaccine was no good.[260] Besides, Cass had ordered that non-treaty peoples not be vaccinated.

In the same letter, Pilcher added that he "continued on to my Agency"—the "Sioux Agency" at Big Bend—"six hundred miles above, and there recevd [sic] from the boat and delivered the annuities due the Yankton & Sante Siouse [sic]."[261] At that point, Pilcher referred Clark to his earlier letters of June 10 and July 1, 1837 for details. Pilcher's June 10 letter gave the arrival date of the annuities at his Sioux Agency as June 5, 1837, adding that they were "immediately paid over to the Yankton & Santee, whose receipts" were forwarded to Captain Hichcock.[262] The letter of July 1 enclosed a "duplicate" abstract of "presents delivered to the Indians of this Agency" in "the quarter ending yesterday," or June 30, 1837.[263] Clearly, annuities and presents were handed out to the Indians at Council Bluffs, Fort Clark, and at Pilcher's Sioux Agency at Big Bend. In view of the epidemic, Hitchcock's letter of March 21, 1838 becomes chilling, in suggesting that high-plains annuity blankets, left-over from 1837, be distributed to the Pottawattomis in 1838.

It is worth pausing a moment to consider just what Majors Dougherty, Fulkerson, and Pilcher thought they were doing in distributing presents and annuities when, as Pilcher reported to Clark on June 10, 1837, "The Small Pox broke out on board the steamboat before she passed for[t] Leavenworth" with the disease "still" continuing "to rage" as of the date of his letter.[264] The fact that the Mackinaw boats were deliberately separated from the *St. Peter's* was of little consequence, since the separation was not effected until Fort McKenzie, a stop well after Fort Leavenworth and, indeed, the terminus of the run.[265] Separating the Mackinaws at that late date could not have protected anyone. No documents exist opening a window on the agents' thought processes, here, but later plausible deniability for starting the epidemic does spring to mind.

On June 28, 1837, Major Fulkerson made his distribution at Fort Clark.[266] On July 14, 1837, the first recorded smallpox victim, a "young Mandan," died at Fort Clark.[267]

From all the descriptions of the 1837–1838 epidemic, the type of smallpox involved was hemorrhagic, with a death rate among the unvaccinated of 95 percent.[268] According to Catlin's 1841 account, for instance, the "disease became so malignant that death ensued in a few hours after its attacks," so rapidly in fact, that "very many died in two or three hours after their attack, and in many cases without the appearance of the disease upon the skin."[269] It is with hemorrhagic smallpox that death can occur before the first rash appears, as well as any time after it does.[270] The smallpox rash typically appears 12 to 14 days after the disease is caught, although it can appear as late as 17 days from first exposure.[271]

Counting the day of the distribution, the time elapsed between Fulkerson's June 28, distribution of presents and the first known death from smallpox on July 14 was 17 days. This is within the standard incubation period, and conservatively assumes that the Mandan victim in question *immediately* partook of presents actually given to the Arikaras, not the Mandans. In all probability, the young Mandan shared in the "gift" one to three days later. This still places events within the standard incubation period.

Aside from incubation periods, other circumstantial evidence of a deliberate spread of smallpox should also include Chardon's nervousness surrounding the *St. Peter's* run in 1837. Not only did he assiduously track water levels in the Missouri that spring—the steamboat could not travel in water too shallow—but he also repeatedly and anxiously sent out for "news" or "discoveries." It is true that the steamboat was at least three weeks late, but Chardon's news anxiety continued *after* the *St. Peter's* had arrived, only to slacken, and suddenly, with the first death at Mandan.

As the incubation period of smallpox was closing after Fulkerson's distribution, Chardon's news quest peaked. On July10, he sent Toussaint Charbonneau to "collect news"; again on July 12, he noted "Nothing stirring, No News"; and on July 13, he "Sent Garreau out on discovery."[272] The next day, the Mandan died, and Chardon's news anxiety collapsed, with no further interest evinced until a report of smallpox was brought in on July 20, not coincidentally by Bill May.[273] After this, news reports sporadically indicated the levels of smallpox among the various Native nations, but Chardon's news lust had abated, with his entries incidental rather than sought.

Chardon was always an unapologetic Indian hater, as his journal showed, for instance noting the "sweet revenge" he took on them for his dead dog and calling the Arikaras the "horrid tribe."[274] As though the Arikaras did not have enough disease to contend with by February 6, 1838, Chardon cynically sent one of his men "down to the Ree camp, to be cured of the Venerial."[275] (This was a sneering reference to the Native American commonplace that being among the well could help cure the sick, especially through sexual relations.) Chardon certainly did not mourn the massive death rates that the epidemic occasioned, instead noting on September 19, 1837, with seeming satisfaction, "What a bande of RASCALS has been used up—" (as in original).[276] The effects of the epidemic on the surrounding nations did not unduly upset him.

The *St. Peter's* ran up to Fort Union, at the mouth of the Yellowstone River, where it connects with the Missouri. At that fort, fur company steamboats reversed course for the return trip to St. Louis. The fort bookkeeper, E. T. Denig, made some scattered references to the smallpox events, mostly ignored by scholars in favor of the primary source, Charles Larpenteur, a fur company employee at the fort. Larpenteur wrote both the occasional Fort Union journal, not kept daily in 1837, and a narrative of the 1837 epidemic, which he inserted into the journal. The original 1898 Elliot Coues edition, followed by the 1933 edition of Coues' version of Larpenteur's narrative, have been *the* sources for 20th-century scholars writing on the epidemic around Fort Union. In 2001, however, R. G. Robertson importantly discovered that Larpenteur's hard-to-access manuscript does not tell the same story as the easily acquired printed versions.

In the introduction to his 1898 offering, Coues claimed to have received a copy of the manuscript from a Dr. Washington Matthews (a U.S. Army surgeon), who had received it from Larpenteur's nephew.[277] Coues seemed to have had a guilty conscience about his changes, since he addressed the issue of editorial tinkering twice in his introduction. Following a noble gloss on the necessity of primary sources as a "great antiseptic to the ptomaine of tradition," Coues insisted that all he had done to the Larpenteur manuscript was "helped the author to express himself" grammatically, asserting that "the sense and sentiments" of the result were Larpenteur's "own, if the style [wa]s not."[278] However, Coues next admitted that, in fact, Washington Matthews had also made alterations, courtesy of "his long experience on the Upper Missouri, of his keen criticism and wise counsel: so that if any points be left obscure or dubious, it is because our united intellects were unequal to the emergency."[279] Although the introduction of the 1933 edition of the journal noted that Coues's "editorial practices were not in harmony with the principles of historical scholarship," for he "exercised a freedom which no careful scholar would permit himself to indulge," it inexplicably went forward as an "almost literal reprint" of the Coues version.[280]

The differences between the faithful typescript of Larpenteur's manuscript and the 1898 and 1933 editions are heart-stopping, and must be canvassed here, for they greatly impact the story. Noting that the "steamer" arrived "late in June" 1837 (a date Coues gave as June 24, 1837), the two published versions describe the epidemic this way:[281]

> The mirth usual on such occasions was not of long duration, for immediately on the landing of the boat we learned that smallpox was on board. Mr. J. Halsey, the gentleman who was to take charge this summer, had the disease, of which several of the hands had died; but it had subsided, and this was the only case on board. Our only apprehensions were that the disease might spread among the Indians, for Mr. Halsey had been vaccinated, and soon recovered. Prompt measures were adopted to prevent an epidemic. As we had no vaccine matter we decided to inoculate with the smallpox itself; and after the systems of those

who were to be inoculated had been prepared according to Dr. Thomas' medical book, the operation was performed upon about 30 Indian squaws and a few white men. This was done with the view to have it all over and everything cleaned up before any Indians should come in, on their fall trade, which commenced early in September. The smallpox matter should have been taken from a very healthy person; but, unfortunately, Mr. Halsey was not sound, and the operation proved fatal to most of our patients.[282]

By contrast, Larpenteur's manuscript, which is too long to quote in its entirety here, says that the *St. Peter's*, having suffered smallpox deaths (plural) during its journey, arrived on June 20, 1837—*not* 24 June, as Coues and Matthews had it. Moreover, the boat carried active cases of smallpox onboard, of which Jacob Halsey's was but one. Halsey's "halfbreed" wife had died of smallpox on board while giving birth to a daughter. Larpenteur explained to his reader that the fur "business oblidges" traders to "take Squaws such as the Daugters [sic] of Chieves or of desent [sic] indian families," so that "a halfbreed" like Mrs. Halsey was "one step more toward civilization."[283] For unprimed readers, "squaw" is an obscenity, from the Iroquoian root word for human genitals. As such, it means "cunt," not "Indian woman."[284]

Upon arrival at Fort Union, the previously vaccinated Mr. Halsey was "not at his worse [sic]," because he had "distinct" smallpox, or a less virulent form than hemorrhagic smallpox. Confining himself to a room in hopes of containing the smallpox, Halsey was waited upon only by "those who had had it or that was well vaxinated and shoud [showed] good marks." There is no indication that the other active cases were similarly confined. Either because of this or because he was with his father, Mr. Halsey's son fell ill. Then, Edwin Thompson Denig took sick, and "from that every Souls were frightnd to death."[285] Contrary to the published account's assertion that "there was no vaccine matter" at the fort, there were in fact "seven Assiniboins Squaws at the time in the fort besides some half breeds who all had been vaxinated," but the vaccine matrix "was not good," so that the vaccinations had not taken. Denig recovered, and was thus thought to have been ill from some other cause, although, as the son of a physician, it is my guess that he had been vaccinated properly by his father at an earlier time.[286]

Larpenteur stated that Robert Thomas's "Medical Book" was "braught down from the Library" with its "treatment of small Pox vaxination read over and over," from which it was gleaned that inoculation would cause a "lighter" and less dangerous epidemic, as long as the "system" had been prepared "well before the opperation." Everyone but Larpenteur consented to be inoculated, although he did note that "what [h]as been done was intended for the good of the company and the one of the Tribe," the "Tribe" to have been spared presumably being the Assiniboins, mentioned later. As Larpenteur explained the reasoning, "prehaps it was better to looze two squaws than to inflict this outrageous desease amongst the Tribe which probably might have had been the case if my plan had ben

adopted." Because "the desease" had been kept "much confined," Larpenteur supposed that it was "not likely that the desease was at this time in their system," that
is, that none of the Assiniboins had yet been exposed.[287]

Consequently, as soon as Halsey's son and Denig fell ill, Larpenteur planned to
"ship off all the Assiniboine Squaws to their camp," two days' march from the fort,
since he realized that "it was very dangerous to expose an indian life" to smallpox,
lest all "the whites" be "blamed and must pay." Unfortunately, Larpenteur's plan
was scuttled by the fact that "the mother in law and Brother of one of the squaws
had Left the fort" about six days before, so that Larpenteur abandoned his plan
to "ship off" the Assiniboin women.[288]

Instead, "it was agreed that they should all be noculated" after their "systems"
were first "prepaired," a procedure not actually canvassed in Thomas's *Domestic
Medicine* entry on smallpox and thus left to the reader's imagination. Larpenteur
felt that "only behold the greates most skillful phisition in the present wourld
would not have ventured the like to give the small Pox to seventeen persons
whom were all obliged to rised [reside?] within the Limits of about one hundred
feet" (brackets as in the typescript). Nevertheless, they were all variolated on
July 12, 1837. Along with the rest of the Indian women in the fort, Larpenteur's
"squaw" came "to get death put in to her harm [arm]" (brackets mine).[289]

On the evening of July 20, everyone was down "with the fever and that of the
hotest kind." Despite expecting the "mildest kind" of smallpox, four of the cases
"proved of the worse," that is, the hemorrhagic "kind," then called "confluent."
The rest were so severe as to have been "scarcely" distinct from hemorrhagic.[290]
Of course, Thomas's recommended treatments at that point would hardly have
helped: leeches, blisters, emetics, expectorants, calomel (powdered mercury),
nitre (an ingredient of gunpowder), opium, antimonial powder (one part oxide of
antimony and two parts phosphate of calcium), camphor, ether, muriatic acid (a
hydrogen-chloride solution), and/or sulfuric acid.[291]

I had thought that, by this point in my research, nothing could shock me further, but the reprehensible liberties taken by Coues and Matthews with Larpenteur's account did shock me. Their published version, which became the standard
account, compared with Larpenteur in the raw, greatly reformulated events. No
mention was made in Coues and Matthews of the known deaths and the active
cases aboard the *St. Peter's* when it docked, let alone the attempted isolation of
Halsey, the deaths of his son and wife, the attendants on Halsey (who otherwise had the run of the fort), or the bad vaccine with which the Indians had
been previously vaccinated. Nothing in Coues and Matthews mentioned the non-
fort-associated Assiniboins there at the time of the *St. Peter's* arrival, Larpenteur's
planned expulsion of the Assiniboin women, or the departure of the relatives of
one woman, after they had been well exposed but before they knew of their danger. Larpenteur's well-founded fears that inoculation was a bad idea are absent
from Coues and Matthews, whereas Coues's flattering reference to the humanitarian concerns of company officials for the wellbeing of the Indians was a fabrication. Larpenteur honestly admitted that his fear of reprisals alone sparked his

flawed attempts at containment, and that the company was concerned that but one nation survive, not all the Upper Missouri peoples.

Worst of all, vitally absent from Larpenteur's actual journal was the Coues and Matthews account of warding off visiting Indians who had come in to trade. Coues and Matthews asserted:

> While the epidemic was at its height a party of about 40 Indians came in, not exactly on a trade, but more on a begging visit, under the celebrated old chief Co-han; and the word was, "Hurry up! Open the door!" which had been locked for many days, to keep the crazy folks in. Nothing else would do—we must open the door; but on showing him a little boy who had not recovered, and whose face was still one solid scab, by holding him above the pickets, the Indians finally concluded to leave.[292]

Absolutely nothing of the sort appears in Larpenteur's manuscript. The story of warding off the Indians is a complete lie, perhaps suggested to the imaginations of Coues and Matthews by the fact of Halsey's sick son. Moreover, in full racist form, Coues and Matthews not only presented the 40 Indians as beggars but also as led by the Assiniboin chief Cohan (meaning "Hurry Up," also called Gauché), whom they had carefully positioned earlier as a drunken schemer.[293]

What Larpenteur recounted, instead, was that, while the disease was at its "most critical" stage and the traders "did not whish to see no one," about 200 Indians of unnamed nation "came to trade." After "a great deal of talk" through "the Best interpretter" on the Missouri River, the Natives agreed "to trade out side the Fort." Far from Coues's and Matthews's band of 40 beggars, shooed away by a scabby face glimpsed from a safe distance, the whole 200 who showed up to trade were exposed to hemorrhagic smallpox by the traders who left the fort to set up trade. Denig's independently corroborating account put the distance at one mile.[294] Neither Larpenteur nor Denig made mention of Chief Cohan (Gauché).

Larpenteur assumed that the Indians must have been offended either by having been kept out of the fort or by the quality of the goods traded, because, as negotiations closed, "there were four or five indians got over the Picketts of the old fort." Mounting "two of the best horses," they swung open the fort gate preparatory to driving out all the horses before they were "discovered." Instead, they made off with the two horses "they had mounted while in the Fort" and, apparently, others.[295] (The manuscript is confusing and vague about the number of horses taken.) Not willing to lose those horses, four of "our activest men," that is, four of the fort's most ambulatory hands, took the fastest horses remaining, and with "the assistance of some good Indians," raced off in pursuit, managing to recover all but five of the horses, which Indian members of the posse took north, presumably as bride payments. Four days later, "B Contois a half Breed from the red river who had taken an active part in getting Back the Horses" came down with hemorrhagic smallpox. Meanwhile, on August 4, 1837, Larpenteur's "squaw expired," and on

August 12, "Poor Contois Was Put in to his earthly dwelling." On August 16, another Indian concubine died in the fort.[296] There "for you," Larpenteur quipped acidly, was the "one case out of six hundred" that Thomas predicted as the death rate of "inoculation," if the patient were "afterward treated properly."[297]

In other words, everyone in the fort when Halsey and his son arrived were exposed, especially those who were his attendants while he was confined. Since not only Halsey but others arrived sick, those within the fort were necessarily exposed through them. Two non-fort Assiniboins left after they had been exposed but before they showed symptoms. Over Larpenteur's objections after two more people fell frighteningly ill, all 17 unaffected people still in the fort were variolated using live smallpox from Halsey. Everyone fell deathly ill. When 200 local Indians came to trade, the fort was at its sickest. Nevertheless, the most ambulatory *engagés* in the fort set up trade a mile outside it, effectively exposing all 200 Indians in the party. (The mile as ensuring safety was based on the miasma theory of disease, which claimed that bad air in a particular location caused epidemics, so that moving outside of the area of bad air solved the problem of contagion. This is, of course, nonsense. Infection travels with the infected, so that the sick traders brought the infection to the site in their persons to pass along to the Indians during the trade.)

In addition, young men entered the fort, stealing horses, with four *engagés* and some of the Natives from inside the fort giving chase. The posse physically caught the culprits, meaning that the incubating Contois, along with unnamed others, passed on the infection to these outsiders, as well. Certain Indians in the posse then proceeded north with five of the reclaimed horses, exposing yet others more distant. All Indians involved took their exposure home with them to their nations. Afterwards, one of the pursuing Indians, Larpenteur's wife, and a third Indian woman died in the fort.

All versions of Larpenteur showcase Robert Thomas's 1822 *Domestic Medicine,* a standard medical text of the day. What Thomas said is that "by applying variolous matter to a scratch or wound," smallpox "shall be absorbed into the constitution, a much milder disease and fewer eruptions will be the results, than when the smallpox takes place in the natural way; and therefore inoculation has pretty generally been adopted throughout every civilized part of the world." Thomas went on to state that the death rate of smallpox caught "the natural way" was 33 percent, but that among the inoculated, "the proportion of deaths does not exceed one in six or seven hundred."[298] In his discussions, Thomas did not distinguish carefully among vaccination, inoculation, and variolation. He was, however, very direct in his caution that:

> inoculation is highly beneficial to *individuals*, by lessening the danger; but it may, at the same time, be asserted that it has not proved of benefit to *mankind* in general, but the reverse; as the bills of mortality provide that the smallpox has increased, in England alone, in the proportion of nineteen to every hundred, since the introduction of inoculation. This has been owing to the want of proper

laws to prohibit inoculated personal from appearing in public, and intermixing with persons who never had had the disease. The smallpox is thereby propagated afresh, and often extends far and wide, committing dreadful and extensive ravages.[299] (Italics in the original)

One thinks of the ambulatory fort staff, going outside the fort to trade with 200 Indians, and subsequently forming a posse with "good" Indians to run down the "bad ones."

A paragraph later, Thomas reinforced his opinion. "Disapproving, as I do, of keeping up the smallpox by inoculation, I shall refrain from laying down any rules for its performance, and do strongly recommend vaccine inoculation in its stead" because "in 999 cases out of a thousand," cowpox vaccine was effective.[300] This is hardly a ringing endorsement of inoculation, still less of variolation, and it is no doubt what made Larpenteur refuse to go along with the inoculation scheme at first.

Just who did the inoculating is unclear. Some infer that Larpenteur did it, but his deep reservations in the original manuscript make that very unlikely. The most attractive possibility is the quickly recovered E. T. Denig. The fort's "bookkeeper, who understood some little surgery," Denig fancied himself a doctor, among other things.[301] In 1851, a black employee described him as "a hard man, liked by nobody," who kept "two Indian wives" on whom he "squandere[d]" all he had, that he "begrudge[d] anything paid the employees, oppresse[d] the engagees [sic] with too much work, [wa]s never satisfied, etc.," a disgust that another employee, Rudolph Kurz, came to share after a brief honeymoon period.[302] Kurz recorded Denig's rambling denigrations of Indians, noting that Denig "would be supremely happy to be put in command of at least 100,000 men and empowered to make them do some sort of work" for to "command" was "his greatest pleasure; desire to command his most characteristic trait."[303] Such a presumptuous man, safe himself from smallpox, might throw himself into the variolation of others where potential victims ran around 100,000.

Sixteen years later, Denig revealingly described the 1837–1838 smallpox epidemic, broadly hinting at his prowess as a physician:

We have personally tried experiments on nearly 200 cases according to Thomas's Domestic Medicine, varying the treatment in every possible form, but have always failed, or in the few instances of success the disease had assumed such a mild form that medicines were unnecessary. It generally takes the confluent turn of the most malignant kind (when the patient does not die before the eruption), which in 95 cases out of 100 is fatal.[304]

This same passage is riddled with defensive misrepresentations featuring Assiniboins as foolishly refusing European vaccination; smallpox as the "natural curse of the red men," and innocent settlers as thereafter falsely targeted by Indians, who charged them with having deliberately spread the disease.[305]

Denig's reference to Thomas's *Domestic Medicine* leads me to speculate that the copy at Fort Union was his, cadged from his father. I will also bet my lunch money that Denig played doctor by variolating those 200 Indians at the trading spot a mile from the fort, which he had probably been the one to recommend as a safe distance from the miasma. The faux medical tone of this passage leads me to suspect that he performed the fatal variolations inside the fort, as well.

Some pages earlier, Denig had voiced another settler myth about this epidemic, common to the telling long afterwards, that "every precaution had been used" to prevent it, that despite the *St. Peter's* having been "cleansed, and no appearance of the disease for a long time aboard, yet it in some way broke out among the Indians."[306] No document of the time mentions anything of the sort.

Another exculpatory passage in another of his "ethnographies" stated:

> This disease made its appearance in Fort Union when the steamboat arrived in the month of June with the annual supplies of the post. No Indians were then near except the wives of the engagées [sic] of the Fur Company in the fort, every one of whom caught the infection. In a short time 30 persons were laid up. When the first band came, they were met a mile from the place by good interpreters who represented to them the danger of going near and goods were brought out with the view of trading with them at a distance. All efforts of the kind, however, proved unavailing. They would not listen, and passed on to the fort.[307]

Denig was an infamous drunkard, and his passages sound to me like the ramblings of a long-time alcoholic making right on paper what had gone wrong on the ground.[308] Nevertheless, his publications offered a sideways confirmation of Larpenteur's account, omitting the fatal variolations (another reason I suspect that the "doctor" was he) and rounding up the number of those inside the fort at the outbreak, but nevertheless acknowledging that trade was set up outside the fort. The horse-stealing invasion is misrepresented as a general entry into the fort, but still echoes the story line in Larpenteur's credible manuscript.

Later settler accounts of the 1837–1838 epidemic seemed to delight in its horrific physical effects on the Indians. Part and parcel of this trend was a wholly contrived section inserted by Coues and Matthews, featuring one John Brazo, for whom tossing dead Indians into the bushes was presented as "fun."[309] (The name "John Brazo" appeared nowhere in Larpenteur's actual manuscript.) By the same token, while short-shrifting the causes, the most popular accounts dwelt in loving detail on the miseries that hemorrhagic smallpox visited on the plains peoples. I do not go into those sadistic accounts here, because they strike me as nothing quite so much as snuff pornography, luxuriating in the gory details of the suffering and death of helpless "Others."[310] Suffice it to say that the population losses among the high plains peoples were staggering, averaging between 50 and 95 percent of those affected, depending on nation and prior vaccination.[311]

The temptation for modern Americans faced with a story such as this is to sweep it under the rug to turn to something more pleasant. However, truth and justice require an unflinching assessment. At the most, the smallpox epidemic was a conspiracy encompassing U.S. Indian agents, Generals Cass and Gaines, and all top fur company executives in St. Louis, who deliberately planned and executed it as a path-clearer for U.S. territorial expansion and a booster shot to failing fur companies. At the very least, it showed those same actors as guilty, all around, of criminally reckless disregard for human life:

- Lewis Cass did not have to order that Upper Missouri peoples not be vaccinated;
- The vaccine at Fort Pierre, at least some of which was known to have been bad, did not have to go unreplaced and unused.
- The bad vaccine at Fort Union did not have to go unreplaced, nor did the vaccine possibly at Fort Clark.
- The *St. Peter's* did not have to run up the Missouri in 1837, knowingly carrying smallpox the whole way.
- American Fur Company officials did not have to variolate the Natives in, or trade with the Indians around, Fort Union.
- Three U.S. Indian Agents, all of them holding commissions as majors in the U.S. Army, did not have to distribute gifts and annuities from loads known to have been infected with smallpox.

Nevertheless, U.S. government and American Fur Company officials *chose* to do all those things.

∾

CHAPTER 4

"How Many Times Are You Going to Talk?": The Accusation of Poisoning against Marcus Whitman

On November 29, 1847, Marcus Whitman, his wife Narcissa, and 12 other settlers at Waiilatpu, Oregon, were executed by the Cayuses for alleged crimes, the foremost of which was having deliberately poisoned the Cayuse, Nez Percé, and Walla Walla peoples to facilitate the seizure of Oregon Territory by settlers from the United States. The poisoning was held to have occurred by two methods. One was in lacing melons with tartar emetic and meat with strychnine. The other was by giving Cayuse victims of the 1847 measles epidemic poisonous doses of tartar emetic and *nux vomica*, the 19th-century "medical" form of strychnine. In addition, the Cayuses charged the Whitmans and the mission's settlers with the grand theft of Native labor, land, lumber, water, fish, and animals.

To date, these allegations of deliberate poisoning have been sidetracked in historical accounts of the "Whitman massacre," while the charge of theft is never examined at all. Whitman's elite status as a mission doctor has so far stood as prima facie proof against the claims of Cayuse tradition. Typically, the Cayuse accusations are waved off as "difficult to believe" of Dr. Whitman, evidence in themselves of Cayuse "superstition."[1] Occasional critiques of the missionaries pop up, but ultimately, it is the Cayuses who are drubbed for their "overreliance on a supernatural framework to interpret all phenomena."[2] Apparently, the Whitmans' overreliance on their own supernatural framework of Christianity to interpret all phenomena does not count. However, it is well past time for racism and missionary zeal to stand as the sole assessment tools in examining the Cayuse allegations. Let us, instead, try basing assessment on the historical and traditional record.

In the 19th century, the utter unconstitutionality of using missions as political wedges was not even a blip on the settler radar. Bringing Christianity to the supposedly benighted savages was a spin that worked magically upon the average American mind to rationalize land seizure and genocide. As George E. Tinker so forthrightly demonstrated in *Missionary Conquest,* "patriotic" missionaries typically conflated their "gospel message" with the "doctrine of Manifest Destiny," to public acclaim.[3] Thus, regardless of whether they personally grasped the fact, missionaries were entirely complicit with empire.[4] As often as the fur traders, they supplied the advance guard of first entry into the next lands coveted by the settlers and their government.

Native American political analysts had always been perfectly aware of this. In 1762, for instance, a Lenape speaker was dispatched by his governing council to missionary and spy, Frederick Post, to outline, and by thus exposing it, end, the progression of missionary entry:

> Brother! last year you asked our leave to come and live with us, for the purpose of instructing us and our children, to which we consented; and now being come on, we are glad to see you!
>
> Brother! It appears to us that you must since have changed your mind, for instead of instructing us or our children, you are cutting trees down on our land! you have marked out a large spot of ground for a plantation, as the white people do everywhere; and bye and bye another, and another, may come and do the same; and the next thing will be, that a fort will be built for the protection of these intruders, and thus our country will be claimed by the white people, and we driven further back, as has been the case ever since the white people first came into this country. Say! do we not speak the truth?[5]

This speech neatly summed up the missionary method of frontier advance, enacted over and over, from the Atlantic to the Pacific coast:

1. Preachers invited themselves into the country, purportedly on a spiritual mission;
2. They cleared off farmland, helping themselves to Indian assets;
3. They became a way station for an influx of new settlers;
4. Their government erected a fort to protect its setters;
5. Their government claimed the land; and,
6. The original Native inhabitants were driven out.

This is exactly what transpired in Oregon.

The opening salvo of any missionary conquest was identifying "the call." Each sect cherished up a "call," or invitation, to come convert the "savages," which purportedly justified trespassing on Indian land. Although, as in the Lenape case, the missionaries often invited themselves in, occasionally there were genuine invitations, typically issued by a fringe element of the nation. Most frequently, however, far from conversion to Christianity, the motive behind the invitation was to secure physical protection from well-oiled settlers, who knew that they could kill Indians on a whim without facing any retribution. From the first, Indians observed that missions could sometimes forestall, or at least mitigate, settler crimes against them. Thus, when the Cayuga chief, Shikellimy, invited missionaries into Shamokin, Pennsylvania, in the 18th century, it was because Shikellimy was a colonial agent who hoped that material gain and protection for his town would result. Conversion to Christianity was not his object.[6]

Frequently, in deciding whether to issue a call, the point of contention among the Native factions was over which group, Indian or European, was the physically *safe* group to back.[7] This only looks hypocritical to westerners. In Native North American cultures, the first law is the Law of Innocence, which absolutely guarantees safety and security to women, children, elders, and the mentally ill. It is the *obligation* of elders and the Young Men they dispatch to ensure, before all else, that the Innocents are safe.[8]

Moreover, Native groups did not understand what conversion meant to the Europeans, because it was against Indian law for anyone to force a spiritual belief system on anyone else. The closest convention to conversion in Native culture was "adoption," which meant the acceptance of citizenship in a group other than one's birth group. Thus, when "adopted" by one or the other of the clans (sects) of the "Christian nation," as settlers were wont to term themselves, the adoptees (converts) thought that they had become *citizens* of the settler state. At the same time, they had a firm expectation of absolute freedom of conscience, so that the heavy-handed dogmas imposed on them post-adoption usually came as an unwelcome and resisted surprise. Finally, having accepted adoption, Indian converts were typically stunned to discover that the missionaries still considered them Mahicans, or Pawnees, or Cayuses, and not U.S., or British, or French citizens.[9]

Christian settlers had a totally different take on the matter, which let them simultaneously impose racist imperatives and Christian dogma in the process of seizing land. They had entire organizations set up for just those purposes, including the American Board of Commissioners of Foreign Missions (ABCFM). In 1820, the Presbyterians, Congregationalists, and Dutch Reformed Church joined forces as the ABCFM to fling missionaries into whatever far corners of the earth the United States was then eyeing. It was through the ABCFM that the Whitmans wound up in Oregon in 1836, but the "call" that put them there needed considerable massaging before the ABCFM felt empowered to elbow out the Methodists and the Catholics, who responded to the same "call," quickly popularized as that of the "Four Wise Men of the West."

Primary sources mentioning the original "call" are scarce and scattered, and they certainly do not justify most of the subsequent hype. What can be confidently asserted is that, with Removal heating up, the head of the Indian Department of the Western District headquartered in St. Louis, General William Clark, found himself "surrounded" by "hundreds of Indians," including some from "*West of the Rocky Mountains*" (italics in the original), as he stated on November 20, 1831, in his "1830 Report on the Fur Trade."[10] One of the Indians was William Walker, a Wyandot-turned-Methodist minister, who headed a six-man Wyandot delegation to St. Louis in the fall of 1831, to confer with Clark on the upcoming Removal of his people from their capital of Upper Sandusky, Ohio, to Indian Territory.[11]

Meanwhile, four Indian emissaries from Oregon traveled east to St. Louis along the fur trade route that same fall.[12] The two elder emissaries, both Salish, were Narcisse and Paul.[13] The two younger emissaries were Nez Percés named Hee-oh'ks-te-kin and H'co-a-h'co-a-h'cotes-min.[14] None of the four was Cayuse, and none of them spoke English or French.[15] These four men were the western Indians Clark mentioned and whom Walker immortalized as the "Flat-Head Indians." Of the four, who had had come to see a Catholic church, Narcisse and Paul died of disease in St. Louis, attended by local Catholic priests.[16] The two younger of them, Hee-oh'ks-te-kin and H'co-a-h'co-a-h'cotes-min, returned to Oregon along the American Fur Company steamer route in the spring of 1832. Artist George Catlin was also on board, seizing the opportunity to take names and draw portraits.[17]

En route home, H'co-a-h'co-a-h'cotes-min died "near the mouth of the Yellow Stone River" of a disease contracted in St. Louis.[18] Hee-oh'ks-te-kin, alone, made it home.[19] Clark did speak with the four Oregon emissaries, and summarized the conversation at least twice, during the separate visits of William Walker and George Catlin, although Clark later called Walker's recital of his exchange with the Oregonians "highly wrought" and "incorrect."[20]

This conversation, as supposedly repeated to, and then certainly written down by, Walker, became the source material of the ABCFM's "call." Addressed to Gabriel P. Disosway, a devout merchant in New York, Walker's letter recounted, secondhand, the meeting between General William Clark and the four emissaries. Apparently without permission or further research, Disosway straightaway transmitted the letter to the *Christian Advocate and Journal and Zion's Herald,* along with superfluous commentary of his own. First printed in the March 1, 1833, issue of *The Christian Advocate* under the title, "The Flat-Head Indians," Walker's letter broke the spine-tingling news of the Wise Men of the West, a delegation of four "Flat-Head Indians" who had journeyed valiantly from Oregon, across the Rocky Mountains, across the Great Plains, to St. Louis, all in search of a Bible.[21] (At the time, the reference to "Four Wise Men of the West" resonated with devout Christians as a cutesy allusion to the "Three Wise Men of the East" of the Jesus nativity story.)

It is worth pausing here to recall that William Walker was a Wyandot, whose people were on the brink of being Removed under the auspices of General Clark. For all their posturing, the Methodist missionaries had proven themselves totally ineffectual in preventing the Wyandots' cruel Removal from their Ohio homeland. Straight-faced jokes were and remain a favorite Iroquoian form of clowning, pulled in the service of deflating distended egos or exposing wrongdoing. All things considered, missionary uselessness atop Christian gullibility might just have formed too tempting a target for the Wyandot in Walker to have resisted. I suspect that Walker was pulling the humor-impaired Disosway's leg. Once his private joke spun out of control, it is understandable that Walker might have bitten his lip, glanced nervously to and fro, and decided that his continued silence on the provenance of his tale was probably the safest policy.

Walker's letter is riotously absurd on its face. First, Walker waited until the spring of 1833, a full year, to write up his secondhand account of the emissaries' visit.

Then, he got the date wrong, a slap at western historiography. Second, his letter included a ridiculous drawing of an Indian with a head flattened to a conical point, in an early image of The Coneheads. This image neatly encapsulated the minstrel stereotype of "Flat-Head Indians" then in vogue among the settlers. Third, Walker had the emissaries, who spoke no settler language, sitting primly through a pompous, drawn-out disquisition on Christianity, starting with THE BEGINNING OF TIME, continuing through the (to Indians) inscrutable crucifixion, and ending on the (to Indians) utterly alien laws of the Decalogue of the Jews, who, of course, do not accept the divinity of Jesus.

Finally, as for the call, itself, Walker related that a mysterious "white man" had happened upon one of the Indians' ceremonies, only to criticize it as so "radically wrong" as to have been offensive to some unknown yet "great Spirit." Not to worry, however, since the settlers "had a book" of "directions," a how-to guide on currying favor with this exotic "Spirit." Accordingly, the Indians dispatched emissaries in search of "their great father," oddly not the U.S. president, but William Clark (whom they recalled from his visit to them during the Lewis and Clark expedition), feeling safe that he would "tell them the whole truth" of the matter. For their trouble, two emissaries died before they could return to the west (a reward that screamed "Wrinkled Spirit").[22]

From there, the story took on a life of its own as one of the major urban legends of 19th-century America. The motivation behind the Indians' visit, the personal and national identities of the emissaries, and just who had said what to whom began shifting about quite a bit. The sordid results would hardly have made for a historical footnote, had not the climax of the grim comedy proven so lethal to so many. Whole tracts, treatises, and two governmental reports were published, most of them stuffed with irresponsible and even deceitful versions of the events that followed. Rival sects clamored that *they* had been the ones *really* called by the "Flat-Heads," with each adjusting the story to suit its individual purposes. Meanwhile, erstwhile (and self-appointed) "Friends of the Indian" gleefully bruited the tale about as proof positive of "the absurdity of the assertion" common among the settlers that the Indian could "never be civilized or christianized."[23]

At this point, consulting Catholic archives instates some sanity into the discussion. Joseph Rosati, Bishop of St. Louis, recounted the visit of the emissaries in a December 31, 1831, letter sent from St. Louis to the editor of the Catholic publication, *Annales de l'Association de la Propagation de la Foi*. Because the original letter is difficult to procure and always alluded to secondhand, with any quotes in English, no less, I am providing Rosati's original French text followed by my translation of it:

Il y a quelques mois, quatre sauvages qui habitent de l'autre côté de monts Rocheaux, près du fleuve Colombia, sont arrivés à Saint-Louis, après avoir visité le général Clarke [sic], qui dans son célèbre voyage avait vu la nation à laquelle ils appartiennent et en avait été bien traité; ils vinrent voir notre église et parurent en être extrêmement

satisfaits; malheureusement il n'y avait personne qui entendît leur langage. Quelques
temps après deux d'entr'eux tombèrent dangereusement malades. J'étais alors absent
de Saint-Louis. Deux de nos Prêtres les visitèrent, et ces pauvres Indiens parurent en-
chantés de leur visite. Ils firent des signes de croix et d'autres signes qui semblaient
avoir quelque rapport au Baptême. On leur administra ce sacrement; ils en témoig-
nèrent leur contentement. On leur présenta un petit croix, ils la saisirent avec empress-
ment, la baisaient souvent, en on ne put la leur ôter des mains qu'après leur mort. Il
était bien affligeant de ne pas pouvoir leur parler. On porta leurs corps à l' église pour
l'enterrement qui fut fait avoic toutes les cérémonies catholiques. Les deux autres sau-
vages y assistèrent avec une très-grande modestie. Ils sont retournés dans leur pays.
Nous von appris depuis, par un canadien qui a traversé la contrée qu'ils habitent, qu'ils
appartiennent à la nation des Têtes-Plates, laquelle, ainsi qu'une autre appelée les
Pieds-Noirs, a reçu des notions de la Religion catholique de deux sauvages qui avaient
été au Canada et qui leur avaient raconté en détail ce qu'ils avaient vu, faisant des
descriptions frappantes des belles cérémonies du culte catholique, leur disant que c'était
aussi la Religion des Blancs; ils en ont retenu ce qu'ils on pu, ils ont appris à faire le
signe de croix et à prier. Ces nations n'ont pas encore été corrumpues par le commerce
des autres; elles ont des moeurs douces et sont très-nombreuses. Nous avons conçu le
désir le plus vif de ne pas laisser perdre une si belle occasion. M. Condamine s'est offert
pour y aller au printemps prochain avec un autre. (Italics in the original)[24]

[A few months ago, four savages who inhabit the far side of the Rocky Mountains, near the Columbia River, arrived in St. Louis. After having visited General
Clark, who, during his celebrated travels, had seen the nation to which they belonged and where he had been treated well, they came to see our church and appeared to have been extremely satisfied with it. Unfortunately, there was no one
who understood their language. Some time afterwards, two of them fell danger-
ously ill. I was then absent from St. Louis. Two of our priests visited them, and
these poor Indians seemed delighted by their visit. They made signs of the cross
and other signs that seemed to indicate some acquaintance with the sacraments.
They were administered the sacrament; they expressed their satisfaction with it.
They were presented with a small cross; they took it eagerly, kissed it frequently,
and it could only be taken from their hands after their death. It was a great affliction not to have been able to speak with them. Their corpses were carried to
the church for interment, which was done with all the Catholic ceremonies. The
two other savages assisted in this with very great propriety. They have returned to
their country. We have since learned, from a Canadian who has traveled through
the country they inhabit, that they belonged to the *Flat-Head* nation, which, also
called the *Blackfeet*, received some smattering of the Catholic religion from two
savages who had been to Canada and who had recounted to them what they had
seen in detail, giving striking descriptions of the beautiful rites of the Catholic sect,

telling them that it was moreover the religion of the whites. They have retained what they could of it. They have learned to make the sign of the cross and to pray. These nations have not been as corrupted by trade as the others; they have gentle manners and are very numerous. We have conceived the most urgent desire not to allow this lovely opportunity to be lost. Mr. Condamine has volunteered to go out there next spring, along with one other. (Italics in the original)]

Very importantly in this account, the "call," such as it was, went *to the Catholics* and no one else. Moreover, Rosati twice stated that no one understood the Indians' language, nor did the emissaries understand the settlers', making Clark's fabled catechism impossible to have been accomplished. Rosati also stated that the emissaries had visited Clark simply because they knew his name. The implication was that they were totally lost in a strange city and in need of a guide around St. Louis. Furthermore, the visit was mainly prompted by a curiosity to see the Catholic church, with their possibly having been shown the brand new St. Louis cathedral, whose *"première Pierre,"* or cornerstone, Rosati had just that year *"bénit et posé,"* or "blessed and set.[25] Obtaining a Bible was *not* on the agenda.

Other Catholic records show a complicated and nuanced genesis of the embassy nowhere evident in Walker, Catlin, or Clark's melodramatic sketches. According to Catholic archives, between 1812 and 1820, a group of 24 Catholic Mohawks, under the leadership of Ignace Le Mousse, traveled from Caughnawaga near Montreal to the Flathead Valley in northwestern Montana. Moving in with the Salish ("Flat-Head") people, they intermarried and remained with their hosts, tutoring interested Salish people in Catholic catechism. Eventually desiring actual priests to attend to them, the Catholics among the Mohawk-Salishes sent the fabled embassy to St. Louis, but there were so many Native embassies in the city in the fall of 1831 that the four had a hard time catching anyone's attention. The fact that none of them could communicate with anyone around them greatly hampered their efforts. A little desperate, they remembered William Clark, and, with that name, finally managed to find both him and the Catholic church. Shortly after their visit to Clark, the two elder emissaries died and were buried, Narcisse on October 31, 1831, and Paul on November 17, 1831, in the St. Louis Catholic cemetery.[26] By 1839, only four of the original two dozen Mohawk Catholics were still alive among the Salishes.[27]

The Catholic response was not as rapid as Father Condamine's immediate volunteering might have suggested. Nothing much happened for years, although Ignace La Mousse seemed to have had some communication with the Catholics in the east. In 1835, La Mousse took two of his Salish sons east to St. Louis.[28] In the fall of 1837, the Salishes sent another delegation, in search of a priest, but all members of that embassy were killed by Lakotas at Ash Hollow. In 1839, yet another embassy was sent to St. Louis, and ultimately, after some back-and-forthing, Father P. J. De Smet set up his St. Mary's Mission at present-day Stevensville, Montana, on October 3, 1841.[29]

These facts of the matter were, however, twisted out of all recognition, in a battle of the titans between, first, Catholics and Protestants and, second, warring Protestant sects, particularly the Presbyterians and the Methodists. Facilitating this battle, at least in the minds of the Protestants, was a minstrel version of events that was concocted by the Presbyterian missionary, Henry Harmon Spalding, who cooked up a spurious speech and attributed it to the speaker among the Four Wise Men of the West.[30] Despite its completely specious provenance and ridiculous text, which was repeatedly exposed as a fraud throughout the 19th century, the speech continued appearing as authentic, if occasionally rewritten, in major historical biographies of Marcus Whitman.[31] Disturbingly enough, the internet is now giving Spalding's hoax a second life as legitimate in the 21st century.[32]

Spalding dexterously pushed all of the right Protestant buttons by having footsore Indians piteously pleading for a Bible. A code for "Catholic" that would have been instantly recognized by all readers of the *Christian Advocate* in 1833 was any mention of a Bible's having been refused to a seeker. Catholics sent priests, not Bibles, which were to have been interpreted for the multitudes by the Catholic hierarchy. By contrast, the necessity of each lay reader's interpreting the Bible for him- or herself was an ardently held Protestant tenet. Thus, when Spalding mentioned that the emissaries were returning home Bibleless, readers were to have leapt to the conclusion that Catholicism was nefariously involved. In addition, by mentioning Clark in the same breath as the hapless Bible seekers, Spalding seeded a long-standing rumor that William Clark was a closet Catholic, which, in *Christian Advocate* circles, was roughly equivalent to having been fingered by the House Un-American Activities Committee as a secret Soviet agent in 1952. It was sure to have sent shivers up the spine of Protestant America.

If less intentionally so, the Wise Man speech seeded by Spalding is just as ridiculous as Walker's "call," being pure mumbo-jumbo, with pseudo-Indian metaphors gone wild:

> I came to you over a trail of many moons from the settling sun. You were the friend of my fathers who have all gone the long way. I came with one eye partly opened, for more light for my people who sit in darkness. I go back with both eyes closed. How can I go back with both eyes closed? How can I go back blind to my blind people? I made my way to you with strong arms, through many enemies and strange lands, that I might carry back much to them. I go back with both arms broken and empty. The two fathers who came with us—the braves of many winters and wars—we leave asleep by your great water and wigwam. They were tired in many moons and their moccasins wore out. My people sent me to get the white man's book of Heaven. You took me where you allowed your women to dance, as we do not ours, and the book was not there; you showed me the images of good spirits and pictures of the good land beyond, but the book was not among them to tell us the way. I am going back the long sad trail to my people of the dark land. You make my feet heavy with burdens of gifts, and my

moccasins will grow old in carrying them, but the book is not among them. When I tell my poor blind people, after one more snow, in the big council, that I did not bring the Book, no word will be spoken by our old men of by our young braves. One by one they will rise up and go out in silence. My people will die in darkness, and they will go on the long path to the other hunting grounds. No white man will go with them and no whiteman's book will make the way plain. I have no more words.[33]

I walk around with my eyes closed. How do I get anywhere with my eyes closed? Braille? Maybe that how-to book on the White Spirit will help, except that, for all the advance billing on the subject, it does not seem to be in evidence. I marvel that anyone could ever have taken this text seriously, still more that anyone today could entertain it as genuine.

Although only the Catholics had actually been invited, and then, only by a small cadre of the already-Catholic Canadian Mohawks among the Salishes, the ABCFM considered itself in a footrace to Oregon with both the Catholic and Methodist missionaries.[34] To establish its own toehold in Oregon, the ABCFM first sent Samuel Parker and Marcus Whitman on a scouting expedition to the Pacific Northwest in 1835. Given Parker's favorable report, the ABCFM dispatched Henry Spalding and his wife, Eliza, to the Nez Percés, and Marcus Whitman and his wife, Narcissa, to the Cayuses. These four were joined in 1837 by the Elkanah Walkers, the Cushing Eellses, and the Asa B. Smiths, all missionaries, along with some mission laborers. Once everyone was in Oregon, they immediately set to brawling with one another, to the decided detriment of all of their missions.

The particular feud that pertains here was the continual open season that Marcus Whitman and Henry Spalding declared on each other, each man apparently despising the other with a passion. Contributory sideswipes were taken both by and at William Gray, a Whitman booster. Narcissa Whitman was likewise dragged into the fray. Marcus Whitman was fond of firing off incendiary diatribes against Spalding to their mutual ABCFM superiors in Boston, culminating in his unauthorized ride east in the fall of 1842. The entire debacle did no credit to anyone involved, and, today, the furious letters and irate diary entries read like competing blogs posted by rival middle-school cliques.[35] Marcus Whitman seemed to have been the primary instigator.

In encapsulated form, the rub between Spalding and Whitman was named Narcissa. A refined eastern, upper-class lady, and something of a drama queen, Narcissa Prentiss was obviously considered a prize by her home circle and seemed to have so considered herself. Despite later biographers' smoothing away of her sharp edges, her surviving letters show that she had a fairly large ego and felt herself to have been reserved by Providence to some great purpose. Consequently, when courted by the colorless yet intense and socially awkward Spalding, she deigned not to throw herself away on his marriage proposal. There is some suspicion that his illegitimate birth might further have rendered his attentions unacceptable to Narcissa.[36] Thus rebuffed, in October 1833, Spalding married Eliza Hart, a delicate, humorless lady with missionary ambitions of her own.

Enter Marcus Whitman, a flashy, poised, and educated male diva, another center of nervous gravity. Like Narcissa, he liked to keep the dramatic pot boiling. Although he had not initially intended to do so, he took the full course for his medical doctor's certificate, finishing in 1825. His entire course of study consisted of two, 16-week medical classes and a two-year' ride-along with a practicing physician, Dr. Ira Bryant, of Rushville, Massachusetts.[37] While a medical student, Whitman had been engaged to a Miss Persía Saunders, who died in 1830, presumably before their marriage could take place.[38] Thus, in 1835, he was a footloose, newly-minted physician on the look-out for a woman as flamboyant as himself to complete the tableau. Although always and only a doctor, he had missionary urges. Apparently against her family's preferences, Narcissa accepted Marcus, marrying him in February 1836, preparatory to leaving for missionary assignment in Oregon.[39]

Narcissa was no unwilling combatant in the Whitman-Spalding war. Throughout her literate and often entertaining journal-letter home covering her trip west to Oregon in 1836, Narcissa made catty comments about Eliza Spalding's ill health, along with passive-aggressive swipes at Eliza's "having the right temperment [sic] to match" Spalding's, with the implication of failure left dangling just below the surface.[40] For his part, in explaining why his own mission at Lapwai was situated so far from Whitman's Waiilatpu mission, Spalding rather spitefully quipped to Elkanah Walker, "Do you suppose I would have come off here all alone a hundred & twenty miles if I could have lived with him [Marcus] or Mrs. Whitman?," a comment that Walker recorded in a letter of October 14, 1840.[41] This remark probably came in response to a diagnosis that Whitman had sent in September 1840, to their mutual bosses in Boston, that "Spalding was suffering from a disease of the head which was liable to make him insane, 'especially if excited by external circumstances,'" as William Marshall summarized the letter in 1911.[42]

It is true that missionaries did sometimes go gloriously insane, as did the "self-supporting" missionary Asahel Munger over the winter of 1840–1841, nailing one hand to a mantelpiece in a botched replication of the crucifixion, apparently in the expectation of a subsequent resurrection.[43] However, Spalding's alleged madness was nothing quite so spectacular. It consisted of untoward comments that he had made about Narcissa Whitman, at which the Whitmans took unremitting umbrage. In his diary entry of July 9, 1840, Spalding recorded that "the root of all the difficulties in the Mission lay between us, viz., in an expression I made while in the States respecting his wife before she was married to Doct. Whitman, viz., that I would not go into the same Mission with her, questioning her judgment." (Said bad judgment was presumably displayed in refusing his hand.) Spalding continued that, although he had thought the matter behind them, Whitman had informed him in July 1840 "that either himself or me [sic] must leave the mission."[44] The matter had not cooled down by that fall. In a letter of September 3, 1840, to the secretary of the ABCFM, Asa B. Smith recounted that Whitman had generally accused Spalding of gossiping about Narcissa "from town to town before he left the States," declaring that "he would not go on a mission" that included her.[45]

Just why the ABCFM would send couples with this fraught history on a far mission together is a mystery. Perhaps no one in Boston quite realized the fragility of their relationship. Even more perplexing is why the ABCFM would send out as missionaries people like the Whitmans, who were so magnificently unqualified for the task in either personality or preparation. Their unsuitability was no secret at the time. In fact, on October 19, 1849, the Reverend H.K.W. Perkins's reaction to the massacre was, basically, that the Whitmans had set themselves up for it. Perkins told Narcissa's sister that both Whitmans "were out of their proper sphere" and "not adapted to their work." The Cayuses *"feared* the Doctor" but "they did not *love* him," nor did they "love" Narcissa, whom they "always considered *haughty*" (italics in the original).[46] Perkins was quite right: Both Whitmans belonged in the elite east, where shooting off one's mouth did not incite one's neighbors to shoot back with anything more lethal.

The Spalding-Whitman feud had boiled to a head when Whitman decided to ride back east, leaving for Boston on October 3, 1842, mainly to demand that the ABCFM *do something,* although, from the very laconic records kept of the commissioners' meetings with Whitman, just *what* is hard to tell. After hobnobbing a bit in Washington, D.C., Whitman arrived at the Boston headquarters of the ABCFM on March 30, 1843.[47] The Commissioners were quite startled by Whitman's presumption in coming so far, since he had not been authorized to leave his post in Oregon. He was apparently scolded for having come.[48] Although the ABCFM's meeting notes were fairly hush-mouthed about the personnel problems in Oregon, based on the decision recorded, the hostilities were clearly the object of the discussion. The commissioners ordered a continuation of Spalding's and Whitman's separate missions, while releasing from missionary service Waiilatpu's much disliked mechanic-carpenter, William Gray, along with his wife.[49]

Although mostly spurred by the missionaries' adolescent squabbling, like the "Four Wise Men" story of the "call," Whitman's ride east ballooned into an enduring myth, here that Whitman had dashed east to "save Oregon" from the fell clutches of the British, on the one hand, and the Catholics, on the other. This version of events was heavily promulgated from the time of Whitman's death until it was deftly expunged from the record by William Isaac Marshall's excruciatingly detailed study of the issue in 1911.[50] No one today seriously proposes that Whitman, colorfully regaled in his buckskins and fresh from a grueling trek across the trackless prairies, single-handedly persuaded President John Tyler, his Cabinet, and Congress to annex Oregon territory.

Oddly enough, the story of Whitman, Martyred Savior of Oregon, was primarily invented and promoted by his old rival, Spalding, although the ABCFM cooperated with the push, probably for its public-relations value. After the Whitmans' death, Spalding capitalized on the massacre by presenting himself as the great defender of the Whitman memory, in a series of rash articles printed in the California Congregationalist publication, *The Pacific,* from 1864 to 1865. In the 10th of these, appearing on October 19, 1865, Spalding puffed the story of Whitman's riding east to spread the dire word that Britain was out to seize Oregon.[51]

In fact, aside from settling the internecine spats, Whitman had ridden east to beef up settler emigration to his section of Oregon. Enticing settlement was the reason behind his layover at Washington, D.C., probably in March of 1843, but what transpired there is, once more, fairly sketchy in the record. Whitman claimed to have conferred with President John Tyler and key members of the cabinet and Congress on the necessity of the United States' seizing of Oregon forthwith. Whitman did thereafter send a letter to James M. Porter, the Secretary of War, which was received by Porter's office on June 22, 1844, in which Whitman claimed to have been complying with Porter's request to see the text of Whitman's proposed bill to annex Oregon.[52]

Notwithstanding, the president at the time of Whitman's ride, John Tyler, had a different recollection of events. What Whitman proposed to Tyler, and all he proposed, was taking a wagon train of settlers back to Oregon in 1843. In letters of December 11, 1845, December 23, 1845, and January 1, 1846, Tyler emphatically refuted simplistic notions that Whitman was the prime mover of the Oregon annexation by recounting the long and intricate negotiations with England under U.S. policies set in 1818, as worked up by John Quincy Adams, Secretary of State under James Monroe, and then again in 1826 under Quincy Adams's own presidency, as well as through later, internal politics involving James K. Polk.[53]

Tyler was correct. National policy on Oregon had been in the crafting stages since at least 1818, when Britain and the United States had signed an agreement to share the territory. Talks to renew the agreement in 1827 stipulated that neither could grant lands in the territory and that each entity must give the other 12 months' notice of intent to abrogate the treaty.[54] The next president, James K. Polk, had campaigned on an expansionist program and did pursue the acquisition of Oregon. In his first inaugural address, on March 4, 1845, he pressed to abrogate the treaty with Britain, and he did eventually force the Oregon Treaty of 1846.[55] Obviously, this was a land-grab in the political works since 1818, not one materializing suddenly from Whitman's dash east in the fall of 1842.

In riding east, Whitman was riding a trend. Oregon had beckoned settlers ever since Samuel Parker's glowing descriptions of it in his 1838 *Journal of an Exploring Tour beyond the Rocky Mountains*.[56] The rumor of its being a disease-free destination enticed disease-ravaged settlers.[57] By the 1840s, settlers were quite literally pouring in, 900 of them in 1843, with 1,200 more surging across Cayuse land in 1844. In 1845, a whopping 3,000 raced across Cayuse territory, and in 1847, even more, 4,500, swept in.[58] By contrast, there were, perhaps, 1,500 Cayuses there in this same decade.[59] In the entire territory of Oregon in 1845, the total Indian population was estimated at 27,000.[60] The land grab was on, and the settlers were restless, and, in response to the massacre, burning the Indians' homes and killing them at will, without repercussions, according to the August 10, 1849, report of the Indian subagent, Robert Newell.[61]

There is no doubt that Whitman was intent upon enticing new settlers to Oregon. In a letter to Myron Eells dated February 10, 1880, Whitman's nephew, Perrin Whitman, gave the Whitman spin on the adventure:

> While crossing the plains I repeatedly heard the Doctor express himself as being very anxious to succeed in opening a wagon road across the continent to the Columbia River, and thereby stay, if not entirely prevent, the trading of this northwest coast, then pending between the United States and the British government. In after years the Doctor, with much pride and satisfaction, reverted to his success in bringing the immigration across the plains, and thought it one of the means of saving Oregon to his government."[62]

Drumming up settlers was hardly a novel purpose. In 1837, William Gray had made a similar ride east, bringing back the Eellses, the Walkers, and the Smiths, all of whom promptly set up more missions.[63] Whitman was not interested in more missionaries who would siphon off incoming settlers through their own missions, however. He wanted settlers coming through *his* mission.

There is some indication that, while in Washington, Whitman was scrounging up governmental funding to drag more settlers to Oregon. On May 27 and 28, 1843, Whitman wrote two letters chatting up the 200 "immigrants to Oregon" he was personally taking back with him, in company with a 30-man U.S. Army Corps of Engineers scouting party under "Lieut. Fremont" (John Charles Fremont), sent "to explore for the government." Claiming that it was "now decided in my mind that Oregon will be occupied by American citizens," Whitman also planned "to impress the Secretary of War" with the need for sheep as "indispensable for Oregon," being "more important to Oregon's interest than soldiers." Whitman's plans were "to get sheep and stock from government [sic] for Indians instead of money for their lands."

In addition to Whitman's proposed "bill," he also mentioned "a private letler [sic] touching some particular" but unspecified "interests."[64] This probably pertained to the 200-strong wagon train that Whitman took back with him in 1843. The effort was encouraged by Tyler's Secretary of State, Daniel Webster, probably because it formed a timely and expedient public relations move for the United States in long-extant plans to take over Oregon.[65] It was the first, large-scale wagon train to Oregon.[66]

ABCFM notes dated April 4, 1843 also document Whitman's purpose of securing new U.S. settlers for Oregon, a request that the ABCFM granted on the condition that it did not have to pay for anything connected with the venture.[67] The ABCFM saw it as problematic that Whitman's Waiilatpu mission was being used as a way station by settlers, most of whom continued on to the nearby Willamette Valley rather than staying put at his mission. The commissioners were not about to support a generalized Oregon settlement using mission funds. Even though, during Whitman's visit, the commissioners had sanctioned his plans to import "business men 'to settle at or near the mission station,'" Whitman's own turn away from religious to very secular—and lucrative—concerns seemed to have troubled his superiors.[68] In fact, they were concerned that Whitman's and their purposes were diverging. In a later communication, David Greene, the ABCFM's secretary, warned Whitman against becoming "a man of business."[69]

In 1843, the ABCFM demanded an update from Whitman, resulting in his report, "Oregon Indians." In it, perhaps responding to ABCFM uneasiness, Whitman spun his business decisions as spiritually motivated. He stressed the detriment to new settlers, just then "crossing the Rocky Mountains in companies containing, sometimes, hundreds of souls," should they be greeted by "nothing better than heathenism or Romanism." Whitman presented the happy solution to this problem as "to procure additional laborers" as well as "to induce christian families to emigrate and settle in the vicinity" of the ABCFM missions. Probably to allay the commissioners' concern over his business activities, Whitman contended that such laborers would not only "relieve" him of his "secular responsibilities," but also "contribute directly, in various ways, to the social and moral improvement of the Indians."[70]

The ABCFM's concern over Whitman's business activities deserves scrutiny it seldom receives, for he was clearly in the business of business, using the ABCFM funding as his seed money. The Whitmans' mission had become a major hub of settlement, boarding incoming settlers or the children of settlers in difficulty; mountain men, fur traders, and their children; "self-supporting" missionaries, who never managed to support themselves; and new "associates" for their mission.[71] On May 2, 1840, Narcissa boasted to her mother that "We are emphatically situated on the highway between the states and the Columbia river, and are a resting place for the weary travelers, consequently a greater burden rests upon us than upon any of our associates—always to be ready."[72] The Whitmans even developed the gall to require settlers as well as Indians to call them "Mother" and "Father" Whitman.[73] In a sort of poetic comeuppance, by 1844, the main route into Oregon lay to the Whitmans' south, leaving Waiilatpu to host the poorest of the incoming settlers, but Whitman was still making money on them as well as on his lumber mill.[74] Undaunted, in 1844, Whitman told the eastern Prentisses that it would not "surprise" him to see their "whole family in this country in two years."[75]

Obviously, Marcus Whitman worked intensively to make his mission the gateway to Oregon, and he stood to become comparatively rich in the process. This was why, for instance, he was so intent upon acquiring, and did acquire, the nearby Methodist mission called The Dalles, a docking point of ships from Boston.[76] (*Les dalles* is French for flagstones or paving-stones, referencing the stone outcroppings at this narrows of the Columbia River.) The Dalles was also a prize fishery of the Oregon Natives, and thus, of the incoming settlers.[77] Whitman certainly did not want The Dalles because it was successful as a mission. In 1847, the Methodists abandoned it as an expensive failure, having cost their sponsorship $250,000 without converting anyone.[78]

The invasion of Oregon that Whitman helped to spur resulted in three problems that collided and then reverberated. First, following the missionary model, the settlers simply took anything they wanted—trees, game, water—as the presumed fat of the land, free-of-charge to all comers. Second, although Oregon was not annexed as a U.S. territory until 1848, U.S. settlers there formed their own government in 1843, the year Whitman dragged in his large wagon train.[79] Third, in the wake of the settlers, disease ran rampant. Once all of these factors converged, a disaster was unavoidable.

As already noted, some of the settlers who came through the Hudson's Bay Company were Iroquois and Algonkin. Their number included the 24 Catholic Mohawks who sent to St. Louis in 1831 for a priest and at least one Lenape, Tom Hill.[80] Such eastern Native Americans brought more than European religion. They also carried with them the traditions of what had happened to their own peoples as a direct result of settler invasion. Hill recounted that "a few Americans had come at first to settle on the lands of the Shawnees, but when they were strong enough they had driven the Shawnees away, so that the Shawnees had no land left," assuring the Oregon peoples that "the Americans would treat them in the same way."[81] Another eastern Native, Joseph Lewis, fully apprised the Cayuse of the Haudenosaunee Holocaust.[82]

The histories alluded to here involve deeply traumatic Native experiences. The Iroquois were almost destroyed by Revolutionary armies and militias that were making total war on civilian Indian populations in pursuit of prize lands in upstate New York, Western Pennsylvania, and Ohio. To this day, the events of 1779–1782 are called "The Holocaust" by the Iroquois for the genocidal attacks ordered by the Town Destroyer, General George Washington.[83] Fiercely assaulted, the Ohio Lenapes and Mahicans also retain traditions of genocide, especially the horrifying massacre of March 8, 1782, when 96 of them, most of them starving women and children including 90 Moravian converts, were hideously killed at Goschochking, Ohio, by a Revolutionary militia after lucrative booty, scalp bounties, and land.[84] The Shawnees fared only slightly better than the Lenapes and Mahicans, but they, too, were starved, dispossessed, and driven to death by the Revolutionary militias.[85]

The Cayuses did not, however, need the prodding of the incoming Iroquois and Lenapes to see the land-grab in progress, as the ABCFM missionaries simply set themselves up on Indian land, took down trees, and planted gardens. The Cayuses watched the missionaries help themselves to fish and game while damming up streams for mills and buzzing through the lumber supply like nightmarish beavers. According to Christian missionary ideology, the "Flat-Heads" had invited them in, which justified their taking anything they wanted as the honest cost of bringing the rumored good news of their gospel.[86] The missionaries even assumed that the Indians existed as their built-in labor pool, airily dismissing Cayuse resistance to becoming their "slaves."[87] In his 1843 report, Whitman opined that a Cayuse refusal to convert justified taking Cayuse land.[88] It seemed never to have occurred to the missionaries, or to the majority of the settlers flocking in behind them, that there was anything untoward about such wholesale appropriation of the Indians' land, labor, water, lumber, fish, and game.

It occurred to the Indians, though, especially the Cayuses. Their speakers directly confronted Whitman about it, and more than once. After insisting upon being freely admitted to the Whitmans' house, and fed once there (as was the Cayuse custom with visitors), they "murmured still and said we must pay them for their land we lived on," Narcissa complained. She added in disgust that "something of this kind is occurring almost all the time when certain individuals" were present, that is, the Cayuse speakers deputed to tell the Whitmans that they had worn out their welcome.[89] In a joint letter, Marcus and Narcissa Whitman characterized the Cayuses as "these selfish Indians" for demanding fair pay for their labor and for their general countenance of the Whitmans' undesired presence on their land.[90]

The Whitmans' obduracy escalated difficulties, calling forth an instructional response. A standing tactic of behavior modification common to North American Natives is to do unto the other the objectionable thing that is being done unto the self, in a practical demonstration of just what feels like to be on the receiving end of said bad behavior. Once *that* point is made, elders typically sum up the lesson thus: *If you don't like it, then don't do it to anyone else.* All Native children raised in anything like a traditional household are quite familiar with this tactic.

Accordingly, the Cayuses began to pasture their horses in missionary cornfields on the land that Whitman had just boasted that he had never paid for, and never would.[91] They also quipped that "it would be good" to kill Whitman's cattle, burn his mill, or take some of the melons he had grown on their usurped lands.[92] Instead of grasping the object lesson, Whitman remarked that the "greatest fear" of the mission farmers was that the unconverted Indians would "steal from them."[93] Obviously, behavior modification failed to get through to Whitman, so the Cayuses directly warned him that, should he stay, he would be killed.[94]

Throughout their tenure in Oregon, the Whitmans demonstrated an astounding monoculturalism, which is, unfortunately, often still shared by western historians. Nevertheless, it is vital that readers grasp what was going on from a Native perspective. When the Whitmans first arrived on the scene, the Cayuse, Walla Walla, and Nez Percé clan mothers welcomed Narcissa, while the councils of male elders listened to Marcus's message because this was what Native American etiquette called for.[95] International relations had long been established across Turtle Island (North America), along with the protocols of emissaries. If one group wanted to open relations with a distant group, the council elders of the first group sent their speakers with a message for the council elders of the second group.

Speakers were usually young men and women, physically up to an arduous trip and mentally alert enough to learn new languages in which to convey complex messages. Upon the arrival of peaceful emissaries, the host group dispatched a welcome wagon, typically composed of official women, to find out who the emissaries' elders were. Once the emissaries were officially welcomed by the women, councils (male with male emissaries and female with female emissaries) listened to the messages sent by the faraway elders. During this interchange, the emissaries were housed and fed. However, emissaries had no speaking rights in the host councils, and once those councils had crafted their answer, the emissaries were supposed to *head back home with the reply.*

Across Native America, this was what the councils thought was occurring when they first saw arriving missionaries and U.S. scouting expeditions, like that of Lewis and Clark in 1804–1806 and, specific to Oregon, those of Horatio Hale and Joseph Drayton in 1841 and Lt. John Charles Fremont in 1843.[96] This was, by the way, why General Clark was well thought of by Native nations: He and Meriwether Lewis actually *had* gone home again. By the time of Hale, Drayton, and Fremont, the Indians were becoming disgusted, but, since those three, anyway, also went home again, the Natives felt that an embassy, however botched, had just occurred.

Emissaries from great distances were mostly young people, which broaches another important Native American convention, that of the proper interface of youth and age. Elders are *always* in charge. Youngers *never* talk back to elders and certainly *never* criticize or order them about, yet here were the youthful Whitman emissaries, sassing local elders and "always talking bad to them."[97] When Whitman obstinately refused take their point, the elders' speakers confronted him dramatically, with Tilakanik accosting Whitman to demand "how many times" he "was going to talk." Striking Whitman "twice severely" in the chest, Tilakanik "commanded" Whitman "to stop talking." Instead of understanding this direct reproach for talking over the elders, Whitman laid the message to the fact that Tilakanik had been "practicing the ceremonies of the Papists."[98] Tilakanik also "took hold" of Whitman's "ear and pulled it and struck" him on the breastbone, "ordering" him "to hear."[99] Pulling the ears of errant children, while tapping them firmly on the breastbone and ordering them to listen constitutes a last-chance admonition that naughty Native children dread to this day. Unfortunately, pulling Whitman's ear to command his attention proved useless, for he was profoundly deaf to cultural tones other than his own and too self-righteously white supremacist to suspect that his own behavior might have been at fault.

Thus, the atmosphere around Waiilatpu in the fall of 1847 was already decidedly strained when the worst hit. That year's bevy of settlers had brought in the measles with accompanying dysentery and influenza. The measles might have come in from two directions, the west and the east. On July 22, 1847, at Fort Walla Walla, the artist Paul Kane recorded an account of an ill-fated Walla Walla and Cayuse expedition just then returning from California. It had encountered "the disease," meaning the measles, which had claimed around 15 percent in fatalities, or "upwards of thirty" of the party's original "200 men."[100] Thus, some have suggested that the measles arrived that summer from California.[101] However, the measles had already run its course through the joint expedition by the time it returned to Oregon, thus making the eastern settlers just then coming in the more likely agents of the measles' entry.

Dysentery had long plagued the area, killing many Indians, but now both dysentery and influenza hitchhiked on the lowered resistances wrought by the measles, laying some settlers and most Indians low.[102] The Oregon Natives soon noticed that they were dying in larger numbers than the settlers from the combined forces of measles, dysentery, and influenza. In an 1878 manuscript, a British physician, Dr. William Tolmie, recounted that, on December 20, 1847, a "fugitive Indian conjurer or curer of the sick, flying for his life from the Sinahomish country" claimed that "the Whites had brought the measles to exterminate the Indians."[103] This allegation was absolutely accepted by all of the Oregon Natives. Among the stories brought west and recounted to the Cayuse by other Indians was that of James Beckwourth's having deliberately infected the Blackfeet with smallpox just 10 years earlier.[104]

Furthermore, the Oregon peoples had already had their own confrontation with the deliberate spread of disease long before Whitman arrived. Catholic sources identified the disease of this tradition as the smallpox epidemic of 1830.[105] In a different and more specific take, possibly of a different event, Tolmie recorded that "it was firmly believed by the natives that the remittent fever of 1828 and after, so decimating them, had been left by a Boston shipmaster, Dominis, because they had not sold him all their furs."[106] Not coincidentally, 1828 was also the year that the British-American treaty on Oregon was extended. The British were determined to stay until the fur had been traded out of Oregon, at which point conceding the territory to the United States would not pose a problem for England. This suggests that, in introducing the fever, the Bostonian might have been retaliating spitefully against the Indians for preferring to trade with British agents more generous than himself.

Regardless of whether the settlers deliberately spread the measles, it was Whitman's attendance on those Cayuses sickened by the disease that culminated in the massacre. The Cayuses charged, and continue to charge, that Whitman deliberately poisoned them under the guise of helping them. The standard dismissal of the allegation hangs on a very interesting commentary originally provided by Dr. Tolmie in 1884. As father-in-law to a Spokane-descended daughter of settler John Work, Tolmie acquired some grasp of (and sympathy for) an Indian perspective.[107] By contrast, the longer he knew the missionaries, the lower his opinion of them dropped. His acquaintance with them, begun cordially in 1836, had soured by 1841, when he concluded that, "Missionary labor amongst the Indians was impracticable and fruitless in good results either to the teachers, or taught," so that labor "among the poor of some of the large cities at home" seemed to him a better use of missionary time than imposing upon the Indians.[108]

Appointed the medical officer at the British Forts Nisqually and Vancouver, Dr. Tolmie quickly came to realize that physicians were held to high standards by the Oregon peoples.[109] Among the Oregon nations, *tewats,* or healers, needed to exercise caution in their cures, for when the patient died, so might the *tewat.* Tolmie learned this from talk of assassinating him after he had lost a patient.[110] Thereafter, he was very careful whom he took on as a patient, for instance, refusing medical attention on January 22, 1835 to a patient "affected with vomiting of blood for some days past," fearing that "should he die his friends might demand payment as is the custom in the interior of the Columbia," that is, the payment of Tolmie's life.[111] Accordingly, in 1884, Tolmie suggested that, between the Indian impatience with incompetent healers and the measles epidemic, whose Cayuse fatalities had been assiduously tended by Whitman, the massacre at Waiilatpu was a totally foreseeable event. The Cayuses were killing a failed *tewat*.[112]

This is certainly a winsome explanation from an attractive source. Since it was widely confirmed in settler diaries and letters of the time that being a *tewat* was a dangerous career choice, Tolmie's suggestion goes down well with western historians.[113] There are, however, three difficulties with it:

1. It requires sheer ignorance of *tewat* protocol on the part of Whitman.
2. It obviates the differentials in death rates between those in and not in Whitman's area.
3. It assumes without question that the accusations of poisoning by Whitman were unfounded, based on nothing but Cayuse "superstition."

First, there is no reason to assume that Whitman was naive enough not to understand the Cayuse custom of killing incompetent doctors. He was not. In a May 3 entry in a diary letter dated March 30 1837—ten-and-a-half years before the measles epidemic—Narcissa Whitman informed her brothers and sisters that badly performing *tewats* were killed. In full knowledge of this, Whitman had taken on a "very sick" Cayuse, and Narcissa bragged that "the medicine given soon relieved him," in contrast to the *tewat*'s remedies, which had failed him.[114] Thus, Whitman was entirely aware of the custom and seemed to take an adrenalin junkie's delight in competing with the *tewats*. Furthermore, showing up Native American healers was a hoary tactic of settler bravado. Missionaries and lay settlers alike typically saw Indian medicine people as Christianity's chief rivals, so they concluded that publicly shaming Indian medical personnel would show those superstitious Indians just whose spirits were superior to whose.[115]

Second, statistically, there was a strangely higher rate of death among the Indians in Whitman's area than among people outside of his area. The common fatality rate from measles was 10 percent, but around Whitman in the Willamette Valley, that death rate stood five times higher, at 50 percent.[116] Robert Boyd put this down to a "virgin soil" epidemic, but Oregon Natives had already been raked over by disease, starting with the earliest contacts with the fur traders. Given, at highest, the 15 percent death rate experienced by the Cayuse and Walla Walla expedition to California, in a measles outbreak not tended by Whitman, the 50 percent death rate in his area needs explaining. Interestingly, by December 24, 1847, with Whitman dead, settler George Roberts recorded, "The disease does not seem to spread so quickly as was expected."[117] The deep destructiveness of the 1847 epidemic among the Indians attended by Dr. Whitman was considered quite important by local Natives, as shown by a Cayuse account recorded by William Craig in 1848.[118] It was not lost on the Cayuses that 197 of them died in the measles epidemic, and those were only the Cayuse deaths recorded by the settlers.[119]

Third, Whitman's long track record of funny business when it came to dispensing medicine must be considered. If only one incident were involved, then charges of poisoning by Whitman might reasonably be dismissed as egregious, but more exist than just one isolated incident. If the charges were vague, then they might be credibly discounted, but the charges are quite specific. If the charges came from only one, unreliable source, then they might be considered feeble, but there are numerous, mutually reinforcing testimonies from independent sources. If the charges came only from Cayuse oral tradition, then they might be questionable, but corroborating settler accounts from the time are on record. Thus, the allegations of deliberate poisoning deserve to be laid out and weighed.

Cayuse suspicious first arose in 1840. In a report of July 6, 1840 to ABCFM, Whitman noted an epidemic that he was attending.[120] The results were not favorable, so that this 1840 epidemic became an important part of Cayuse oral tradition concerning Whitman.[121] Then, in 1841, came the melon poisonings. Whitman's mechanic-carpenter, William Gray, openly reminisced about them as comic.[122] Indeed, settlers' chronicles are full of what passed for "humorous" tales of the settlers feeding Indians various noxious and toxic substances, such as liquor laced with laudanum or gunpowder dispensed as medicine.[123] This was obviously not an unprecedented antic.

The story goes that, annoyed that the Cayuses took melons from his garden, Whitman hit upon the hilarious solution of injecting ripe melons with one of his medicines, "tartar emetic," to teach those thieving redskins a lesson. Archibald McKinley, the commander at Fort Walla Walla near Waiilatpu, dated this event to 1841, in the "two epistles" dated April 28, 1884 and May 12, 1884 that he wrote to Tolmie about the "drugging of the melons." Thereafter, McKinley concluded, "Whitman was suspected of being a dangerous *medicine man*" (italics in the original).[124]

According to a deposition by Augustine Raymond on September 12, 1848, Raymond had personally heard Gray's boast of poisoning the melons. Moreover, Raymond had, himself, eaten melons given to him by Gray.[125] John Young likewise testified that Gray, "who was then living with" Whitman,

> offered us as many melons to eat as we liked; but he warned us at the time not to eat them indiscriminately, as some of them were poisoned. "The Indians," said he, "are continually stealing our melons; to stop them *we* have to put a little poison on the bigger ones, in order that the Indians who eat them might be a little sick; *we* did not put on enough of it to kill them, but only enough to make them a little sick." (Italics added)[126]

Tartar emetic (antimony potassium tartrate) will make people more than "a little sick." An urban legend of the day viewed antimony poisoning as harmless, the stuff of a practical joke, but that did not stop the victims of it from dying.[127] In the 19th century, tartar emetic was frequently used in conjunction with strychnine to commit outright murder.[128] Indeed, tartar emetic, alone, was used to murder people.[129]

Because the melon story came partially through Gray, 19th- and 20th-century historians typically fobbed the melon poisoning off on Gray, even claiming that the

Whitmans had disapproved of the tactic.[130] However, the "we" in John Young's affidavit clearly goes beyond just Gray's culpability. In fact, Gray was probably trying to cash in on some of Whitman's glory with his "we." He liked to pass himself off as a doctor, and even got himself identified as "W. H. Gray, *Physician* and *Mechanic*" in an 1839 article in the *Missionary Herald*.[131] In a letter of October 22, 1839 to the ABCFM, Whitman strenuously protested this printed portrayal of Gray as a doctor.[132] Whitman was jealous of his status as THE DOCTOR and thus disapproved of Gray's masquerade, but Whitman's displeasure did not keep Gray from impersonating a doctor long enough to bleed a Spokane chief to death in 1839.[133] Physicians of the day regularly bled patients, but the real doctors knew when to stop.

There was clearly a strain between Gray and Whitman over Gray's medical pretensions, but the fact remains that it was Whitman alone who owned and had access to the medicine chest containing the tartar emetic (antimony), a standard western "medicine" of the day.[134] Importantly, McKinley, the commander at Fort Walla Walla, attributed the melon poisoning to Whitman.[135]

McKinley also noted that the melon matter was "little thought of at the time" by the settlers, who clearly saw it as a joke; Gray later "boasted" to McKinley of his "clever method" of preventing melon theft. Not so the Natives of the area, however. They "frequently referred to it," not only to McKinley but also to Whitman.[136] The reason that the poisoning was so little thought of by the settlers was that the victims were just Indians, and nothing that happened to people who were already "doomed" mattered much.

The idea of Indians as "doomed" was much on the minds of missionaries. As Mary Walker, Elkanah's wife, noted in her diary on November 17, 1839, the Indians "all seem doomed to melt away like the snow on the approach of summer & all we can do seems only calculated to hasten their doom."[137] Whitman spoke just as breezily about the necessity of the Oregon Indians' giving way in favor of the settlers, for instance, here, in a letter to his in-laws dated May 16, 1844:

I am fully convinced that when a people refuse or neglect to fill the designs of Providence, they ought not to complain at the results; and so it is equally useless for Christians to be anxious on their account. The Indians have in no case obeyed the command to multiply and replenish the earth, and they cannot stand in the way of others doing so. A place will be left them to do this as fully as their ability to obey will permit, and the more we can do for them the more fully will this be realized. No exclusiveness can be asked for any portion of the human family. The exercise of his rights are all that can be desired. In order for this to its proper extent in regard to the Indians, it is necessary that they seek to preserve their rights by peaceable means only. Any violation of this rule will be visited with only evil results to themselves.

Whitman noted the Indian anxiety "about the consequences of settlers among them," ending on a "hope" that "no acts of violence" would result "on either hand," but the sentiment rang very hollow in view of what he had just asserted.[138] It was a not a hope, but a wink-and-nod forecast.

Narcissa Whitman's recorded sentiments jibed with Marcus's racist attitude. Having already wished that the inconvenient Cayuse chiefs might "all die" during an 1837 epidemic, in 1841, she quoted, without dispute, her mother's characterization of the Indians as "perishing heathens," pausing only long enough to question her own, obviously lacking qualifications as a missionary.[139] Despising the Indians as filthy, selfish, and hopeless of improvement, she deeply resented cleaning up after Indian visitors to the mission, snapping that she had come "to elevate them" and not "to sink down to their standard."[140] When her door latch was jiggled the night of October 7, 1842, she immediately concluded that it was an Indian rapist, although no Indian was in the house and no rape ensued.[141]

The Indians were quite aware of this missionary prediction of their quick demise. In a letter of November 25, 1845, Whitman wrote that Wawatowe accused the settlers of "having a design" to seize Indian lands in Oregon, "being prepared with poison and infection to accomplish their purpose."[142] The Oregon Indians strongly suspected that, in addition to scaring up more settlers, Whitman had gone east in 1842–1843 "to get a bottle of poisen [*sic*] for us."[143] The Indians had already seen the missionaries truck in drugs. In 1838, Gray and Smith purchased large quantities of settler medicine to bring to Oregon.[144]

The Catholic account flatly stated that Whitman was poisoning the Indians.[145] Father Jean Baptiste Abraham Brouillet, the priest on the spot just after the massacre, recounted a shocking story in 1853 that he had had from John Young. Working for Whitman over the winter of 1846, Young saw Whitman regularly order two of his other employees to put out poisoned meat, ostensibly to kill wolves. Once, Whitman ordered Young himself to put out the poisoned meat, which he did:

> Some Indians who happened to pass there took the meat and ate it; three of them
> were very sick and were dying. Some days afterwards the Doctor [Whitman] told
> me, laughing, that they would have certainly died if they had not drunk a great
> quantity of water to excite vomiting. "I had told them very often," said he, "not
> to eat of that meat which we distributed for the wolves, that it would kill them;
> they will take care now, I suppose."[146]

Apparently, not only poisoned melons, but also poisoned meat eaten by the Cayuses was pretty doggone funny. In this instance, the supposed target of poisoning was a wolf pack, but Whitman obviously knew perfectly well that the starving Cayuses would eat the meat, and did not seem disturbed when they did. Importantly, Gray was not implicated in this poisoning. Young directly identified Whitman, alone, as the poisoner.

In 1973, Clifford Drury found it "difficult to believe that Whitman would have treated so serious an incident as lightly as John Young claimed, for he surely knew his own life would have been in danger had any of the Indians died from eating poisoned meat."[147] On the contrary, it is not at all difficult to believe Whitman's airy ridicule, given his easy dismissal of an 1836 Nez Percé warning that it was dangerous for him to enter Cayuse lands and his later contests with the *tewats* undertaken after he knew that the Cayuses sometimes killed those who lost patients.[148] When combined with the not inconsiderable clout of the local settler forts, especially Fort Walla Walla, whose commander obligingly threatened the Natives on Whitman's behalf, it is clear that Whitman did not fear the Cayuses. The Whitmans' cozy relationship with the fort also helps explain why the Cayuses believed that Whitman was attempting to bring the U.S. Army in to kill them all.[149] In fact, the Natives on the ground at the time were scared to death of Whitman, as he acknowledged in a letter of March 12, 1838.[150]

In testimony before a grand jury, Tawatoe confirmed that, well before the massacre, the Cayuses had "suspected that Doctor Whitman might be poisoning their sick." Not knowing what to do, they appealed to an unnamed Catholic priest in the area, who advised them to attempt a scientific experiment under which one patient would be given into the care of their own *tewat,* but another of the sick would be given over to Whitman to treat. Whitman's patient died, whereas the *tewat*'s patient lived.[151] This test helped to confirm the general Cayuse suspicion of deliberate poisoning.

Starting on May 21, 1850, the Oregon settlers conducted a four-day murder trial of the five Cayuses accused of having murdered the Whitmans. During trial testimony, witnesses brought up Joseph Lewis, an Indian originally from Maine but employed by and living at Waiilatpu.[152] (Having fled after the massacre and evaded capture, Lewis himself was not in evidence.[153]) In one deposition, William Craig reported that Lewis had told him of overhearing the Whitmans and Spalding in private conversation one evening, plotting the demise of the local Cayuses and Nez Percés, with Narcissa talking of poisoning them quickly and Marcus urging that they be done away with by degrees. Lewis further stated that Whitman and Spalding "had been writing for two years to their friends in the East, where Jos. Lewis lived, to send them poison to kill off the Cayuses and the Nez Perces; and they had sent them some that was not good, and they wrote for more that would kill them off quick, and that the medicine had come this summer," meaning the summer of 1847.[154] Another deposition, this one from Daniel Young, confirmed the same story.[155]

A similar account was given by the Catholic missionary, Brouillet, in 1853. The Cayuse chiefs told Brouillet that an unnamed "young Indian" conversant in English "who slept in Dr. Whitman's room, heard the Doctor, his wife and Mr. Spalding express their desire of possessing the Indian lands and their animals." In this account, Spalding urged Marcus Whitman, "Hurry, give medicines to the Indian[s] that they may soon die." The chiefs continued, "That the same Indian told the Cayuses, 'If you do not kill the Doctor, soon you will all be dead before spring.'" According to Brouillet, when the measles epidemic hit in 1847, with its disproportionately high death rate among them, the chiefs believed the story and attacked Waiilatpu in self-defense.[156]

Confirmation from yet another source was included in a November 30, 1847 letter by William McBean from Fort Nez Percés to officials at Fort Vancouver. Andrew Rodgers was a young teacher recycled from Spalding's mission, which he had left for Whitman's after having been unable to get along with the Spaldings.[157] Rodgers was killed at Waiilatpu during the massacre. McBean stated that Nicholas Finley, a "half-breed living in an Indian lodge on mission grounds," informed him that Rodgers had told the Waiilatpu Natives of having "overheard Whitman and Spalding plotting to poison them." One evening, while Rodgers was "lying down," he had overheard "the Doctor telling Rev. Mr. Spalding that it was best" that the Indians "be all poisoned at once; but that the latter told him it was best to continue slowly and cautiously, and between this and spring not a soul would remain," after which the settlers could "take possession" of the Cayuses' "lands, cattle, and horses."[158] Further testimony on this came from Tamsucky, one of the Cayuses personally attacking Waiilatpu on November 29. As the Waiilatpu massacre was in progress, Tamsucky demanded of Rodgers whether it were true that Whitman had been poisoning the Cayuses. Rodgers answered *yes*.[159]

In courts of law, deathbed confessions are given weight as the truth. The counterargument, first broached by McBean in his November 30, 1847 letter, that Rodgers would have said anything at that point to save his life, vastly underestimates the conscience of a convinced 19th-century Christian like Rodgers, who would have been less in fear of his physical demise than of his immortal soul should he lie before his god. Besides, as McBean made clear later in his letter, Rodgers did not believe he was marked for death when he made this recital, nor was he. It was only a miscommunication between Tamsucky and his Young Men that later led to Rodgers' mistaken execution.[160]

In a letter dated April 7, 1848, massacre survivor Josiah Osborne supported these accounts by claiming that Tamsucky had explained the reason for the massacre to its targets, declaring that "Doctor and Mrs. Whitman were scattering poison into the air," that is, spreading disease, to "kill them [the Cayuses] all off;" and that Whitman "knew they would all die and he would get their wheat and all they had."[161]

In his affidavit, the defendant Telokite stated that, during the measles epidemic, Whitman had "administered medicines" to the Cayuse, with a "large number of them" dying thereafter, "including the wives and children of some of these defendants," that is, Innocents, whom it was the obligation of elders and young men to protect. Telokite also mentioned a "certain Joseph Lewis," confirming that Lewis had, "a few days before" the attack, told the Cayuses that Whitman was poisoning them deliberately, with the intention of killing them all off by the next spring so that he could appropriate Cayuse land.[162] Whitman was quoted as having replied to Spalding's questions of why he "did not kill the Indians off faster" that "they are dying fast enough; the young ones will die off this winter, and the old ones next spring."[163]

A favorite dodge of 19th- and 20th-century historians for denying Whitman's culpability was to off-load all accusations of poisoning onto supposedly unreliable narrators, the "half-breeds" Joe Lewis, Nicholas Finley, and Tom Hill.[164] Due to the frequency with which his name arose, the favorite whipping boy of these was Joe Lewis, the "half-breed" usually credited by hagiographers with having brought about the massacre by lying to the Cayuses about Whitman.[165] Joe Lewis was, however, mentioned by *none* of the chroniclers of the melon or the meat incidents, whereas Wawatowe, Raymond, The Youngs, Craig, Tamsucky, Finley, Lewis, Telokite, Brouillet, and Rodgers, as well as the secondary accounts of McKinley and McBean, all mutually confirm one another. They go well beyond just Lewis, and all indicate something deeply untoward about Whitman's use of known poisons. The Lewis objection consists of rather disgraceful smoke and mirrors.

The key word in the Lewis smokescreen, likely to be missed by modern readers, is "half-breed," in references derived from the pseudoscience of race.[166] Widespread from the mid-18th through to the mid-20th century, race science was considered unchallengeable until it was thoroughly discredited by the Jewish Holocaust in the mid-20th century. The science of race posited western Europeans as the top of the racial hierarchy, with the "lesser" races degenerating from the Exalted Caucasian Pinnacle of Being down to the lowest rungs of Africans and Native Americans. Nineteenth-century polygeneticists held that Africans, Asians, and Native Americans were not even of the same *species* as Europeans. The monogeneticists disputed this, but nevertheless concurred that only Europeans were fully developed human beings capable of civilization.[167]

Under the rubrics of such race science, it was obvious that, as Indians, the Cayuses, Walla Wallas, and Nez Percés possessed a natural "disposition to murder."[168] The only thing lower or more dangerous than a primitive, "full-blooded" African or Native American was a "half-blood," with one half contributed by its respective "lower race" and the other half contributed by the "superior" European race. It was well known that "half-breeds" exhibited the worst traits of both races and possessed an irresistible impulse toward criminality. This was why, well into the 20th century, it was sufficient to mention Lewis, Finley, and Hill's mixed ancestry to prove that they were liars and murderers from the womb. Mentioning that they were Catholics, besides, just sealed the deal. That their racial identities are *still* mentioned in modern texts on the Whitman saga takes my breath away.[169]

For the record, Joe Lewis's mixed heritage did not make him a monster at the moment of conception. Neither did the silly allegation that he was working with the Mormons against the incoming Protestant settlers, nor did his interest in the "Dreamer" religion of Smohalla, which leaned on Catholic ritual while rejecting Christianity.[170] Of course, "none" of the incoming Protestant settlers "liked him," and, of course, Whitman only "reluctantly gave him some work." Lewis was, after all, a Catholic "half-breed," and they were devout bigots. The Protestant settlers' disrespect for a Catholic "half-breed" no doubt preceded and precipitated Lewis's "surly and morose" behavior on the wagon train and at Waiilatpu.[171] However surly and morose Lewis might have appeared to the settlers, however, the salient information about him is that Whitman *did* employ Lewis, and that, like Rodgers, Lewis *did* live in the compound at Waiilatpu, where he, like Rodgers, could easily have overheard the missionaries' conversations.

Interestingly, since no one could accuse Rodgers of being a "half-breed," his story was just quietly omitted from tellings of the Whitman saga, where it might otherwise have begged for equal time. It should be obvious by now that this whole "half-breed" tack is nothing but an antique conspiracy theory, with the "half-breed" troublemakers purportedly put up to no good by steely-eyed Catholic puppet-masters out to destroy Protestantism in Oregon. As such, it depends for its success on a shameful level of anti-Catholic and racist bigotry being present in the audience. Hopefully, the days are past when that expectation might have been borne out.

The flip side of the racist strategy to dismiss the Cayuse allegations was that the supposed poisoner was an elite, Euro-American missionary doctor, who could never have done such a thing. As William McBean put it in 1848, the Cayuse accusations were "only Indian reports," whereas "no person" could "believe the Doctor capable of such an action without being as ignorant and brutal as the Indians themselves."[172] Although the diction has been updated, this same character reference for Whitman is simply waved through as counterevidence, without serious examination.

Let us examine it here.

During the trial following the massacre, settlers testified that Whitman was ad-ministering drugs to the sick Cayuses. When the defendants' lawyer asked witness Eliza Hall whether Whitman gave the Cayuses medicines for their measles, she answered, "Oh, yes."[173] Witness Elizabeth Sager agreed that Whitman had given the Cayuses medicines.[174] A third witness, Josiah Osborne, testified that Whitman gave the Cayuses the same medicine that he gave the settlers, but that the morning of the massacre, Whitman had told him that the Cayuses had accused him of being a "sorcerer" who had given them different medicines.[175]

It is well known that Whitman had inordinate amounts of strychnine on hand, which he used in an "exceedingly careless way."[176] The standing rationale for this is that he was using it to poison out-of-control wolves. To be sure, strychnine was sold by the factor at Fort Vancouver, John McLoughlin, for the purpose of killing wolves. A letter dated December 13, 1839 to McLoughlin from the Hudson Bay Company enclosed "a small quantity of Strychnine made up in dozes [sic] for the destruction of Wolves," along with instructions that "it should be inserted in pieces of raw meat placed in such situations that the shepherd's dogs may not have ac-cess to them."[177]

Deducing the apparent size of the wolf menace from Whitman's supply of strych-nine, I assumed that his mission must have been inundated by wolves, but in re-searching, I was actually hard-pressed to find more than fleeting mentions of these animals. In a letter of April 7, 1846 to Joel Palmer, written by Henry Spalding and edited by Whitman, the possibility of sheep farming in Oregon was mentioned as a lure to settlers. Whitman noted that, at the time, one shepherd per 1,000 sheep would be required to fend off wolves in the winter. "But Strycknine [sic] is a sure poison with which to destroy them," Whitman concluded.[178] Elkanah Walker's di-ary entry of February 12, 1841 recorded, "Went in the evening and put out some poison." The next day, he wrote, "The wolves paid my poison a visit last night, but did not eat it." Henry Spalding's diary for January 5, 1841 mentioned that he had found "a wolf dead from poison this morning."[179]

Then, Spalding's diary for August 18, 1841 recorded "a most severe affliction" due to "the loss of the large, white, and spotted cow, both American," apparently "poisoned," since "we found a piece of meat I had given to an Indian containing *nux vomica* to kill a dog," but "being salt the cows ate it." In the second cow, Spalding "could find nothing." Nevertheless, he asserted confidently that both cows had "died of the same cause." At that point, Spalding darkly hoped that the "Indian" actually had put the meat out "for the dogs," that is, that the Nez Percés had not turned the tables on the missionaries by feeding the poisoned meat to their cows "by design."[180]

It is worth noting that, in the passage just quoted, Spalding referred to strychnine as *nux vomica*, the term then applied to strychnine used medicinally. In July 1838, William Gray complained of duplicative expenditures on "medicine," stating that he had already brought "from Cincinnati all the medicines necessary to the company," in fact, "twice as much" as he had "thought necessary." When Asa B. Smith "came on he was supplied with more than double the quantity, to the amount of $22.75, when six or ten dollars would have been an abundance," so that in 1838, the missionaries had "$30 dollars worth" of drugs, a huge supply at the time.[181] Not all of this was tartar emetic and *nux vomica*, but they would have been present as staples of every physician's medicine chest.

Furthermore, in the 1843 supply shipment to Fort Vancouver, Hudson Bay Company officials attempted to reduce "the quantity of Strychnine from 6 oz. valued at £27.12 to 1 oz." going out to Oregon, because the previous shipment was reported to have been "perfectly useless." A company official opined that, should the strychnine "be useless as represented," the company had "much better expose the concern to the loss of one ounce than six, until it be ascertained whether the drug be efficacious or not."[182] In reply, McLoughlin, responded on November 18, 1843 that "the 6 oz. Strychnine is for sale except about 1/4 oz. for ourselves," explaining his earlier complaint of "inferior quality" as having been meant to spur an increase, not a decrease, in supply, because the fort sold a "large quantity" of "medicine." The "American Settlers," as well as "our own," made "large demands" for the strychnine.[183]

This exchange is a mite inscrutable, unless the reader knows that the standard strength of *nux vomica*, the form in which strychnine as medicine was then distributed, fluctuated from 0.5 percent to 1 percent of the preparation. A preparation containing 7.4 percent, or half a grain per ounce of strychnine, was not created until 1890.[184] Thus, when the percentage of strychnine in *nux vomica* fluctuated down nearer to half a percent than to a full percent, the settlers complained that the drug was ineffective. Due to settler demand, McLoughlin was angling for the supplies containing the highest percentage of strychnine then available.

McLoughlin's strychnine letter of November 18, 1843 never mentioned wolves. Instead, he specifically referred to the strychnine as a "drug" and a "medicine," which is how the settlers seemed to have been using it. Not a little important in this regard is the account by Istacus (also called Stikas) saying that, after the massacre, the Cayuse war party went into Whitman's quarters, dragging the priest Brouillet along with them, so that he could read the inscriptions on Whitman's drug vials. They demanded that Brouillet find the poison that Whitman had been using on them: "After searching some time among the medicines, he found *a vial with something white in it,* and told them, *'Here it is'*" (italics in the original).[185]

Importantly, once Brouillet had found the vial, the Cayuses buried it. Colonel Cornelius Gilliam and his secretary, who recorded Istacus's statement on this episode, said that the interment was supposedly to forestall any settlers who remained after the massacre from finding the poison and finishing off the Cayuses with it.[186] This last sounds like a western interpolation, however. Far from an idiosyncratic security precaution, the act of burying poison is a very authentic tidbit of Indian lore, not commonly known to or understood by westerners.

Traditionally, Our Beloved Mother, the Earth, absorbs wrinkled medicine, recycling it into health, which is why her bones (i.e., rocks, especially any containing, say, uranium) are to be left buried in the ground. Any type of substance, including debris or ash left after cleansing ceremonies, is thus immediately buried to check the unwanted action of any wrinkled energy that it absorbed rather than purified during the ritual. Similarly, if a person has died without passing on his or her medicine-lodge knowledge, any medicine paraphernalia used in life is buried along with the corpse, lest it jump about like downed power lines, doing unintentional damage. The medicine was given only to that person by the spirits, so only that person is qualified to use it. Consequently, burying the white powder found in Whitman's effects argues strongly that the Cayuses did find and bury poison because it was in the medicine pouch of a *tewat* no longer able to use it.

The vial that Brouillet handed over to the Cayuses had "*something white in it.*" Strychnine looks like a white powder, either straight or prepared as *nux vomica.* Tartar emetic (antimony) also looks like a white powder. It is not unlikely that Whitman was using *both* antimony and strychnine on the Cayuses. The standard treatment for measles at the time was "tartarized antimony" (tartar emetic), with "antimonials" used as a secondary treatment of "eruptions" in various stages of the measles.[187] Strychnine was prescribed as a treatment for dysentery, which accompanied the 1847 measles outbreak.[188]

Importantly, from the end of the 18th through the 19th century, and even—for the slow learners in the autopsy room—into the early 20th century, strychnine was regarded as a miracle cure for whatever ailed one. Physicians experimented with various dosages of it, both alone and in combination with other lethal substances.[189] Moreover, despite its 1847 Code of Ethics, the medical profession was not overly nice in its protocols for experimentation on human beings. Doctors, many of them only barely trained, experimented away, often without the patients' permission and, in some instances, without their knowledge. The class standing of the physicians involved protected them from any perception of criminality.[190]

Marcus Whitman had taken his medical degree and begun practicing at the height of medical strychno-mania, when strychnine was even tried out on cholera patients.[191] By the mid-1830s, some "physicians were administering stupendous amounts of nux vomica power in a regimen of gradually increasing doses," so that the patient's survival depended upon his or her body's ability to absorb the poison.[192] Other physicians had just gone over to using straight strychnine.[193] As an up-to-date doctor, Whitman knew all of this. As far as he would have been concerned, the problem was in the dosage, not in the strychnine itself.

Finally, it would have tickled Whitman's overweening ego to have made a great medical breakthrough in the treatment of measles, and he had at his literal disposal a throw-away population of Cayuses, for whom he had no use and whom he had openly opined should die on Manifestly Destined schedule. Whitman might easily have been experimenting upon the Cayuses to see whether strychnine were as effective against the measles as the medical science of his day claimed that it was against so many other diseases. He might have been testing it against the standard antimonial treatment in control subjects, accounting for the charge that he gave the Cayuses different medicines from what he gave the settlers. He might also have been testing strychnine in combination with tartar emetic. All three possibilities were then standard medical approaches, and massive doses of strychnine alone or in combination with antimony potassium tartrate would certainly have accounted for the startling death rate of 50 percent in the Willamette region, as opposed to the 10 to 15 percent death rate from the measles epidemic elsewhere.

In short, the vindication of Whitman based on character witnesses falls flat. It was Whitman's very identity as an elite physician in 1847 that makes the Cayuse allegations against him of poisoning credible. He was, moreover, unquestionably guilty as charged of land and asset theft from the Cayuses, as were all the settlers involved in the missionary conquest of Oregon.

Notes

❦

INTRODUCTION

1. Hiram Martin Chittenden, *The American Fur Trade of the Far West* (1902; repr., New York: The Press of the Pioneers, Inc., 1935), 1: 12–13.

CHAPTER 1

1. J[ohn] C[uthbert] Long, *Lord Jeffrey Amherst, A Soldier of the King* (New York: The Macmillan Company, 1933), 187.

2. Pierre Pouchot, *Memoirs on the Late War in North America between France and England,* ed. Brian Leigh Dunnigan, trans. Michael Cardy (1781; repr., Youngstown, NY: Old Fort Niagara Association, Inc., 1994), 180.

3. For the secrecy of the plan, see Pouchot, *Memoirs on the Late War in North America,* 181–82.

4. William Stone, ed., *The Life and Times of Sir William Johnson, Bart.* (Albany, NY: J. Munsell, 1865), 2: 64–65. I was quite delighted to learn that, when Francis Parkman plied the Onondagas with cigars and pipes in 1845 to pump them for information, they stonewalled him in the traditional way by simply agreeing to anything and everything he said. Mason Wade, ed., *The Journals of Francis Parkman* (New York: Harper & Brothers Publishers, 1947), 1: 315.

5. Stone, *Life and Times of Sir William Johnson,* 2: 82.

6. Stone, *Life and Times of Sir William Johnson,* 2: 83–84.

7. Richard White, *The Middle Ground: Indians, Empires, and Republics in the Great Lakes Region, 1650–1815* (Cambridge: Cambridge University Press, 1991), 257–58.

8. Milton W. Hamilton, ed., *The Papers of Sir William Johnson* (Albany: The University of the State of New York, 1951), 10: 615.

9. Barbara Alice Mann, *Iroquoian Women: The Gantowisas* (New York: Peter Lang Publishing, 2006), 197–228.

10. The classic on Iroquoian agriculture is Arthur Caswell Parker, "The Iroquois Uses of Maize and Other Food Plants," in *Parker on the Iroquois,* ed. William N. Fenton (1913;

repr., Syracuse: Syracuse University Press, 1968), 5–119. For the astonishment of Europeans upon personally witnessing the depth and breadth of Native agriculture, see, for instance, on Denonville, Louis Armand, Baron de Lahontan, *New Voyages to North America,* ed. Reuben Gold Thwaites (1703; repr., Chicago: A. C. McClure & Co., 1905), 1: 130; E. B. O'Callaghan, ed., "Letter from M. de Denonville to the Minister [of France]," *Documentary History of the State of New-York* (Albany, NY: Weed, Parsons & Co., 1850), 1: 147; for Sullivan, see Frederick Cook, *Journals of the Military Expedition of Major General John sullivan against the Six Nations of Indians in 1779* (1887; repr., Freeport, NY: Books for Libraries, 1972), 34, 40, 75, 91, 99, 101, 163, 165, 166, 176, 235, 272, 303; for an extended discussion of the Sullivan rampage and the numbers, types, sizes, and extent of Iroquoian crops destroyed, see Barbara Alice Mann, *George Washington's War on Native America* (Westport, CT: Praeger, 2005), 67–77.

11. For a longer discussion of the Two cosmology (as contrasted with the ONE cosmology, see Barbara Alice Mann, *Native Americans, Archaeologists, and the Mounds* (New York: Peter Lang Publishing, 2003), 176–238.

12. Arthur Caswell Parker, "The Constitution of the Five Nations, or the Iroquois Book of the Great Law," *New York State Museum Bulletin* 184 (April 1916): 54.

13. Mann, *Iroquoian Women,* 231–37. There is a burgeoning literature on the topic of gift-economies, much of it French, but it is important to note its status as a defining, and perhaps *the* defining, feature of matriarchies. See, especially, Genevieve Vaughn, ed., *Women and the Gift Economy: A Radically Different Worldview Is Possible* (Toronto: Inanna Publications and Education, Inc., 2007).

14. Hamilton, *The Papers of Sir William Johnson,* 4: 134.

15. Stone, *Life and Times of Sir William Johnson,* 2: 123.

16. Hamilton, *The Papers of Sir William Johnson,* 10: 645.

17. Parker, "The Constitution of the Five Nations," 45, 103; John Heckewelder, *The History, Manners, and Customs of the Indian Nations Who Once Inhabited Pennsylvania and the Neighboring States,* The First American Frontier Series (1820, 1876; repr., New York: Arno Press and *The New York Times,* 1971), 270 n. 1. For a book-long examination of the "same bowl" metaphor, see Lisa Brooks, *The Common Pot: The Recovery of Native Space in the Northeast* (Minneapolis: University of Minnesota Press, 2008.)

18. For "tying up the clothes," see Harriet Maxwell Converse, *Myths and Legends of the New York State Iroquois,* ed. Arthur C. Parker, New York State Museum Bulletin 125, Education Department Bulletin no. 437 (Albany: University of the State of New York Press, 1908), 133; Henry Lewis Morgan, *League of the Haudenosaunee, or Iroquois* (1851; repr., New York: Burt Franklin, 1901), 1: 228; Arthur Caswell Parker, *The Life of General Ely S. Parker: Last Grand Sachem of the Iroquois and General Grant's Military Secretary* (Buffalo: The Buffalo Historical Society, 1919), 254.

19. For some expressions of this philosophy, see Michel Eyquem de Montaigne, "*Des cannibales,*" *Essais* (1580; repr., Paris: Éditions Garnier Frères, 1962), 1: 244–45; for Milky Way Trail, Gabriel Sagard, *The Long Journey to the Country of the Hurons,* ed. George M. Wrong (1632; repr., Toronto: The Champlain Society, 1939), 88–89; for Lenape spirits, Jonathan Edwards, ed., *David Brainerd: His Life and Journal* (1749; Edingburgh: H.S. Baynes, 1826) 314.

20. Hamilton, *The Papers of Sir William Johnson,* 10: 647.

21. Hamilton, *The Papers of Sir William Johnson,* 10: 465.

22. Hamilton, *The Papers of Sir William Johnson,* 10: 658–59.

23. Hamilton, *The Papers of Sir William Johnson,* 10: 857.

24. Stone, *Life and Times of Sir William Johnson,* 2: 136.

25. Stone, *Life and Times of Sir William Johnson,* 2: 136, 390–91; Sharon Block, *Rape and Sexual Power in Early America* (Chapel Hill: University of North Carolina Press, 2006), 3, 83–84.

26. Stone, *Life and Times of Sir William Johnson,* 2: 136–37.

27. E. B. O'Callaghan, ed., *Documents Relative to the Colonial History of the State of New York* (Albany: Weed, Parsons, Printers, 1853–1887), 7: 530.

28. The Board of Regulations outlined a new plan of trade, and Amherst entertained opening "a Trade, under proper Regulations." For quotation, see Hamilton, *The Papers of Sir William Johnson,* 10: 857; for Board of Trade, see O'Callaghan, *Documents Relative to the Colonial History of the State of New York,* 7: 535, 548–49, 560, 572–84, 599–602; Hamilton, *The Papers of Sir William Johnson,* 4: 106, 454, 556–63.

29. Stone, *Life and Times of Sir William Johnson,* 2: 40.

30. Stone, *Life and Times of Sir William Johnson,* 2: 12.

31. Hamilton, *The Papers of Sir William Johnson,* 4: 202.

32. Hamilton, *The Papers of Sir William Johnson,* 10: 461.

33. Stone, *Life and Times of Sir William Johnson,* 2: 136.

34. Mann, *Iroquoian Women,* 179–82.

35. For enslavement fears, see Hamilton, *The Papers of Sir William Johnson,* 4: 95, 125; for official denial of planned forts, Hamilton, *The Papers of Sir William Johnson,* 4:128; for settlers seizing the land anyway, see Hamilton, *The Papers of Sir William Johnson,* 4: 132.

36. Hamilton, *The Papers of Sir William Johnson,* 10: 505–6.

37. Stone, *Life and Times of Sir William Johnson,* 2: 176–78, 185–88; Hamilton, *The Papers of Sir William Johnson,* 4: 108, 112–17, 141–46.

38. O'Callaghan, *Documents Relative to the Colonial History of the State of New York,* 7: 544. For a discussion of European legalities of so-called right by conquest, see Robert J. Miller, *Native America, Discovered and Conquered: Thomas Jefferson, Lewis & Clark, and Manifest Destiny* (Westport, CT: Praeger, 2006), 4–5, 36, 40–41, 46, 66.

39. It was the Miamis entrusted with the woodlands legal requirement of notifying the enemy of impending attack. See Hamilton, *The Papers of Sir William Johnson,* 4: 97, 98–99.

40. Hamilton, *The Papers of Sir William Johnson,* 10: 689; O'Callaghan, *Documents Relative to the Colonial History of the State of New York,* 7: 543.

41. Joseph Doddridge, "The War of 1763," in *Notes on the Settlement and Indian Wars of the Western Parts of Virginia and Pennsylvania* (1824; repr., New York: Garland Publishing, Inc., 1977), 217.

42. Thomas Mante, *The History of the Late War in North America, and the Islands of the West Indies* (London: W. Strahan and T. Cadell, 1772), 482; William Smith, *An Historical Account of the Expedition against the Ohio Indians in the Year 1764* (London: T. Jeffries, Geographer to His Majesty, 1766), iii.

43. Doddridge, "The War of 1763," 217. After the war, the surviving traders, including William Trent, howled for restitution and were compensated by the British for their losses in the war. O'Callaghan, *Documents Relative to the Colonial History of the State of New York,* 7: 613–15; Hamilton, *The Papers of Sir William Johnson,* 4: 264–66, 270–71.

44. Hamilton, *The Papers of Sir William Johnson,* 4: 99.

45. Hamilton, *The Papers of Sir William Johnson,* 4: 187; Doddridge, "The War of 1763," 214–15.

46. Hamilton, *The Papers of Sir William Johnson,* 4: 166–67.

47. John Grier Varner and Jennette Johnson Varner, *Dogs of Conquest* (Norman: University of Oklahoma Press, 1983), 36–39, 192–93.

48. Louis M. Waddell, ed., *The Papers of Henry Bouquet* (Harrisburg: The Pennsylvania Historical and Museum Commission, 1994), 6: 304–5.

49. Waddell, *The Papers of Henry Bouquet,* 6: 315; Francis Parkman, *The Conspiracy of Pontiac and the Indian War after the Conquest of Canada* (1851, 1870; repr., Lincoln: University of Nebraska Press, 1994), 2: 40.

50. Smith, *An Historical Account of the Expedition,* 50.

51. Stone, *Life and Times of Sir William Johnson,* 2: 129.

52. Waddell, *The Papers of Henry Bouquet,* 6: 244–45.

53. Waddell, *The Papers of Henry Bouquet,* 6: 327.

54. Matthew C. Ward, "The Microbes of War: The British Army and Epidemic Disease among the Ohio Indians, 1758–1765," In *The Sixty Year's War for the Great Lakes, 1754–1814,* ed. David Curtis Skaggs and Larry L. Nelson (East Lansing: Michigan State University Press, 2001), 64.

55. Wilbur J. Jacobs, ed., *The Letters of Francis Parkman* (Norman: University of Oklahoma Press, 1960), 2: 148.

56. Stone, *Life and Times of Sir William Johnson,* for New York, 2: 115; for Quebec, 2: 120.

57. Stone, *Life and Times of Sir William Johnson,* 2: 200–201; Hamilton, *The Papers of Sir William Johnson,* 4: 139; Mante, *The History of the Late War in North America,* 489–90.

58. Pouchot, *Memoirs on the Late War in North America between France and England,* 162, 162 n. 482, 425, 425 n. 1331; Wade, *The Journals of Francis Parkman,* 2: 606, 606 n. 15.

59. Waddell, *The Papers of Henry Bouquet,* 6: 229. Trans. B. Mann.

60. Mary Carson Darlington, *Fort Pitt and Letters from the Frontier* (Pittsburgh: J. R. Weldin & Co., 1892), 145–46; Hamilton, *The Papers of Sir William Johnson,* 4: 197.

61. Waddell, *The Papers of Henry Bouquet,* 6: 251.

62. Carson. *Fort Pitt and Letters from the Frontier,* 182.

63. Thomas Lynch Montgomery, ed., *Frontier Forts of Pennsylvania* (Harrisburg, PA: William Stanley Ray, State Printer, 1916), 2: 276.

64. Alexander Scott Withers, *Chronicles of Border Warfare, or, a History of the Settlement by the Whites, of Northwestern Virginia, and of the Indian Wars and Massacres in that Section of the State* (1895; repr., New York: Arno Press, 1971), 291.

65. Darlington, *Fort Pitt and Letters from the Frontier,* 136; Waddell, *The Papers of Henry Bouquet,* 6: 259.

66. Waddell, *The Papers of Henry Bouquet,* 6: 228, 233 n. 1.

67. Darlington, *Fort Pitt and Letters from the Frontier,* 129.

68. Darlington, *Fort Pitt and Letters from the Frontier,* 155.

69. Darlington, *Fort Pitt and Letters from the Frontier,* 157

70. Darlington, *Fort Pitt and Letters from the Frontier,* 136.

71. Darlington, *Fort Pitt and Letters from the Frontier,* 136.

72. For a biography of McKee, see Larry L. Nelson, *A Man of Distinction among Them: Alexander McKee and British-Indian Affairs along the Ohio Country Frontier, 1754–1799* (Kent, OH: Kent State University Press, 1999).

73. Hamilton, *The Papers of Sir William Johnson,* 10: 743.

74. Hamilton, *The Papers of Sir William Johnson,* 4: 197.

75. Darlington, *Fort Pitt and Letters from the Frontier,* quotations, 92–93; same account in "William Trent's Journal at Fort Pitt, 1763: Notes and Documents," *Mississippi Valley Historical Review* 11 (1924): 400.

76. "William Trent's Journal at Fort Pitt," 400.

77. John Heckewelder, *The History, Manners, and Customs,* xxix–xxx, 58.

78. From the inception of their interaction with woodlanders, Europeans had been beside themselves over what they saw as homosexual practices. See, for instance, Lafitau's hysterical section titled, "Men Dressed as Women [Transvestites]," in Joseph Francois Lafitau, *Customs of the American Indians Compared with the Customs of Primitive Times,* ed. William N. Fenton and Elizabeth L. Moore (1724; repr., Toronto: The Champlain Society, 1974), 1: 57–58. Some commentators did grasp the political structure of gendered jobs, however grudgingly. See, Heckewelder, *History Manners, and Customs,* 56–57.

79. Stone, *Life and Times of Sir William Johnson,* 2: 13.

80. Heckewelder, *History, Manners, and Customs,* 70.

81. Darlington, *Fort Pitt and Letters from the Frontier,* 86.

82. Darlington, *Fort Pitt and Letters from the Frontier,* 93.

83. Darlington, *Fort Pitt and Letters from the Frontier,* 93; Waddell, *The Papers of Henry Bouquet,* 6: 262.

84. Waddell, *The Papers of Henry Bouquet,* 6: 258. Amherst referred simply to a trader, but the letter could only have come from Trent, as the General would not have replied personally to anyone of lower standing. Amherst steered clear of any promises in reply. Waddell, *The Papers of Henry Bouquet,* 6: 258 n. 4. Given this letter and the restlessness of the colonists, it was perhaps not surprising that Amherst began rethinking trade regulation in September 1763. Hamilton, *The Papers of Sir William Johnson,* 10: 857.

85. "William Trent's Journal at Fort Pitt," 400.

86. Mann, *George Washington's War on Native America,* 100. The identical originals of soldiers' journal entries are found in Frederick Cook, *Journals of the Military expedition of Major General John Sullivan against the six Nations of Indians in 1779* (1887; repr., Freeport, NY: Books for Libraries, 1972), 75, 91, 235.

87. Darlington, *Fort Pitt and Letters from the Frontier,* 182.

88. Waddell, *The Papers of Henry Bouquet,* 6: 264.

89. Hamilton, *The Papers of Sir William Johnson,* as Deputy Agent, 4: 111; for lost in a fire, 4: 272. Although some blame the fire at Croghan Hall for the loss of Croghan's report, this fire occurred before the smallpox gift, and thus cannot account for why the report is missing.

90. For McKee's position, see Hamilton, *The Papers of Sir William Johnson,* 4: 110.

91. Alexander McKee, "Report of Speeches of the Delaware Indians," Fort Pitt, June 24, 1763, in *The Papers of Col. Henry Bouquet,* ed. Sylvester K. Stevens et al., Series 21655. B.M., Add. MSS 21655, f. 216, D. 1943, 210, Ohio Valley-Great Lakes Ethnohistory Archives: The Miami Collection. This report is also glossed in Waddell, *The Papers of Henry Bouquet,* 6: 262.

92. C. M. Barbeau, *Huron and Wyandot Mythology,* Memoir 80. No. 11, Anthropological Series (Ottawa: Government Printing Bureau, 1915), 270.

93. Barbeau, *Huron and Wyandot Mythology,* 81.

94. Waddell, *The Papers of Henry Bouquet,* 6: 254.

95. Waddell, *The Papers of Henry Bouquet,* 6: 251.

96. Waddell, *The Papers of Henry Bouquet,* 6: 256.

97. Waddell, *The Papers of Henry Bouquet,* 6: 277.

98. Waddell, *The Papers of Henry Bouquet,* 6: 259. Trans. B. Mann.

99. Waddell, *The Papers of Henry Bouquet,* 6: 264.

100. Waddell, *The Papers of Henry Bouquet,* 6: 327, 341, 342 n. 2.

101. Smith, *An Historical Account of the Expedition against the Ohio Indians,* viii–xii.

102. O'Callaghan, *Documents Relative to the Colonial History of the State of New York,* 7: 546.

103. O'Callaghan, *Documents Relative to the Colonial History of the State of New York,* 7: 550.

104. Waddell, *The Papers of Henry Bouquet,* 6. 301.

105. Waddell, *The Papers of Henry Bouquet,* 6: 301 n. 1.

106. Long, *Lord Jeffrey Amherst,* 187. Long was quoting Parkman, The *Conspiracy of Pontiac,* 2: 40. Too squeamish to print "bastards," Parkman had dashed out the word. For some reason, Waddell omitted this letter from his compilation, although Parkman saw the letter "among the manuscripts of the British Museum," *Bouquet and Haldimand Papers,* No. 21,634. This was the same letter that conveyed the dogging plan to Amherst.

107. Parkman, *The Conspiracy of Pontiac,* 2: n. 40. Parkman had been generally research-ing when he visited London for the first time in 1845 (Jacobs, *The Letters of Francis Parkman,* 1: 31), although his London journal of 1845 did not mention a trip to the British Museum: Wade, *The Journals of Francis Parkman,* 1: 220–27. It is possible that he saw a copy of this letter in materials he acquired from Lyman Draper (Jacobs, *The Letters of Francis Parkman,* 1: 31), or in a specific Bouquet letter collection he recorded having accessed at the Historical Society in Philadelphia in 1845: Wade, *The Journals of Francis Parkman,* 1: 294. During a side trip to Canada (Wade, *The Journals of Francis Parkman,* 1: 309–10), he might also have seen the letter in the Canadian Archives, which (at least in 1928) had a copy of the letter under "Bouquet Papers, Series A," as documented in John J. Heagerty, *Four Centuries of Medical History in Canada* (Toronto: The Macmillan Company of Canada, Ltd., 1928), 1: 43 n. 20.

108. Waddell, *The Papers of Henry Bouquet,* 6: 315.

109. Waddell, *The Papers of Henry Bouquet,* 6: 316.

110. Waddell, *The Papers of Henry Bouquet,* 6:327, 327 n. 1.

111. Waddell, *The Papers of Henry Bouquet,* 6: 315.

112. Waddell, *The Papers of Henry Bouquet,* 6: 315 n 1.

113. Waddell, *The Papers of Henry Bouquet,* 6: 325.

114. Waddell, *The Papers of Henry Bouquet,* 6: 300.

115. Darlington, *Fort Pitt and Letters from the Frontier,* 170.

116. Waddell, *The Papers of Henry Bouquet,* 6: 378.

117. For repair of Fort Pitt, see Mante, *The History of the Late War in North America,* 484; for cannonshot, see Waddell, *The Papers of Henry Bouquet,* 6: 314, 327; for feuding with Trent, see Darlington, *Fort Pitt and Letters from the Frontier,* 155, 157; for exaggerating illness, see Waddell, *The Papers of Henry Bouquet,* 6: 462–63; for deserting, see Waddell, *The Papers of Henry Bouquet,* 6: 496, 497.

118. Hamilton, *The Papers of Sir William Johnson,* 10: Pottawattomis, 526; Miamis and Kickapoos, 572.

119. Hamilton, *The Papers of Sir William Johnson,* 4: 299.

120. Waddell, *The Papers of Henry Bouquet,* 6: 515.

121. Waddell, *The Papers of Henry Bouquet,* 6: 523.

122. John Duffy, "Smallpox and the Indians in the American Colonies," in *Biological Consequences of European Expansion, 1450–1800,* ed. Kenneth F. Kiple and Stephen V. Beck (1951; repr., Brookfield, VT: Ashgate Publishing Company, 1997), 249.

123. Sylvester K. Stevens and Donald H. Kent, eds., *The Papers of Henry Bouquet* (Har-risburgh, PA: 1940–41) Series 21650, Part 2, 127; Waddell, *The Papers of Henry Bouquet,* 262, 263 n.4.

124. Heagerty, *Four Centuries of Medical History in Canada,* 1: 43.

125. O'Callaghan, *Documents Relative to the Colonial History of the State of New York,* 7: 535, 548–49, 560, 572–84, 599–602; Hamilton, *The Papers of Sir William Johnson,* 4: 106, 454, 556–63.

126. For Fort Stanwix Treaty, see Barbara Alice Mann, "The Greenville Treaty of 1795: Pen-and-Ink Witchcraft in the Struggle for the Old Northwest," in *Enduring Legacies: Native American Treaties and Contemporary Controversies,* ed. Bruce E. Johansen (Westport, CT: Praeger Press, 2004), 140–44. The Treaty of Pittsburgh followed Lord Dunmore's War of 1774, a failed settler attempt to grab Ohio.

CHAPTER 2

1. See my discussion of the exculpatory dancing around the word "genocide," in Barbara Alice Mann, *George Washington's War on Native America* (Westport, CT: Praeger, 2005), 51–55. The term "genocide" was coined by Polish Jurist Raphael Lemkin in *Axis Rule in Occupied Europe: Laws of Occupation, Analysis of Government, Proposals for Redress* (Washington, D.C.: Carnegie Endowment for International Peace, 1944), 79–98.

2. Starting in the mid-18th century, European scholars propounded the crudest racism as irrefutable science. For major original theorizers, see Carolus Linneaeus, *A General System of Nature* (1758; 1806, repr., Ann Arbor: University Microfilms, 1968); Joannes Friedrich Blumenbach, *On the Natural Varieties of Mankind* (1795; 1865, repr., New York: Bergman Publishers, 1969); Samuel George Morton, *Crania Americana* (Philadelphia: J. Dobson, 1839). For smooth, secondary treatments of race pseudoscience and its effects on the development of the United States, see Robert E. Bieder, *Science Encounters the Indian, 1820–1880: The Early Years of American Ethnology* (Norman: University of Oklahoma Press, 1986); David Hurst Thomas, *Skull Wars: Kennewick Man, Archaeology, and the Battle for Native American Identity* (New York: Basic Books, 2000); and Barbara Alice Mann, *Native Americans, Archaeologists, and the Mounds* (New York: Peter Lang, 2003). especially 19–50, 280–83.

3. For the "cult of cultivation," see Ben Kiernan, *Blood and Soil: A World History of Genocide and Extermination from Sparta to Darfur* (New Haven: Yale University Press, 2007), 213–48, 310–63.

4. Mann, *George Washington's War on Native America,* 54–55.

5. Mann, *George Washington's War on Native America,* 38, 39, 109–10, 147–48, 177.

6. Robert J. Miller, *Native America, Discovered and Conquered: Thomas Jefferson, Lewis & Clark, and Manifest Destiny* (Westport, CT: Praeger, 2006), 58–59, 78–79, 90–91.

7. The best study of settler misuse of the land remains William Cronon, *Changes in the Land: Indians, Colonists, and the Ecology of New England* (New York: Hill and Wang, 1983). Dedicated studies of southern plantation land frenzies cry out to be done.

8. James Fenimore Cooper, *The Pioneers, or the Sources of the Susquehanna; A Descriptive Tale,* ed. James Franklin Beard (1823; repr., Albany, NY: State University of New York Press, 1980), especially chapter 22, 242–50, and chapter 23, 251–61. This novel was wildly popular when it came out.

9. For "wasty ways," see Cooper, *The Pioneers,* 248.

10. Bruce E. Johansen, *Shapers of the Great Debate on Native Americans: Land, Spirit, and Power* (Westport, CT: Greenwood Press, 2000), 79–80.

11. See, for instance, Robert E., Wright and David J. Cowen, *Financial Founding Fathers: The Men Who Made America Rich* (Chicago: University of Chicago Press, 2006), 169. The only mention of "Indians" in regards to Jackson was his attack on the Muskogees

in 1813 (167), which so glossed the actual history of the Fort Mims attack as to present Indians as the aggressors, rightly deserving to have been scorched later.

12. See Donna L. Akers, *Living in the Land of Death: The Choctaw Nation, 1830–1860* (East Lansing: Michigan State Press, 2004), and "Removing the Heart of the Choctaw People: Indian Removal from a Native Perspective," *American Indian Culture and Research Journal* 23, no. 3 (1999): 63–76. The article was recently reprinted in *Medicine Ways: Disease, Health, and Survival among Native Americans,* ed. Clifford E. Trafzer and Diane Weiner (Walnut Creek, CA: Altamira Press, 2001), 1–15.

13. Abraham H. Maslow, "A Theory of Human Motivation," *Psychological Review* 50 (1943): 370–96.

14. James D. Richardson, ed., *A Compilation of the Messages and Papers of the Presidents* (Washington, D.C.: Bureau of National Literature, 1897), 2: 1084.

15. Ralph Waldo Emerson, *Essays by Ralph Waldo Emerson* (New York: Thomas Y. Crowell, 1926), on history, 1–30; on self-reliance, 31–66.

16. Ernest Thompson Seton, *The Gospel of the Red Man: An Indian Bible* (Garden City, NY: Doubleday, Doran & Company, 1936), quoting a Crow named Curley, 58.

17. Akers, "Removing the Heart of the Choctaw People," 67, 68.

18. Akers, "Removing the Heart of the Choctaw People," 69.

19. For extended discussions of the two spirits (blood/earth and breath/sky) indwelling every person, see Barbara Alice Mann, *Iroquoian Women: The Gantowisas* (New York: Peter Lang Publishing, 2006), 327–32; and Mann, *Native Americans, Archaeologists, and the Mounds,* 180–96. Interestingly, the Lenapes sent their breath spirits south.

20. Akers, "Removing the Heart of the Choctaw People," 70, 74.

21. See, for instance, a complaint about their presence in *Correspondence on the Subject of the Emigration of Indians, between the 30th of November, 1831, and 27th December 1833.* Document 512 (Washington, D.C.: Duff Green, 1831–1835), 1: 944–45, 2: 307–8.

22. Akers, "Removing the Heart of the Choctaw People," 74.

23. *Correspondence on the Subject of the Emigration of Indians,* Document 512; for Peter Pitchlyn's miserable commute, see, 1: 406, 436, 500, 756–58; for Joel Nail's experiences, see, 1: 374–76, *passim,* 401, 573, 575, 610, 611–12, 650. These were just the experiences of the rescued, hence recorded, commuters. Both Pitchlyn and Nail were Choctaw-elected chiefs.

24. *Correspondence on the Subject of the Emigration of Indians,* Document 512, as "lamented," 1: 255; pork as "re-brined," 1: 837; letter exchanges, 1: 33, 220, 255, 831, 837, 842–43, 846, 849, 840, 853, 858.

25. Akers, "Removing the Heart of the Choctaw People," for the 1000, 74; for "Land of Death," 73.

26. Akers, "Removing the Heart of the Choctaw People, 64–65; Arthur H. DeRosier, Jr., "Andrew Jackson and Negotiations for the Removal of the Choctaw Indians" *The Historian* 29, no. 3 (1967): 343.

27. Robert B. Ferguson, "Treaties between the United States and the Choctaw Nation," in *The Choctaw before Removal,* ed. Carolyn Keller Reeves (Jackson: University of Mississippi Press, 1985) 214–18.

28. Barbara Alice Mann, "The Greenville Treaty of 1795: Pen-and-Ink Witchcraft in the Struggle for the Old Northwest," *Enduring Legacies: Native American Treaties and Contemporary Controversies,* ed. Bruce E. Johansen (Westport, CT: Praeger Press, 2004), 135–202. Ohio Indians coined the term, "pen-and-ink witchcraft" in 1791. See Alexander McKee, "Minutes of Debates in Council on the Banks of the Ottawa River, (Commonly

Called the Miami of the lake), November, 1791," (Philadelphia: William Young, Bookseller, 1792), 11.

29. J.F.H. Claiborne, *Mississippi, as a Province, Territory, and State* (Jackson, MI: Power & Barksdale, Publishers and Printers, 1880), Choctaw people as opposed to treaty, 506, 508; two-thirds of delegates as having left treaty council, 509–10, 521. Arthur H. DeRosier, Jr., *The Removal of the Choctaw Indians* (Knoxville: The University of Tennessee Press, 1970), 126; Ferguson, "Treaties between the United States and the Choctaw Nation," 222–23; Anthony Winston Dillard, "The Treaty of Dancing Rabbit Creek between the United States and the Choctaw Indians in 1830," *Transactions of the Alabama Historical Society* 3 (1899): 104–5.

30. Claiborne, *Mississippi, as a Province, Territory, and State,* 509–10, 516, 521; Akers, *Living in the Land of Death,* 91–93; Ferguson, "Treaties between the United States and the Choctaw Nation," 220–24; *Correspondence on the Subject of the Emigration of Indians,* Document 512, 1: 369. For a smooth rendition of the whole, shameful process, see Dillard, "The Treaty of Dancing Rabbit Creek," 99–106.

31. Wright, "The Removal of the Choctaws to the Indian Territory, 1830–1833," 105–6. The treaty was signed on September 27, 1830, and ratified by Senate on February 24, 1831. *Correspondence on the Subject of the Emigration of Indians,* Document 512, 2: 304.

32. *Correspondence on the Subject of the Emigration of Indians,* Document 512, 2: 185, 251–55, 256.

33. *Correspondence on the Subject of the Emigration of Indians,* Document 512, 1: 5–6.

34. Russell Booker, a Virginia State Registrar, coined the term "documentary genocide." J. David Smith, *The Eugenic Assault on America: Scenes in Red, White, and Black* (Fairfax, VA: George Mason University Press, 1993), term coined, 111; act of defined and explored, 89–100.

35. *Correspondence on the Subject of the Emigration of Indians,* Document 512, 2: 256–57; Claiborne, *Mississippi, as a Province, Territory, and State,* 521.

36. Pamela Coe, "Choctaw Saga," *Indian Affairs* 34 (1959): 6; Ferguson, "Treaties between the United States and the Choctaw Nation," 225.

37. Charles J. Kappler, "Treaty of Dancing Rabbit Creek," in *Indian Affairs: Laws and Treaties* (Washington, D.C.: Government Printing Office, 1904), 2: 314–15.

38. Kappler, "Treaty of Dancing Rabbit Creek," 313; Akers, *Living in the Land of Death,* 93.

39. Claiborne, *Mississippi, as a Province, Territory, and State,* 510; Ferguson, "Treaties between the United States and the Choctaw Nation," 223–25; Akers, *Living in the Land of Death,* 93; Arthur H. de Rosier, Jr., *The Removal of the Choctaw Indians* (Knoxville: The University of Tennessee Press, 1970) 135.

40. *Correspondence on the Subject of the Emigration of Indians,* Document 512, 3: 202; 4: 144–45, 498–500, 556, 559–67 passim, 578–79; *Letters Received by the Office of Indian Affairs, 1824–1881,* The National Archives and Records Service, General Services Administration, 1959, Microcopy No. 234, Roll 184, frames 0197–98.

41. *Correspondence on the Subject of the Emigration of Indians,* Document 512, dismissal, 4: 539–40; cattle, 1: 48, 2: 197, 1: 579, 1: 618–19, 2: 312–13, 2: 351, 2: 357–58, 2: 363–64, 2: 384, 3: 288, 3: 299, 3: 395, 3: 401; annuities, 1: 377–79, 2: 196, 2: 295, 2: 304–305, 3: 266, 3: 380, 3: 659; land, 1: 189, 1: 416, 1: 418, 1: 578–79, 1: 605, 2: 304–305, 2: 307, 2: 374, 2: 392–93, 3: 202, 3: 210, 3: 215, 3: 226–27, 3: 266, 3: 360–63, 3: 379–80, 3: 384–85, 3: 387, 3: 402, 3: 406, 3: 456, 3: 458, 3: 484, 3: 502–3, 3: 503, 3: 573, 3: 666, 4: 2–3, 4: 65–66, 4: 144–47, 4: 156, 4: 196–97, 4: 470–71, 4: 498–500, 4: 504–5, 4: 521–22, 4: 530–31, 4: 556–67, 4: 578–79, 4: 613–14, 4: 748–50.

42. Grant Foreman, *Indian Removal: The Emigration off the Five Civilized Tribes of Indians* (1932; repr., Norman: The University of Oklahoma Press, 1972), 31–37.

43. Foreman, *Indian Removal,* 46–54.

44. *Correspondence on the Subject of the Emigration of Indians,* Document 512, 1: quote, 77; 182.

45. *Correspondence on the Subject of the Emigration of Indians,* Document 512, 3: 303.

46. *Correspondence on the Subject of the Emigration of Indians,* Document 512, 1: 27, 156–57, 171.

47. *Correspondence on the Subject of the Emigration of Indians,* Document 512, 1: 27, 156–57.

48. *Correspondence on the Subject of the Emigration of Indians,* Document 512, 1: 171, 344.

49. *Correspondence on the Subject of the Emigration of Indians,* Document 512, 1: 620; Jackson as setting, *Correspondence on the Subject of the Emigration of Indians,* Document 512, 1: 153.

50. *Correspondence on the Subject of the Emigration of Indians,* Document 512, 1: 210, 289.

51. *Correspondence on the Subject of the Emigration of Indians,* Document 512, 1: 858.

52. *Correspondence on the Subject of the Emigration of Indians,* Document 512, 1: 215.

53. *Correspondence on the Subject of the Emigration of Indians,* Document 512, 1: 53.

54. *Correspondence on the Subject of the Emigration of Indians,* Document 512, 1: 54.

55. *Correspondence on the Subject of the Emigration of Indians,* Document 512, double-dipping, 1: 190; speculating, 1: 379–81.

56. *Correspondence on the Subject of the Emigration of Indians,* Document 512, 1: 243.

57. *Correspondence on the Subject of the Emigration of Indians,* Document 512, 1: 156–57, 421, 583, 587, 590.

58. *Correspondence on the Subject of the Emigration of Indians,* Document 512, estimates, 1: 471, 603–4; insufficient commutation, 1: 607.

59. *Correspondence on the Subject of the Emigration of Indians,* Document 512, for 1832, it is hard to secure an exact head count due to Ward's manipulations, but from reports at starting rendezvous and headcounts of arrivals, 5,000 looks like a solid number; see 1: 395, 603, 768, 837. In 1928, Muriel Wright counted up 5,217. See Wright, "The Removal of the Choctaws," 120–21.

60. *Correspondence on the Subject of the Emigration of Indians,* Document 512, 1: 254.

61. For stacks of problems caused by Ward's miserably kept registers, see *Correspondence on the Subject of the Emigration of Indians,* Document 512, 4: 565–67. 4: 2–3, 65–66, 144–47, 498–500, 504–51, 530–31, 539–40, 556–67, 578–79, 588, 599, 613–14, 748–50.

62. J. Diane Pearson, "Lewis Cass and the Politics of Disease: The Indian Vaccination Act of 1832," *Wacazo-Sa Review* 18, no, 2 (2003): to embed, 10; to punish, 20.

63. Elbert Herring, "Report from the Office of Indian Affairs," 22nd Cong., 2nd sess. House Document 2, 1832, Vaccination Act, 162; doubt, 163.

64. Herring, "Report from the Office of Indian Affairs," 167; Pearson, "Lewis Cass and the Politics of Disease," 10.

65. *Correspondence on the Subject of the Emigration of Indians,* Document 512, 1: 596.

66. *Correspondence on the Subject of the Emigration of Indians,* Document 512, 1: 372.

67. *Correspondence on the Subject of the Emigration of Indians,* Document 512, 1: 384–85.

68. *Correspondence on the Subject of the Emigration of Indians,* Document 512, ill conductor, 1: 385; for death of physician, 1: 417.

69. *Letters Received by the Office of Indian Affairs, 1824–1881,* The National Archives and Records Service, General Services Administration, 1959, Microcopy No. 234, Roll 170, frames 0091, 0105, 0107, 0108, 0110.

70. *Letters Received by the Office of Indian Affairs, 1824–1881,* letter of 27 July 1832, Roll 170, frames 0111–15.

71. For Gwin and Jackson, see Edwin A. Miles, "Andrew Jackson and Senator George Poindexter," *The Journal of Southern History* 24, no. 1 (1958): 56, 56 n. 33. For Dr. Smith, see *Letters Received by the Office of Indian Affairs, 1824–1881,* Roll 170, frames 0102–3, 0110–11. For a discussion of the pork-barrel, see J. Diane Pearson, "Lewis Cass and the Politics of Disease," 14.

72. *Correspondence on the Subject of the Emigration of Indians,* Document 512, as brothers, 1: 161, 165, 368, 388, 398, 417; appointment of the Armstrongs, 1: 124.

73. *Letters Received by the Office of Indian Affairs, 1824–1881,* Roll 170, frame 0256.

74. Akers, "Removing the Heart of the Choctaw People," 74.

75. R. J. Morris, *Cholera 1832: The Social Response to an Epidemic* (London: Croom Helm, 1976), 15; Charles E. Rosenberg, *The Cholera Years: The United States in 1832, 1849, and 1866* (Chicago: University of Chicago Press, 1962), 3. For "blue death," see Robert D. Morris, *The Blue Death: Disease, Disaster, and the Water We Drink* (New York: HarperCollins, 2007), 13–14.

76. Morris, *The Blue Death,* 11.

77. Charles E. Rosenberg, *The Cholera Bulletin Conducted by an Association of Physicians, Volume I, Numbers 1–24* (1832; repr., New York: Arno Press and *The New York Times,* 1972), 116, 127, 134; Rosenberg, *The Cholera Years,* 13. For steamboat dispersal, see J. S. Chambers, *The Conquest of Cholera, America's Greatest Scourge* (New York: The Macmillan Company, 1938), 47–50, 86–87, 94–95, 104–8, *passim*; Rosenberg, *The Cholera Years,* 21, 36.

78. Morris, *The Blue Death,* 19.

79. Rosenberg, *The Cholera Years,* 66–67; Morris, *The Blue Death,* 18–19;

80. Rosenberg, *The Cholera Years,* 14, 19; Chambers, *The Conquest of Cholera,* 96.

81. Bernhard Joseph Stern, *Society and Medical Progress* (Princeton, NJ: Princeton University Press, 1941), 211.

82. Rosenberg, *The Cholera Bulletin Conducted by an Association of Physicians,* 49; Rosenberg, *The Cholera Years,* 7, 40, 42, 44, 55, 60–61; Chambers, *The Conquest of Cholera,* 60, 70–71.

83. Morris, *Cholera 1832,* 11.

84. Morris, *The Blue Death,* 14.

85. Morris, *The Blue Death,* 15–16.

86. The death rate is 50 percent in virgin populations, declining to around 40 percent if untreated in previously afflicted populations. Morris, *Cholera 1832,* 15.

87. John J. Heagerty, *Four Centuries of Medical History in Canada* (Toronto: The Macmillan Company of Canada, Ltd., 1928), 1: 179; Rosenberg, *The Cholera Years,* 83.

88. Rosenberg, *The Cholera Years,* 19–20.

89. Stern, *Society and Medical Progress,* 207.

90. Chambers, *The Conquest of Cholera,* Great Lakes, 48–49; canals and rivers, 104–8.

91. Rosenberg, *The Cholera Years,* for bathing statistic, 18.

92. Chambers, *The Conquest of Cholera,* 49–51.

93. Wayne Franklin, *James Fenimore Cooper: The Early Years* (New Haven, CT: Yale University Press, 2007), 373.

94. David S. Jones, *Rationalizing Epidemics: Meanings and Uses of American Indian Mortality since 1600* (Cambridge, MA: Harvard University Press, 2004), 77.

95. F. O. M'Cown, *Transactions of the Twelfth Annual Re-Union of the Oregon Pioneer Association for 1884* (Salem, OR: E. M. Waite, 1885), 18.

96. M'Cown, *Transactions,* 20.

97. James Grant Wilson, *The Life and Letters of Fitz-Greene Halleck* (New York: D. Appleton and Company, 1869), 357.

98. Chambers, *The Conquest of Cholera,* October 13, 1832 Proclamation, reproduced facing page 106.

99. Chambers, *The Conquest of Cholera,* 63.

100. Rosenberg, *The Cholera Years,* 37, 37 n. 38.

101. Patrick J. Jung, *The Black Hawk War of 1832* (Norman: University of Oklahoma Press, 2007).

102. Chambers, *The Conquest of Cholera,* 86–90; Jung, *The Black Hawk War of 1832,* 139.

103. *Arkansas Gazette,* "The Cholera," August 15, 1832, 2, c3–4.

104. *Arkansas Gazette,* "The Progress of Cholera," August 29, 1832, 3, c2; *Arkansas Gazette,* "Cholera," September 5, 1832, 4, c1.

105. *Arkansas Gazette,* "Progress of the Cholera," September 12, 1832, 2, c5.

106. *Arkansas Gazette,* "St. Louis, (Mo.) Oct. 16, The Cholera," October 22, 1832, 2 c3.

107. *Arkansas Gazette,* "Little Rock Gazette," October 31, 1832, 3, c1.

108. *Arkansas Gazette,* "CHOLERA!!!—*at last!*" October 31, 1832, 3, c4.

109. *Arkansas Gazette,* "Prevention of Cholera," November 7, 1832, 2, c5.

110. *Arkansas Gazette,* Letter Extract, November 7, 1832, 2, c6.

111. *Correspondence on the Subject of the Emigration of Indians,* Document 512, 1: 378–79.

112. *Correspondence on the Subject of the Emigration of Indians,* Document 512, 1: 31.

113. *Correspondence on the Subject of the Emigration of Indians,* Document 512, 1: 593.

114. *Correspondence on the Subject of the Emigration of Indians,* Document 512, 1: 593, 886.

115. *Correspondence on the Subject of the Emigration of Indians,* Document 512, 1: 1: 160–61, 249, 280–81, 385, 387–89, 409, 417, 527, 700–701.

116. The "seven superficial square feet" were remarked upon in Office of Indian Affairs correspondence during Muskogee Removal, 1837, see Foreman, *Indian Removal,* 187 n. 28. It was not until 1847 that the "Act to Regulate the Carriage of Passengers in Merchant Vessels" began prescribing sufficient space.

117. U.S. Senate, *Report of the Select Committee of the Senate of the United State on the Sickness and Mortality on Board Emigrant Ships* (Washington, D.C.: Beverley Tucker, Senate Printer, 1854), cholera, 5; space requirements, 112.

118. *New York Observer* "Domestic," November 18, 1837.

119. *Correspondence on the Subject of the Emigration of Indians,* Document 512, 1: 107.

120. For Choctaws as "averse to steamboats," see *Correspondence on the Subject of the Emigration of Indians,* Document 512, 1: 603.

121. *Correspondence on the Subject of the Emigration of Indians,* Document 512, 1: 102.

122. *Correspondence on the Subject of the Emigration of Indians,* Document 512, 346. Full regulations are found on 1: 343–49.

123. *Letters Received by the Office of Indian Affairs, 1824–1881,* Roll 184, frame 0123.

124. *Correspondence on the Subject of the Emigration of Indians,* Document 512, 1: 102.

125. *Correspondence on the Subject of the Emigration of Indians,* Document 512, 1: 702.

126. *Correspondence on the Subject of the Emigration of Indians,* Document 512, 1: 131.

127. *Correspondence on the Subject of the Emigration of Indians,* Document 512, 1: 384.

128. *Correspondence on the Subject of the Emigration of Indians,* Document 512, 1: 384.

129. *Correspondence on the Subject of the Emigration of Indians,* Document 512, 1: 392.

130. *Correspondence on the Subject of the Emigration of Indians,* Document 512, 1: 386–87.

131. *Correspondence on the Subject of the Emigration of Indians,* Document 512, 1: 386.

132. *Correspondence on the Subject of the Emigration of Indians,* Document 512, 1: 389.

133. *Correspondence on the Subject of the Emigration of Indians,* Document 512, 1: 389.

134. *Correspondence on the Subject of the Emigration of Indians,* Document 512, 1: 389.

135. *Correspondence on the Subject of the Emigration of Indians,* Document 512, 1: 389.

136. *Correspondence on the Subject of the Emigration of Indians,* Document 512, 1: 390.

137. *Correspondence on the Subject of the Emigration of Indians,* Document 512, 1: 390.

138. *Correspondence on the Subject of the Emigration of Indians,* Document 512, 1: 390.

139. *Correspondence on the Subject of the Emigration of Indians,* Document 512, 1: 394.

140. *Correspondence on the Subject of the Emigration of Indians,* Document 512, 1: 395.

141. *Correspondence on the Subject of the Emigration of Indians,* Document 512, 1: 398.

142. *Correspondence on the Subject of the Emigration of Indians,* Document 512, 1: 398.

143. *Correspondence on the Subject of the Emigration of Indians,* Document 512, 1: 401.

144. *Correspondence on the Subject of the Emigration of Indians,* Document 512, 1: 390.

145. *Correspondence on the Subject of the Emigration of Indians,* Document 512, 1: 391.

146. *Correspondence on the Subject of the Emigration of Indians,* Document 512, 1: 391.

147. *Correspondence on the Subject of the Emigration of Indians,* Document 512, 1: 395.

148. *Correspondence on the Subject of the Emigration of Indians,* Document 512, 1: 395.

149. *Correspondence on the Subject of the Emigration of Indians,* Document 512, 1: 395–96.

150. *Correspondence on the Subject of the Emigration of Indians,* Document 512, 1: 498.

151. *Arkansas Gazette,* "Cholera," November 14, 1832, 2, c4.

152. *Correspondence on the Subject of the Emigration of Indians,* Document 512, 1: 737.

153. *Correspondence on the Subject of the Emigration of Indians,* Document 512, 1: 738.

154. *Correspondence on the Subject of the Emigration of Indians,* Document 512, 1: 398.

155. *Correspondence on the Subject of the Emigration of Indians,* Document 512, 1: 398.

156. *Correspondence on the Subject of the Emigration of Indians,* Document 512, 1: 400.

157. *Correspondence on the Subject of the Emigration of Indians,* Document 512, 1: 400.

158. Foreman, *Indian Removal,* 93.

159. *Correspondence on the Subject of the Emigration of Indians,* Document 512, 1: 401.

160. *Correspondence on the Subject of the Emigration of Indians,* Document 512, 1: 401.

161. *Correspondence on the Subject of the Emigration of Indians,* Document 512, 1: 401.

162. *Correspondence on the Subject of the Emigration of Indians,* Document 512, 1: 402.

163. *Correspondence on the Subject of the Emigration of Indians,* Document 512, appointed, 1: 23; acquainting himself, appointment, 1: 22–23; as posted in Arkansas previously, 1: 831.

164. *Correspondence on the Subject of the Emigration of Indians,* Document 512, 1: 43.

165. *Correspondence on the Subject of the Emigration of Indians,* Document 512, 1: 39.

166. *Correspondence on the Subject of the Emigration of Indians,* Document 512, 1: 31.

167. *Correspondence on the Subject of the Emigration of Indians,* Document 512, 1: 33.

168. *Correspondence on the Subject of the Emigration of Indians,* Document 512, 1: 43–44; Kappler, *Indian Affairs,* 315.

169. *Correspondence on the Subject of the Emigration of Indians,* Document 512, 1: 59.

170. *Correspondence on the Subject of the Emigration of Indians,* Document 512, 1: 82–83.

171. For Gaines, *Correspondence on the Subject of the Emigration of Indians,* Document 512, 1: 258–63, 279, 287–88, 459–79, 631–32, 638–40, 645–46, 650–52, 664, 666, 790–91, 859. For Wright, *Correspondence on the Subject of the Emigration of Indians,* Document 512, 3: 210, 266, 406, 456, 484.

172. *Correspondence on the Subject of the Emigration of Indians,* Document 512, 4: 504–5.

173. *Correspondence on the Subject of the Emigration of Indians,* Document 512, 1: 93, 101, 258, 262, 265, 285, 287, 313–14, 326, 645–46, 618–19, 650–51.

174. *Correspondence on the Subject of the Emigration of Indians,* Document 512, 1: under William Armstrong, 114, as fired by F. W. Armstrong, 195–96.

175. For the size of Colquhoun's party, see *Correspondence on the Subject of the Emigration of Indians,* Document 512, 1: 373.

176. *Correspondence on the Subject of the Emigration of Indians,* Document 512, 1: 628, 885.

177. *Correspondence on the Subject of the Emigration of Indians,* Document 512, 1: 682.

178. *Correspondence on the Subject of the Emigration of Indians,* Document 512, 1: 683.

179. *Correspondence on the Subject of the Emigration of Indians,* Document 512, 1: 405.

180. The moment he saw that the official wind was blowing against Colquhoun, Simonton exculpated himself for the Alston Bluff's fiasco by attributing malfeasance to Colquhoun, *Correspondence on the Subject of the Emigration of Indians,* Document 512, 1: 884–87.

181. *Correspondence on the Subject of the Emigration of Indians,* Document 512, 1: 390.

182. *Correspondence on the Subject of the Emigration of Indians,* Document 512, 1: 405, 885.

183. *Letters Received by the Office of Indian Affairs, 1824–1884,* Roll 184, frame 0152.

184. *Correspondence on the Subject of the Emigration of Indians,* Document 512, 1: 885.

185. *Correspondence on the Subject of the Emigration of Indians,* Document 512, 1: 886.

186. *Correspondence on the Subject of the Emigration of Indians,* Document 512, 1: 628, 886.

187. *Correspondence on the Subject of the Emigration of Indians,* Document 512, 1: 886.

188. *Correspondence on the Subject of the Emigration of Indians,* Document 512, 1: 887.

189. *Correspondence on the Subject of the Emigration of Indians,* Document 512, 1: 400.

190. DeRosier, *The Removal of the Choctaw Indians,* 156.

191. *Correspondence on the Subject of the Emigration of Indians,* Document 512, 4: 504.

192. *Correspondence on the Subject of the Emigration of Indians,* Document 512, 4: 505.

CHAPTER 3

1. The major sources of this standard version of the epidemic include Hiram Martin Chittenden, *The American Fur Trade of the Far West* (1902; repr., New York: The Press of the Pioneers, Inc., 1935); Bernard De Voto, *Across the Wide Missouri* (Boston: Houghton-Mifflin Company, the Riverside Press, 1947); Clyde D. Dollar, "The High Plains Smallpox Epidemic of 1837–38," *Western Historical Quarterly* (January, 1977): 15–38; Michael K. Trimble, "Epidemiology on the Northern Plains: A Cultural Perspective," Diss., University of Missouri-Columbia, 1985; Michael K. Trimble, *An Ethnohistorical Interpretation of the*

Spread of Smallpox in the Northern Plains Utilizing Concepts of Disease Ecology, Reprints in Anthropology, vol. 33 (Lincoln, NB: J&L Reprint Company, 1986); R. G. Robertson, *Rotting Face: Smallpox and the American Indian* (Caldwell, ID: Caxton Press, 2001).

2. John L. O'Sullivan, is credited with coining the actual phrase in O'Sullivan, "Annexation," *The United States Magazine and Democratic Review* 17, no. 85 (1845): manifest destiny, 5; Texas argument, 6–7. Alexis de Tocqueville alluded to the budding doctrine of Manifest Destiny in 1835 when he assured his readers that Euro-Americans were "fulfilling their destinies" by seizing Native lands. Tocqueville's use of the term "destiny" to justify the seize of North America interestingly shows that the articulation of manifest destiny was hatching for more than a decade before John O'Sullivan scratched down its final terminology. Alexis de Tocqueville, *Democracy in America,* 1835 (New York: Vintage Books, 1990), 432. O'Sullivan's exact phrase, "manifest destiny," plus associated doctrine, came in this surrealistically Proustian sentence: "Why, were other reasoning wanting, in favor of now elevating this question of the reception of Texas into the Union, out of the lower region of our past party discussions, up to its proper level of a high and broad nationality, it surely is to be found, found abundantly, in the manner in which other nations have undertaken to intrude themselves into it, between us and the proper parties to the case, in a spirit of hostile interference against us, for the avowed object of thwarting our policy and hampering our power, limiting our greatness and checking the fulfillment of our manifest destiny to overspread the continent allotted by Providence for the free development of our yearly multiplying millions." The term was thus coined in 1845, just in time to be implemented as governmental policy at the outbreak of the Mexican-American War (1846–1848) over the unilateral annexation of Texas by the United States.

3. Barbara Alice Mann, "The Greenville Treaty of 1795: Pen-and-Ink Witchcraft in the Struggle for the Old Northwest," in *Enduring Legacies: Native American Treaties and Contemporary Controversies,* ed. Bruce E. Johansen (Westport, CT: Praeger Press, 2004), 135–202.

4. "The Treaty with the Sioux and Chippewa, Sacs and Fox, Menominie, Ioway, Sioux, Winnebago, and a portion of the Ottawa, Chippewa, and Potawattomie, Tribes., Aug. 19, 1825, 7 STAT., 272; Proclamation 6 February 1826," in Charles J. Kappler, ed., *Indian Affairs: Laws and Treaties* (Washington, D.C.: Government Printing Office, 1904) 2: 250–55; "Treaty Made and Concluded at Prairie du Chien, in the Territory of Michigan, between the United States of America, by their Commissioners, General John McNeil, Colonel Pierre Menard, and Caleb Atwater, Esq. and the United Nations of Chippewa, Ottawa, and Potawatamie Indians, of the waters of the Illinois, Milwaukee, and Manitoouck Rivers, 29 July 1829," in Kappler, *Indian Affairs: Laws and Treaties,* 2: 297–300; "Treaty Made and Concluded at the Village of Prairie du Chien, Michigan Territory, on This First Day of August, in the Year One Thousand Eight Hundred and Twenty-nine, between the United States of America, by Their Commissioner, General John M'Neil, Colonel Pierre Menard, and Caleb Atwater, Esq., for and on Behalf of Said States, of the One Part, and the Nation of Winnebaygo Indians of the Other Part, 1 August 1829, 7 STAT., 323, Proclamation, 2 January 1830," in Kappler, *Indian Affairs: Laws and Treaties,* 2: 300–303; and "The Treaty Made and Concluded by William Clark Superintendent of Indian Affairs and Willoughby Morgan, Col. of the United States 1st Regt. Infantry, Commissioners on Behalf of the United States on the One Part, and the Undersigned Deputations of the Confederated Tribes of the Sacs and Foxes; the Medawah-Kanton, Wahpacoota, Wahpeton and Sissetong Bands or Tribes of Sioux; the Omahas, Ioways, Ottoes and Missourias on the Other Part, 15 July 15, 1830, 7 STAT., 328, Proclamation, 24 February 1831," in Kappler, *Indian Affairs: Laws and*

Treaties, 2: 305–10. With each successive treaty, Native naiveté about treaty-making declined. The first treaty was purely a land concession, offering *no* consideration at all in return for land forfeiture. Article 2 of the second treaty promised the lump sum of "sixteen thousand dollars, annually, forever, in specie," to have been paid "at Chicago," Kappler, *Indian Affairs: Laws and Treaties,* 2: 298. Article 2 of the third treaty required from the United States "eighteen thousand dollars in specie, annually" and as an immediate "present, thirty thousand dollars in goods" along with tobacco and salt, all payable for thirty years, Kappler, *Indian Affairs: Laws and Treaties,* 2: 301. In its Article 4, the last promised a total of $19,000, albeit over but 10 years and parceled out to each nation in specific amounts ranging from $3,000 to $500 each, payable "either in money, merchandise, or domestic animals, at their option." In addition, blacksmith services and farm implements in amounts stipulated by nation totaled another $2,700, Kappler, *Indian Affairs: Laws and Treaties,* 2: 306–7.

    5. See, for instance, support for Christian missionaries in *Annual Report of the Commissioner of Indian Affairs* for 1837–1838 (Washington, D.C.: Blair and Rives, 1838), 13–14; Isaac McCoy, *The Annual Register of Indian Affairs in the Western (or Indian) Territory, 1835–1838* (1835–1838; repr., Springfield, MO: Particular Baptist Press, 1998), especially 248–49; Elbert Herring, "Report from the Office of Indian Affairs," 22nd Cong., 2nd sess. House Document 2, 1832, missionary-run "Indian school" expenses, 159–60, and Attachment C, 167. Many Indian treaties contained forced transfer of funds from Native accounts to support certain missionary churches and schools, thus forcing Native nations to finance their own cultural genocide.

    6. See tourist Francesco Arese's description of "three or four little houses and a few warehouses, the whole enclosed by a poorly built stockade" in, *A Trip to the Prairies and in the Interior of North America [1837–1838]* (New York: The Harbor Press, 1934), 70.

    7. For a handy list with discussion of each fort, see Appendix F, in Chittenden, *The American Fur Trade of the Far West,* 2: 922–48.

    8. Racist depictions of official race science are so commonplace in all the lore of the time as to be too numerous to list, but the entire *Annual Report of the Commissioner of Indian Affairs* for 1837–1838 will suffice as an example of them in the highest reaches of officialdom. For a thorough review of the "race science" sources, see my documentary discussion of the 18th- through 20th-century pseudoscience of race in Barbara Alice Mann, *Native Americans, Archaeologists, and the Mounds* (New York: Lang Publishing, 2003), 9–50.

    9. Robert J. Miller, *Native America, Discovered and Conquered: Thomas Jefferson, Lewis & Clark, and Manifest Destiny* (Westport, CT: Praeger, 2006), 4, 10, 140. Notice that Discovery Doctrine, generally, was founded on Christian definitions of legal rights.

    10. All ineptitudes as in the original, in Waldo R. Wedel, *The Dunbar-Allis Letters on the Pawnee* (New York: Garland Publishing, 1985), 701.

    11. For a representative example of fur trader "battles," see Aubrey L. Haines, ed., *Osborne Russell's Journal of a Trapper* (Lincoln: University of Nebraska Press, 1965), 8, 12, 16–17, 30–32, 40, 48–49, 52–61 *passim;* 86–89, 102, 161–65 *passim;* For American Fur Company cannons, see Catlin, *Letters and Notes,* 1: 23 *on the Manners, Customs, and Condition of the North American Indians* (1841; repr., Edinburgh: John Grant, 1926); Charles Larpenteur, *Forty Years a Fur Trader on the Upper Missouri: The Personal Narrative of Charles Larpenteur,1833–1872* (Chicago: The Lakeside Press, R. R. Donnelley & Sibs Co., 1933), Fort Union armed with cannon, 45; possessing muskets, bayonets, cartridges, and a cannon in 1834, 68; in 1836, cannon, muskets, and ammunition, 81; cannon, 83. Fur company officials threatening and/or delivering "punishment" to Indians, Maria R. Audubon, *Audubon and His Journals,* ed. Elliott Coues (New York: Charles Scribner's Sons, 1897), 2: 43.

12. The term "raw slaughter" belongs to Bernard De Voto in, *Across the Wide Missouri*, 214. For a reference to 1827 and 1856 starvations, see Chester L. Guthrie and Leo L. Gerald, "Upper Missouri Agency: An Account of Indian Administration on the Frontier," *The Pacific Historical Review* 10, no. 1 (1941): 50, and 53, respectively.

13. Catlin, *Letters and Notes,* 1: 53.

14. For "richest man," see Arese, *A Trip to the Prairies,* 54; for Astor's remarks, see Chittenden, *The American Fur Trade,* 1: 365.

15. *The Missouri Republican,* "Old Times: An Interview with Gen. Bernard Pratte," November 24, 1879.

16. *Annual Report of the American Historical Association for the Year 1944, Part I: 1831–1840* (Washington, D.C.: Government Printing Office, 1945) 2: 521.

17. *Annual Report of the American Historical Association for the Year 1944,* 2: 525.

18. *Annual Report of the American Historical Association for the Year 1944,* 2: quotation, 279; 280, 298–99, 339, 341, 346–47, 373.

19. *Annual Report of the American Historical Association for the Year 1944,* 2: "large" shipment, 315, poor sales, 375.

20. Paul Chrisler Phillips, *The Fur Trade* (Norman: University of Oklahoma Press, 1961), 2: 525–26.

21. Annie Heloise Abel, ed., *Chardon's Journal at Fort Clark, 1834–1839* (1932; repr., Freeport, NY: Books for Libraries Press, 1970), respectively, 96, 99, 100.

22. See, for instance, Haines, *Osborne Russell's Journal,* 60–61; and Frances Fuller Victor, *The River of the West* (1870; repr., Oakland, CA: Brooks-Sterling Company, 1974), 93–96.

23. Hiram Martin Chittenden, *History of Early Steamboat Navigation on the Missouri River* (New York: Francis P. Harper, 1903), 1: 37–38.

24. T. D. Bonner, *The Life and Adventures of James P. Beckwourth, Mountaineer, Scout, and Pioneer, and Chief of the Crow Nation of Indians* (1856; repr., New York: Arno Press and The New York Times, 1969), 346–47.

25. *Annual Report of the Commissioner of Indian Affairs* (Washington, D.C.: Blair and Rives, 1838), 68.

26. Guthrie and Gerald, "Upper Missouri Agency," 47–48.

27. Guthrie and Gerald, "Upper Missouri Agency," 48.

28. Guthrie and Gerald, "Upper Missouri Agency," 50–51.

29. *Act of June 30, 1834,* CH 162, Sec. 17, 4 STAT. 735, codified as amended as 25 U.S.C. Sec. 9 (1988). Louise Barry, "The Fort Leavenworth-Fort Gibson Military Road and the Founding of Fort Scott," *Kansas Historical Quarterlies* 11, no. 2 (1942): 115. Intercourse acts had been passed regularly since Washington's presidency, but the 1834 Act set new ground rules.

30. Guthrie and Gerald, "Upper Missouri Agency," 52. The section establishing forts occurs on p. 738 of the 1834 act.

31. Barry, "The Fort Leavenworth-Fort Gibson Military Road and the Founding of Fort Scott," 117.

32. Barry, "The Fort Leavenworth-Fort Gibson Military Road and the Founding of Fort Scott," 118.

33. Barry, "The Fort Leavenworth-Fort Gibson Military Road and the Founding of Fort Scott," 119.

34. Louise Barry, *The Beginning of the West: Annals of the Kansas Gateway to the American West, 1540–1854* (Topeka: Kansas State Historical Society, 1972), 328.

35. Barry, "The Fort Leavenworth-Fort Gibson Military Road and the Founding of Fort Scott," 122.

36. Barry, "The Fort Leavenworth-Fort Gibson Military Road and the Founding of Fort Scott," 123.

37. Guthrie and Gerald, "Upper Missouri Agency," 52.

38. Thomas Jefferson Farnham, *Farnham's Travels, Part I* (1843), in *Early Western Travels,* ed. Reuben Gold Thwaites (Cleveland, OH: Arthur H. Clark Company, 1906), 28: 120 and 120 n. 64. All that scuttled these happy plans was the Panic of 1837, which cut the War Department's funding. However, by 1841, the project was picked up again, with 1,844 troops assigned (679 of them dragoons). The military road thus built burned into the Kansas Territorial Road in 1854, Barry, "The Fort Leavenworth-Fort Gibson Military Road and the Founding of Fort Scott," 127–28.

39. J. Diane Pearson, "Lewis Cass and the Politics of Disease: The Indian Vaccination Act of 1832," *Wacazo-Sa Review* 18, no. 2 (2003): 9–35; J. Diane Pearson, "Medical Diplomacy and the American Indian: Thomas Jefferson, the Lewis and Clark Expedition, and the Subsequent Effects on American Indian Health and Public Policy," *Wacazo-Sa Review* 19, no. 1 (2004): 106.

40. Herring, "Report from the Office of Indian Affairs," 175–76.

41. Isaac McCoy, *History of Baptist Indian Missions* (1840; repr., Springfield, MO: Particular Baptist Press, 2003), 441–42, 443.

42. For mention of Assiniboin traditions of the 1780 smallpox, see Edwin Thompson Denig, *Indian Tribes of the Upper Missouri* (1854), in *Forty-Sixth Annual Report of the Bureau of American Ethnology to the Secretary of the Smithsonian Institution for 1928–1929,* ed. J.N.B. Hewitt (Washington, D.C.: Government Printing Office, 1930), 396, 399.

43. Alice C. Fletcher and Francis La Flesche, *The Omaha Tribe* (1911; repr., Lincoln: University of Nebraska Press, 1972), 2: 622.

44. Edwin Thompson Denig, *Five Indian Tribes of the Upper Missouri: Sioux, Arickaras, Assiniboines, Crees, Crows* (Norman: University of Oklahoma Press, 1961), 72.

45. McCoy, *The Annual Register of Indian Affairs in the Western (or Indian) Territory,* 249.

46. Pearson, "Lewis Cass and the Politics of Disease," 22.

47. For typical ridicule of Indians as "superstitious," see for instance, Rudolph Friedrich Kurz, *Journal of Rudolph Friederich Kurz,* ed. J.N.B. Hewitt (1937; repr., Lincoln: University of Nebraska Press, 1970), 204; John Edward Sunder, *Joshua Pilcher: Fur Trader and Indian Agent* (Norman: University of Oklahoma Press, 1968), 139; Denig, *Indian Tribes of the Upper Missouri,* 397.

48. Denig, *Indian Tribes of the Upper Missouri,* 428.

49. For calomel in action, see Sunder, *Joshua,* 105–6; Abel, *Chardon's Journal at Fort Clark,* for sugar of lead, 132; for calomel, 356; for these and many more mineral medicines, see Robert Thomas, *A Treatise on Domestic Medicine* (New York: Collins & Co., 1822), 452–56; for gunpowder, see Robert A. Rees and Alan Sandy, eds., *The Adventures of Captain Bonneville* (Boston: Twayne Publishers, 1977), 187; for strychnine, see John Buckingham, *Bitter Nemesis: The Intimate History of Strichnine* (New York: CRC Press, 2008).

50. Rees and Sandy, *The Adventures of Captain Bonneville,* 72.

51. Jonathan B. Tucker, *Scourage: The Once and Future Threat of Smallpox* (New York: Atlantic Monthly Press, 2003), 15; for the role of Tibetan nuns, see Donald R. Hopkins, *Princes and Peasants: Smallpox and History* (Chicago: University of Chicago Press, 1983), 109.

52. Joel Shurkin, *The Invisible Fire: The Story of Mankind's Triumph over the Ancient Scourge of Smallpox* (New York: Putnam's, 1979), 121.

53. Thomas, *Domestic Medicine,* 119; David S. Jones, *Rationalizing Epidemics: Meanings and Uses of American Indian Mortality since 1600* (Cambridge, MA: Harvard University Press, 2004), 91; Wagner Stearn and Allen E. Stearn, *The Effects of Smallpox on the Destiny of the Amerindian* (Boston: Bruce Humphries, 1945), 53.

54. Jones, *Rationalizing Epidemics,* 88–89.

55. Jones, *Rationalizing Epidemics,* 91. Stearn and Stearn, *Effects of Smallpox,* give the eighth-day collection, 58, as opposed to Jones' ninth day collection.

56. Stearn and Stearn, *Effects of Smallpox,* 58.

57. Stearn and Stearn, *Effects of Smallpox,* 57–58 n. *.

58. See, for instance, Chardon's use of "vaccinate" for "inoculate," Abel, *Chardon's Journal at Fort Clark,* 133.

59. Denig, *Indian Tribes of the Upper Missouri,* 428; for inoculating 30 Indian women, Larpenteur (1933), *Forty Years a Fur Trader,* 109–10.

60. Sunder, *Joshua Pilcher,* 139.

61. Henry Rowe Schoolcraft, *Outlines of the Life and Character of Gen. Lewis Cass* (Albany: J. Munsell, Printer, 1848), respectively, 8, 9, 19, 18, 31, 49.

62. Abel, *Chardon's Journal at Fort Clark,* 319 n. 507.

63. Abel, *Chardon's Journal at Fort Clark,* vaccine sent, 319 n. 507; Fort Pierre as principal distribution point, xxix; and Larpenteur (1933), *Forty Years a Fur Trader,* 65 n. 31.

64. Pearson, "Lewis Cass and the Politics of Disease," 22.

65. Guthrie and Gerald, "Upper Missouri Agency," 53.

66. For anti-Arikara propaganda, see Catlin, *Letters and Notes,* 229–30; Abel, *Chardon's Journal at Fort Clark,* 110, 123; Wedel, *The Dunbar-Allis Letters,* 701; Sunder, *Joshua Pilcher,* 39, 47–48. For anti-Blackfeet propaganda, see Farnham, *Farnham's Travels, Part I,* 266; John Bradbury, *Travels in the Interior of America in the Years 1809, 1810, and 1811,* 2nd ed., 1819, in Thwaites, *Early Western Travels,* 5: 224–25, 225 n. 120; Catlin, *Letters and Notes,* 1: 48, 59; Larpenteur (1933), *Forty Years a Fur Trader,* 36, 77, 94; Bonner, *The Life and Adventures of James P. Beckwourth,* 101–7, 108–10, 211–12, 214–18, 221–26, 275, 286, 301, 311–17, 327–28, 346–57, 367–69, 372–73, 402.

67. Henry Rowe Schoolcraft, *Information Respecting the History, Condition, and Prospects of the Indian Tribes of the United States* (Philadelphia: Lippincott, Grambo, & Co., 1853–57), 3: 248, 249; Catlin, *Letters and Notes,* 1: 105, 108; Abel, *Chardon's Journal at Fort Clark,* Mandans as peacemakers, 47.

68. For Mandans, see Letter of 28 January 1852 from D. D. Mitchell, then Superintendent of Indian Affairs, to Schoolcraft, *Information Respecting the History, Condition, and Prospects,* 3: 254; and Catlin, *Letters and Notes,* 106. For the Iroquois as light-skinned people, see Adriaen Cornelissen van der Donck, "Description of New Netherland," 1653, in *Mohawk Country: Early Narrative about a Native People,* ed. Dean R. Snow, Charles T. Gehring, and William A. Starna (Syracuse: Syracuse University Press, 1996), 106, 107; Gabriel Sagard, *The Long Journey to the Country of the Hurons,* ed. George M. Wrong (1632; repr., Toronto: The Champlain Society, 1939), 136; Reuben Gold Thwaites, ed., *The Jesuit Relations: Travels and Explorations of the Jesuit Missionaries in New France, 1610–1791* (New York: Pageant Book Company, 1959), 5: 23; Samuel de Champlain, *The Works of Samuel de Champlain,* ed. H. P. Biggar (Toronto: The Champlain Society, 1936), 4: 53; Lafitau, 1: 89; Pierre de Charlevoix, *Journal of a Voyage to North America* (1761; repr., Ann Arbor, MI: University Microfilms, Inc., 1966), 2: 90. Specifically for Cherokees, who are an Iroquoian people, see Benjamin Smith Barton, *New Views of the Origin of the Tribes and Nations of America* (1798; repr., Millwood, NY: Kraus Reprint Co., 1976), xlv. Appallingly,

the pernicious myth of Europeans as the world's only light-skinned people persists, and is especially active among quantum-counters, hang-around-the-forts, and identity police, both European and Native. In fact, the world is *full* of "white"-skinned people who are not European. Aside from the Iroquois, Cherokee, Mandans, and some other Native Americans, there are also such folks as the Sami of Finland, the Kabyle and other Berbers of Africa, the Jews and most Middle Easterners, the Iranians, and the Ainus of Japan. Moreover, the blue-eyed blonds of Europe actually came from *western China*. Europe's original people, the Celts, looked nothing like them. It is well past time for this skin myth, the most degrading of racist contentions, to die.

69. Sunder, *Joshua Pilcher,* 137–38.

70. McCoy, *The Annual Register of Indian Affairs in the Western (or Indian) Territory,* 249.

71. Charles Larpenteur, "White Man Bear (mato Washejoe), Upper Missouri Trader: Journals and Notes of Charles Larpenteur between 1834 and 1872," transcribed by Edwin T. Thompson, National Park Service Library, Denver, CO, photocopy, 160.

72. *Papers of the St. Louis Fur Trade, Part 1: The Chouteau Collection, 1752–1925,* Roll 24 (Bethesda, MD: University Publications of America, 1991) frames 01121.

73. Barry, *The Beginning of the West,* 323. Barry gives "early May?" as the date here.

74. Writing on 31 May 1837, Allis stated that, the Wednesday before, the Pawnees had received annuities and then left for home. The Wednesday preceding was 24 May 1837. Wedel, *Dunbar-Allis Letters,* 713.

75. *Papers of the St. Louis Fur Trade, Part 1: The Chouteau Collection, 1752–1925,* Roll 24, frame 01212–01213; for Cedar Island as Fort Recovery, see Chittenden, *American Fur Trade of the Far West,* 2: 927; Sunder, *Joshua Pilcher,* 34–35. There is an outside possibility this could have been Cedar Fort, Chittenden, *American Fur Trade of the Far West,* 2: 2: 928–29, but Fort Recovery was military.

76. Arese, *A Trip to the Prairies,* 66.

77. Arese, *A Trip to the Prairies,* 70.

78. *Letters Received by the Office of Indian Affairs, 1824–1881,* The National Archives and Records Service, General Services Administration, 1959, Microcopy No. 234, Roll 884, frame 0280.

79. Abel, *Chardon's Journal at Fort Clark,* 118.

80. Larpenteur, "White Man Bear (mato Washejoe), Upper Missouri Trader," 158.

81. Bonner, *Life and Adventures,* 395.

82. *Missouri Republican,* "Old Times."

83. *Missouri Republican,* "Old Times."

84. *Letters Received by the Office of Indian Affairs,* Roll 884, frame 0280.

85. Dollar, "High Plains Smallpox Epidemic of 1837–38," 18; Robertson, *Rotting Face,* 91 n. 6.

86. Barry, *The Beginning of the West,* 323.

87. Marvin G. Ross, *The West of Alfred Jacob Miller (1837)* (Norman: University of Oklahoma Press, 1951), for the year as 1837, xviii; for the painting, "Crossing the Kansas," see Plate 101.

88. Dorothy O. Johansen, *Robert Newell's Memoranda: Travles in the Teritory of Missourie; Travle to the Kayuse War; together with A Report on the Indians South of the Columbia River* (Portland, OR: Campoeg Press, 1959), 34. For "Sublette & Vasques fort," or Fort Vasquez, see Chittenden, *The American Fur Trade of the Far West,* 2: 926.

89. Barry, *The Beginning of the West,* 323.

90. Wedel, *The Dunbar-Allis Letters,* 714.

91. Arese, *A Trip to the Prairies,* 60.

92. *Missouri Republican,* "Old Times"; Bonner, *The Life and Adventures of James P. Beckwourth,* 394; Barry, *The Beginning of the West,* 324.

93. Audubon, *Audubon and His Journals,* 1: 43.

94. Barry, *The Beginning of the West,* 324; Dougherty was first appointed as subagent in 1824, and then made the head agent in 1828, Guthrie and Gerald, "Upper Missouri Agency," 49.

95. Wedel, *The Dunbar-Allis Letters,* 714.

96. Arese, *A Trip to the Prairies,* 65.

97. Abel, *Chardon's Journal at Fort Clark,* 118.

98. Bonner, *The Life and Adventures of James P. Beckwourth,* 377–78 (spelled "Garro"); Abel, *Chardon's Journal at Fort Clark,* 121.

99. Larpenteur, "White Man Bear (mato Washejoe), Upper Missouri Trader," 159; Abel, *Chardon's Journal at Fort Clark,* 394.

100. Abel, *Chardon's Journal at Fort Clark,* 118, 316 n. 481. Since Pierre Didier Papin, American Fur Company agent to the Dakotas, was at Fort Pierre on April 17, 1837 (*Letters Received by the Office of Indian Affairs,* Roll 884, frame 0134) the passenger was his son, who had gone to St. Louis late in 1836; Bonner, *The Life and Adventures of James P. Beckwourth,* 378, 395.

101. Barry, *The Beginning of the West,* 324; Sunder, *Joshua Pilcher,* 122.

102. Arese, *A Trip to the Prairies,* 64; *Missouri Republican,* "Old Times."

103. Arese, *A Trip to the Prairies,* 72–73.

104. Arese, *A Trip to the Prairies,* 66; Report of February 5, 1838 from Joshua Pilcher to William Clark, *Letters Received by the Office of Indian Affairs,* Roll 884, frame 0274.

105. *Missouri Republican,* "Old Times."

106. Abel, *Chardon's Journal at Fort Clark,* 118–19.

107. *Letters Received by the Office of Indian Affairs,* Roll 884, frame 0134. In this letter, Fulkerson stated that once the *St. Peter's* arrived at the Mandan Subagency, which was at Fort Clark, he was informed that the agency "had been discontinued by the President of the U.S." Not wishing to remain there unemployed all winter, he asked for a 60–day leave.

108. Dollar, "High Plains Smallpox Epidemic," 18, 20, 21; Robertson, *Rotting Face,* 15, 17, 20, 21, 32, 62, 68, 70, 71, 73, 75, 81, 83, 84, 88.

109. *Letters Received by the Office of Indian Affairs,* Roll 884, frame 0345.

110. Robertson, *Rotting Face,* 299.

111. *Papers of the St. Louis Fur Trade, Part 1: The Chouteau Collection, 1752–1925,* Roll 24, frame 01212–01213.

112. Barry, *The Beginning of the West,* 328.

113. Arese, *A Trip to the Prairies,* 60.

114. *Letters Received by the Office of Indian Affairs,* Roll 884, frame 0281.

115. *Missouri Republican,* "Old Times"; *Letters Received by the Office of Indian Affairs,* Roll 884, frame 0273.

116. Dollar, "The High Plains Smallpox Epidemic of 1837–38," 20.

117. Robertson, *Rotting Face,* 62, 91 n. 2.

118. *Letters Received by the Office of Indian Affairs,* Roll 884, frame 0273; Dollar, "High Plains Smallpox Epidemic," 20; Robertson, *Rotting Face,* 89. For Pratte as unacquainted with smallpox, *Missouri Republican,* "Old Times."

119. *Missouri Republican,* "Old Times."

120. For stranding passengers as common, see Arese, *A Trip to the Prairies,* 52; it is also worth noting Arese's tale of his steamboat chugging past, rather than stopping to rescue around a dozen passengers left struggling in the water when their steamboat exploded, Arese, *A Trip to the Prairies,* 53. In addition, there is the case of Lt. Colquhoun, detailed in the chapter 2.

121. Robertson, *Rotting Face,* 34 n. 25. The official has been long assumed to have been William Fulkerson, although his letter of August 9, 1837 indicated that he was Fort Clark when the *St. Peter's* arrived. *Letters Received by the Office of Indian Affairs,* Roll 884, frame 0134. In this letter, Fulkerson stated that once the *St. Peter's* arrived at the Mandan Subagency, which was at Fort Clark, he was informed that the agency "had been discontinued by the President of the U.S." Not wishing to remain there unemployed all winter, he asked for a 60-day leave. Apparently unaware of this letter, both Clyde Dollar and R. G. Robertson assumed that Fulkerson had been aboard since St. Louis. Dollar, "High Plains Smallpox Epidemic," 18, 20, 21; Robertson, *Rotting Face,* 15, 17, 20, 21, 32, 62, 68, 70, 71, 73, 75, 81, 83, 84, 88. It is worth noting, however, that Fulkerson was fired around March 1, 1838 for not being at his post in January and February of that year, *Letters Received by the Office of Indian Affairs,* Roll 884, frame 0345. Being AWOL looked to have been a habit with Fulkerson, Robertson, *Rotting Face,* 299. He might well have been aboard the *St. Peter's,* after all, with the letter falsifying his whereabouts for cover.

122. Sunder, *Joshua Pilcher,* 10–11.

123. Alexandra Minna Stern and Howard Markel, "The History of Vaccines and Immunization: Familiar Patterns, New Challenges, Health *Affairs,* 24, no. 3 (2005): 611–21, http://content.healthaffairs.org/cgi/content/full/24/3/611#R33 (accessed August 13, 2008).

124. Larpenteur (1933), *Forty Years a Fur Trader on the Upper Missouri,* 109.

125. Tex Bandera, "When 10,000 Indian Died of Smallpox," *Frontier Times* 15, no. 7 (1938): 321.

126. *Missouri Republican,* "Old Times."; Audubon, *Audubon and His Journals,* 2: 43; John James Audubon, *Writings and Drawings* (New York: The Library of America, 1999), 640.

127. Larpenteur, "White Man Bear (mato Washejoe)," 159.

128. Arese, *A Trip to the Prairies,* 65; for vomiting as a smallpox symptom see Department of Health and Human Services, Centers for Disease Control and Prevention, "Smallpox," http://redcross.tallytown.com/library/Smallpox-Overview.pdf (accessed August 6, 2008).

129. *Missouri Republican,* "Old Times."

130. Audubon, *Audubon and His Journals,* 2: 43; Abel, *Chardon's Journal at Fort Clark,* 31, 43; Audubon, *Writings and Drawings,* 640. Since not only Maria Audubon but also Elliott Coues were famous for freely changing manuscript texts, sometimes dramatically, I double checked the 1897 text against the 1999 version, from the original manuscripts. The texts were the same here.

131. Abel, *Chardon's Journal at Fort Clark,* 118.

132. Abel, *Chardon's Journal at Fort Clark,* 315–16 n. 478; others as accepting it, Dollar, "High Plains Smallpox Epidemic," 21; Robertson, *Rotting Face,* acknowledged as speculation, 34 n. 22; used as fact, 25, 75, 84.

133. Abel, *Chardon's Journal at Fort Clark,* xxi, 109, 315–16 n. 478. Abel misidentified Tchonsumonska's nation as Teton. She was Lakota.

134. Abel, *Chardon's Journal at Fort Clark,* "whippings" from his wife (Tchonsumonska) for "bad behavior," 37, 78; multiple wives, xxi–xxii.

135. "I shall be at the Little Miss Before the arrival of the SB at that place." The Little Missouri was the Bad River, where Fort Pierre was. *Papers of the St. Louis Fur Trade, Part 1: The Chouteau Collection, 1752–1925*, Roll 24, frame 00953.

136. Abel, *Chardon's Journal at Fort Clark*, 319 n. 507.

137. Abel, *Chardon's Journal at Fort Clark*, xxi; his entry of May 18, 1838, mentioned that he had been married one year, 160, 319 n. 506; as Arikara, 160; as Marguerite Marie, xxi.

138. *Missouri Republican*, "Old Times."

139. Abel, *Chardon's Journal at Fort Clark*, 135, 137, 214 n. 53, 302 n. 382.

140. Abel, *Chardon's Journal at Fort Clark*, 118–19.

141. Report of February 5, 1838 from Joshua Pilcher to William Clark, *Letters Received by the Office of Indian Affairs*, Roll 884, frame 0274.

142. *Letters Received by the Office of Indian Affairs*, Roll 884, frame 0274.

143. *Papers of the St. Louis Fur Trade, Part 1: The Chouteau Collection, 1752–1925*, Roll 24, frames 01212–01213.

144. *Letters Received by the Office of Indian Affairs*, Roll 884, frames 0277–0278, 0280.

145. Letter quoted in Landon Y. Jones, *William Clark and the Shaping of the West* (New York: Hill and Wang, 2004), 330.

146. Abel, *Chardon's Journal at Fort Clark*, 394–96.

147. Wedel, *The Dunbar-Allis Letters*, 713–17.

148. *Annual Report of the Commissioner of Indian Affairs*, Arikaras and Mandans, 65; whole Pilcher section, 63–68.

149. *Annual Report of the Commissioner of Indian Affairs*, 68–69.

150. McCoy, *Annual Register*, 248–49, and McCoy, *History*, 554, 597; John Dunbar, Letter Dated June 8, 1838, *The Missionary Herald* 34 (1838): 383–85.

151. Abel, *Chardon's Journal at Fort Clark*, 118–19.

152. Abel, *Chardon's Journal at Fort Clark*, "Seperated from My dear Ree Wife, after a Marriage of one Year," as in the original, May 18, 1838, 160; "found all Well, except my beloved Ree wife, who has deserted my bed & board," as in the original, August 3, 1838, 170.

153. Abel, *Chardon's Journal at Fort Clark*, 118. "Frolic" was the general settler term for drunken, mixed-sex parties, especially as they involved Natives.

154. Abel, *Chardon's Journal at Fort Clark*, 118–19.

155. Dollar, "High Plains Smallpox Epidemic," 21; Trimble, "Epidemiology on the Northern Plains," 193; Trimble, *An Ethnohistorical Interpretation of the Spread of Smallpox*, 35; Robertson, *Rotting Face*, 90.

156. Arese, *A Trip to the Prairies*, 65.

157. Arese, *A Trip to the Prairies*, 65–66.

158. Arese, *A Trip to the Prairies*, 58.

159. *Letters Received by the Office of Indian Affairs*, Roll 884, frame 0284.

160. Letter reproduced in Abel, *Chardon's Journal at Fort Clark*, 394–96.

161. *Papers of the St. Louis Fur Trade, Part 1: The Chouteau Collection, 1752–1925*, Roll 24, frames 01212–01213. *Letters Received by the Office of Indian Affairs*, Roll 884, frames 0277–0278, 0280–0282.

162. Wedel, *The Dunbar-Allis Letters on the Pawnee*, 713–17; John Dunbar letter dated June 8, 1838, 383–85.

163. Larpenteur, "White Man Bear (mato Washejoe)," 162–63.

164. Catlin, *Letters and Notes*, 2: 293.

165. Audubon, *Audubon and His Journals*, 2: 42–43.

166. Farnham, *Farnham's Travels, Part I*, year, 264, as corrected 266 n. 156, same note "correcting" the nation of the blanket-stealer from Blackfeet to Mandan.

167. *Missouri Republican*, "Old Times"; Chittenden, *The American Fur Trade of the Far West*, 2: 614; Bandera, "When 10,000 Indians Died of Smallpox," 320; Glendolin D. Wagner and William A. Allen, *Blankets and Moccasins: Plenty Coups and His People, The Crows* (Caldwell, ID: The Caxton Printers, 1933), 200–211; De Voto, *Across the Wide Missouri*, 281.

168. *Letters Received by the Office of Indian Affairs*, Roll 884, frames 0273–0275, 0336.

169. Dollar, "High Plains Smallpox Epidemic," 33.

170. *Papers of the St. Louis Fur Trade, Part 1: The Chouteau Collection, 1752–1925*, Roll 24, frame 00953.

171. LeRoy R. Hafen, *The Life of Thomas Fitspatrick: Mountain Man, Guide and Indian Agent* (1931; repr., Lincoln: University of Nebraska Press, 1973), 160–61.

172. *Papers of the St. Louis Fur Trade, Part 1: The Chouteau Collection, 1752–1925*, Roll 24, frame 01121.

173. Herbert Heaton, "Benjamin Gott and the Anglo-American Cloth Trade," *Journal of Economic and Business History* 2, no. 1 (1929): 160–61. For French blankets as among the 1837 supplies, see the letter of 16 April 1837, from Pierre Chouteau to P. D. Papin, in *Papers of the St. Louis Fur Trade, Part 1: The Chouteau Collection, 1752–1925*, Roll 24, frame 01121.

174. *Letters Received by the Office of Indian Affairs*, Roll 884, frame 0336; *Papers of the St. Louis Fur Trade, Part 1: The Chouteau Collection, 1752–1925*, Roll 24, frames 00953.

175. *Missouri Republican*, "Old Times."

176. Catlin, *Letters and Notes*, 2: 293.

177. For the door-to-door program, see Council of the Citizens' Association of New York, *Report of the Council of Hygiene and Public Health of the Citizens' Association of New York upon the Sanitary Condition of the City* (New York: D. Appleton and Company, 1865), cxi; Mary M. Meline and Edward F. X. McSweeny, *The Story of the Mountain: Mount St. Mary's College and Seminary, Emmitsburg, Maryland* (Emmitsburg, MD: Weekly Chronicle, 1911), 357.

178. Meline and McSweeny, *The Story of the Mountain*, 357.

179. George Gregory, *Lectures on the Eruptive Fevers* (New York: S. S. & W. Wood, Publishers, 1851), Table VI., Baltimore, 341. For the 1836 hospital fire, see Lighthouse Friends, "Larzaretto Point Lighthouse, MD," http://www.lighthousefriends.com/light.asp?ID=421 (accessed July 30, 2008).

180. Gregory, *Lectures on the Eruptive Fevers*, Table I., New York, 336; Table II., Philadelphia, 338; Table III., Boston, 339.

181. *Missouri Republican*, "Old Times."

182. Abel, *Chardon's Journal at Fort Clark*, 118.

183. *Papers of the St. Louis Fur Trade, Part 1: The Chouteau Collection, 1752–1925*, Roll 25 (Bethesda, MD: University Publications of America, 1991) frame 00267. This is the (solid) English translation of the letter in French, given as frames 00264–00265, with the French text of the quotation appearing on frame 00264.

184. For the charge of seeding infection, see De Voto, *Across the Wide Missouri*, 442–43 n. 1, and Bandera, "When 10,000 Indian Died of Smallpox," 320; for Culbertson, see Chittenden, *The American Fur Trade of the Far West*, 1: 386.

185. Bandera, "When 10,000 Indians Died of Smallpox," 320.

186. *Papers of the St. Louis Fur Trade, Part 1: The Chouteau Collection, 1752–1925*, Roll 24, frame 00496. For McKenzie, see Larpenteur (1933), *Forty Years a Fur Trader*, 38 n24.

187. Abel, *Chardon's Journal at Fort Clark*, 64.

188. Abel, *Chardon's Journal at Fort Clark*, 122.

189. Abel, *Chardon's Journal at Fort Clark*, leave, 128; return, 131.

190. Abel, *Chardon's Journal at Fort Clark*, 132.

191. Abel, *Chardon's Journal at Fort Clark*, 142.

192. Abel, *Chardon's Journal at Fort Clark*, 144.

193. De Voto, *Across the Wide Missouri*, 443 n. 1.

194. *Papers of the St. Louis Fur Trade, Part 1: The Chouteau Collection, 1752–1925*, Roll 24, frame 01121.

195. Abel, *Chardon's Journal at Fort Clark*, 122; De Voto, *Across the Wide Missouri*, 443 n. 1.

196. For "Little Missouri" as Bad River, see, Gary E. Moulton, ed., *The Journals of the Lewis and Clark Expedition*, (Lincoln: University of Nebraska, 2003), http://lewisandclark journals.unl.edu/index.html (accessed July, 30 2008), and Abel, *Chardon's Journal at Fort Clark*, 74.

197. For Fort Pierre as May's starting point, see Robertson, *Rotting Face*, 168.

198. Catlin, *Letters and Notes*, 2: 293.

199. Bandera, "When 10,000 Indians Died of Smallpox," 320.

200. *Annual Report of the American Historical Association for the Year 1944*, 2: 317.

201. *Annual Report of the American Historical Association for the Year 1944*, 2: fears 328, 332; sales, 342, 343–44.

202. *Papers of the St. Louis Fur Trade, Part 1: The Chouteau Collection, 1752–1925*, Roll 25, frame 00185.

203. Bandera, "When 10,000 Indian Died of Smallpox," 320.

204. *Letters Received by the Office of Indian Affairs*, Roll 884, frame 0273.

205. *Missouri Republican*, "Old Times."

206. See, for instance, Victor, *The River of the West*, 232; Sunder, *Joshua Pilcher*, 62; Larpenteur (1933), *Forty Years a Fur Trader*, 88; Bonner, *The Life and Adventures of James P. Beckwourth*, iv–vi.

207. Dollar, "The High Plains Smallpox Epidemic," "primitive mind," 29; "mulatto," 20.

208. Robertson, *Rotting Face*, 300; De Voto, *Across the Wide Missouri*, 295.

209. De Voto, *Across the Wide Missouri*, 295.

210. Katz in the preface to the 1969 reprint of Bonner, *The Life and Adventures of James P. Beckwourth*, iii.

211. Bonner, *The Life and Adventures of James P. Beckwourth*, 13; Answers Corporation, "Biography: Jim Beckwourth," 2006, http://www.answers.com/topic/beckwourth-jim (accessed July 22, 2008).

212. *Missouri Republican*, "Old Times."

213. *Papers of the St. Louis Fur Trade, Part 1: The Chouteau Collection, 1752–1925*, Roll 24, frame 00652.

214. For St. Louis headquarters, see *Annual Report of the American Historical Association*, 2: 522.

215. Abel, *Chardon's Journal at Fort Clark*, 74.

216. Bonner, *The Life and Adventures of James P. Beckwourth*, voucher, 377; St. Louis, 379.

217. Bonner, *The Life and Adventures of James P. Beckwourth*, 374–75.

218. Bonner, *The Life and Adventures of James P. Beckwourth*, to St. Louis, 379; return to Upper Missouri, 395; Florida, 404.

219. Bonner, *The Life and Adventures of James P. Beckwourth*, 381, 390.

220. Bonner, *The Life and Adventures of James P. Beckwourth*, 388.

221. Bonner, *The Life and Adventures of James P. Beckwourth,* 388–90.

222. Bonner, *The Life and Adventures of James P. Beckwourth,* 391–95.

223. Bonner, *The Life and Adventures of James P. Beckwourth,* 395.

224. Bonner, *The Life and Adventures of James P. Beckwourth,* 377.

225. Bonner, *The Life and Adventures of James P. Beckwourth,* 395.

226. Abel, *Chardon's Journal at Fort Clark,* 202–203 n. 20.

227. Abel, *Chardon's Journal at Fort Clark,* 74, 118, 310 n. 430; at Fort Pierre on April 16, 1837, see *Papers of the St. Louis Fur Trade, Part 1: The Chouteau Collection, 1752–1925,* letter of 16 April 1837, from Pierre Chouteau at St. Louis to P.D. Papin at Fort Pierre. Roll 24, frame 01121.

228. Abel, *Chardon's Journal at Fort Clark,* 118.

229. Bonner, *The Life and Adventures of James P. Beckwourth,* 378, 394.

230. Bonner, *The Life and Adventures of James P. Beckwourth,* 395.

231. Abel, *Chardon's Journal at Fort Clark,* 274 n. 269.

232. Abel, *Chardon's Journal at Fort Clark,* 122; Robertson, *Rotting Face,* 168.

233. Bonner, *The Life and Adventures of James P. Beckwourth,* 377–78. Beckwourth spelled his name "Garro."

234. Abel, *Chardon's Journal at Fort Clark,* 121.

235. Beckwourth described Fort Cass as a square fort of 18-foot "hewn logs planted perpendicularly in the ground" with catty-corner blockhouses, claimed to have been founded by himself, Bonner, *The Life and Adventures of James P. Beckwourth,* 212–13, 220, 301, 339, 364–65, 374.

236. For Fort Cass as built in 1832, see Larpenteur (1933), *Forty Years a Fur Trader on the Upper Missouri,* 97; as built by Beckwourth, see Bonner, *The Life and Adventures of James P. Beckwourth,* 212–13, 220; as built by Samuel Tulloch and sometimes called "Tulloch's Fort," see Chittenden, *The American Fur Trade of the Far West,* 2: 938; Larpenteur (1898) *Forty Years a Fur Trader,* 46.

237. Bonner, *The Life and Adventures of James P. Beckwourth,* 395, 396.

238. Bonner, *The Life and Adventures of James P. Beckwourth,* 395.

239. Bonner, *The Life and Adventures of James P. Beckwourth,* to St. Louis, 403–4; Crow wives, 114, 119–20, 148–49, 190, 401; wife and child as "loved," 383; assault on Blackfeet, 402.

240. Bonner, *The Life and Adventures of James P. Beckwourth,* 403.

241. Bonner, *The Life and Adventures of James P. Beckwourth,* 403.

242. Bonner, *The Life and Adventures of James P. Beckwourth,* 404.

243. Bonner, *The Life and Adventures of James P. Beckwourth,* 404.

244. Bonner, *The Life and Adventures of James P. Beckwourth,* 404.

245. For the Gaineses, see Thomas McAdory Owen, ed., *Publications of the Transactions of the Alabama Historical Society, 1898–1899* (Tuscaloosa: Alabama Historical Society, 1899), 3: 106. For General Gaines's celebrity status in St. Louis, see the gala dinner held in his honor, along with toasts, as covered twice, in *Missouri Republican,* "The Dinner to Gen. Gaines," January 24, 1838, and *Missouri Republican,* "The Dinner to Gen. Gaines," January 25, 1838. Toast quoted, *Missouri Republican,* January 25, 1838.

246. *Handbook of Texas,* "Gaines, Edmund Pendleton (1777–1849)," http://tshaon line.org/handbook/online/articles/GG/fga3.html (accessed August 21, 2008).

247. Bonner, *The Life and Adventures of James P. Beckwourth,* 404–5.

248. Victor, *The River of the West,* 231–32. For a more scholarly, 19th-century citation of the same story, see Hubert Howe Bancroft, *The History of the Northwest Coast* (San Francisco: The History Company Publishing, 1884) 2: 602 n. 3.

249. Stanley Vestal, *Jim Bridger: Mountain Man, A Biography* (New York: William Morrow & Company, 1946), as blankets, 221; summary, 129.

250. Stanley Vestal, *Joe Meek: The Merry Mountain Man, A Biography* (Lincoln: University of Nebraska Press, 1952), 221.

251. Elinor Wilson notes as much in her recital of the same story in her *Jim Beckwourth: Black Mountain Man and War Chief of the Crows* (Norman: University of Oklahoma Press, 1972), 80, 81.

252. Vestal, *Joe Meek*, 172; Nolie Mumey, *James Pierson Beckwourth: An Enigmatic Figure of the West, 1856–1866* (Denver: Old West Publishing, 1957), 70–72.

253. *Papers of the St. Louis Fur Trade, Part 1: The Chouteau Collection, 1752–1925*, Roll 24, frame 01121.

254. *Letters Received by the Office of Indian Affairs*, Roll 884, frame 0336.

255. Abel, *Chardon's Journal at Fort Clark*, 118.

256. Abel, *Chardon's Journal at Fort Clark*, 119.

257. *Letters Received by the Office of Indian Affairs*, Roll 884, frames 0273–0274.

258. Wedel, *Dunbar-Allis Letters*, 713.

259. For vaccination, Pearson, "Lewis Cass and the Politics of Disease," 21; for Pawnees as stricken, Dunbar, Letter, 384.

260. McCoy, *Annual Register*, 249; Larpenteur, "White Man Bear (mato Washejoe), Upper Missouri Trader," 160.

261. *Letters Received by the Office of Indian Affairs*, Roll 884, frames 0273–0274; for Pilcher's agency, see Sunder, *Joshua Pilcher*, 121–25.

262. *Letters Received by the Office of Indian Affairs*, Roll 884, frame 0280.

263. *Letters Received by the Office of Indian Affairs*, Roll 884, frame 0277.

264. *Letters Received by the Office of Indian Affairs*, Roll 884, frame 0282.

265. Chittenden, *History of Early Steamboat Navigation on the Missouri River*, 1: 229; Bandera, "When 10,000 Indians Died of Smallpox," 320.

266. Abel, *Chardon's Journal at Fort Clark*, 119.

267. Abel, *Chardon's Journal at Fort Clark*, 121.

268. Denig, *Indian Tribes of the Upper Missouri*, for hemorrhagic symptoms, 399, for 95 percent fatality rate, 428.

269. Catlin, *Letters and Notes*, 2: 293.

270. James M. Goodrich, "Smallpox: Virology, Clinical Presentation, and Prevention," in *Bioterrorism Preparedness: Medicine—Public Health—Policy*, ed. Nancy Khardori (Weinheim: WILEY–VCH Verlag GmbH & Company, 2006), 106.

271. "Smallpox," http://redcross.tallytown.com/library/Smallpox-Overview.pdf.

272. Mission of news trip, Abel, *Chardon's Journal at Fort Clark*, water levels, 106, 107, 111, 114, 115; news discovery, quotations all on 121; also 101, 102, 102–3, 108, 112, 113, 115, 117, 119.

273. Abel, *Chardon's Journal at Fort Clark*, 122, 123.

274. Abel, *Chardon's Journal at Fort Clark*, respectively, 103, 110.

275. Abel, *Chardon's Journal at Fort Clark*, 149.

276. Abel, *Chardon's Journal at Fort Clark*, 137.

277. Charles Larpenteur, *Forty Years a Fur Trader on the Upper Missouri: The Personal Narrative of Charles Larpenteur, 1833–1872*, ed. Elliott Coues (New York: Francis P. Harper, 1898), 1: xx–xxii. Dr. Matthews also wrote a manuscript dated 1869, "The History of Fort Buford, Dakota Territory, and Locality," along with some "sketches" of Fort Union, both of which are held at the Montana Historical Society in Helena. Matthews was primarily known for his work on the Navajos.

278. Larpenteur (1898), *Forty Years a Fur Trader*, gloss, xvi; changes, xxvi.

279. Larpenteur (1898), *Forty Years a Fur Trader*, xxvi.

280. Larpenteur (1933), *Forty Years a Fur Trader*, xx, xxii.

281. For June 24, 1837 as the *St. Peter's* arrival date, see Larpenteur (1898), *Forty Years a Fur Trade*, 132 n. 14.

282. Larpenteur (1898), *Forty Years a Fur Trader*, 131–33; Larpenteur (1933), *Forty Years a Fur Trader*, 109–110.

283. Illiteracies in the original; Charles Larpenteur, "White Man Bear (mato Washejoe)," 158–59.

284. See my longer discussion of this problematic term in Barbara Alice Mann, *Iroquoian Women: The Gantowisas* (New York: Peter Lang Publishing, 2006), 19–22.

285. Illiteracies in the original; Larpenteur, "White Man Bear (mato Washejoe)," 159.

286. Illiteracies in the original; Larpenteur, "White Man Bear (mato Washejoe)," 160. For Denig as the son of a physician, see Edwin Thompson Denig, "Of the Crow Nation," *Anthropological Papers*, Bulletin 151, Smithsonian Institution, Bureau of American Ethnography, Anthropological Papers, no. 33 (Washington, D.C.: Government Printing Office, 1953), 5.

287. Illiteracies in the original; Larpenteur, "White Man Bear (mato Washejoe)," 160.

288. Illiteracies in the original; Larpenteur, "White Man Bear (mato Washejoe)," 160–61.

289. Illiteracies in the original; Larpenteur, "White Man Bear (mato Washejoe)," 161.

290. Brackets in the typescript; illiteracies in the original; Larpenteur, "White Man Bear (mato Washejoe)," 161.

291. Thomas, *Domestic Medicine*, 119–20.

292. Larpenteur (1898), *Forty Years a Fur Trader*, 133; Larpenteur (1933), *Forty Years a Fur Trader*, 110–11.

293. For Cohan-Gauché, see Larpenteur (1898), *Forty Years a Fur Trader*, 55 n. 3, 56–59, 91–94; Larpenteur (1933), *Forty Years a Fur Trader*, 44–47, 76–78.

294. Denig, *Five Indian Tribes of the Upper Missouri*, 71.

295. Illiteracies in the original; Larpenteur, "White Man Bear (mato Washejoe)," 162–63.

296. Illiteracies in the original; Larpenteur, "White Man Bear (mato Washejoe)," 162–63.

297. Larpenteur, "White Man Bear (mato Washejoe)," 163; Thomas, *Domestic Medicine*, 121.

298. Thomas, *Domestic Medicine*, 121.

299. Thomas, *Domestic Medicine*, 121–22.

300. Thomas, *Domestic Medicine*, 122.

301. Larpenteur (1933), *Forty Years a Fur Trader*, 102.

302. Kurz, *Journal of Rudolph Friederich Kurz*, black's experience of Denig, 101; Kurz's experience with Denig's high-handedness, 240–41, following a honeymoon period after he first hired on, 133.

303. Kurz, *Journal of Rudolph Friederich Kurz*, quotations, 226; kindnesses to Kurz, 133; denigrations of Indians, 204–205.

304. Denig, *Indian Tribes of the Upper Missouri*, 428.

305. Denig, *Indian Tribes of the Upper Missouri*, 428.

306. Denig, *Indian Tribes of the Upper Missouri*, 399.

307. Denig, *Five Indian Tribes of the Upper Missouri*, 71.

308. Denig as drunkard, Larpenteur, "White Man Bear (mato Washejoe)," 187. This is the only time that Larpenteur discussed Denig's drinking, describing him as "too full of alcohol to freeze." Coues added another mention and invented the wording on both in Larpenteur (1898), *Forty Years a Trader,* 1: 162, 186, copied in, Larpenteur (1933), *Forty Years a Fur Trader,* 138; Coues addition, 156–57.

309. Larpenteur (1898), *Forty Years a Fur Trader,* 1: 134; copied in, Larpenteur (1933), *Forty Years a Fur Trader,* 111. There was a French trapper family named "Brazeau," but it was unconnected with this lie.

310. Find accounts in, Farnham, *Farnham's Travels, Part I,* 264–66; Audubon, *Audubon and His Journals,* 2: 44–47; Audubon, *Writings and Drawings,* 640–44; See, especially, the June 6, 1838, letter by Denig reproduced in Maximilian, *Part I. Travels in the Interior of North America,* 33–36; Larpenteur (1898), *Forty Years a Fur Trader,* 1: 134–35; Larpenteur (1933), *Forty Years a Fur Trader,* 111–12; Dunbar, Letter, 383–85; Thomas S. Williamson, Letter of May 10, 1838, *The Missionary Herald* 34 (1838): 385; Schoolcraft, *Information Respecting the History, Condition, and Prospects,* 6: 487; Denig, *Five Indian Tribes of the Upper Missouri,* 70–72. Although he showed compassion, Catlin still satisfied the settler taste for Indian misery in Catlin, *Letters and Notes,* 2: 28–29.

311. The standard, modern text on the losses is in Russell Thornton, *American Indian Holocaust and Survival: A Population History since 1492* (Norman: University of Oklahoma Press, 1987), 94–99. Raw statistics beyond Thornton's sources are still scattered throughout the primary sources, and need to be culled. See Denig, *Indian Tribes of the Upper Missouri,* 397, 399–400, 428, 625; Denig, *Five Indian Tribes of the Upper Missouri,* 71–72; Audubon, *Audubon and His Journals,* 2: 47; Schoolcraft, *Information Respecting the History, Condition, and Prospects of the Indian tribes of the United States,* 2: 239, 3: 250, 3: 254, 6: 487; Catlin, *Letters and Notes,* 1: 59, 60 n. *, 61, 92, 150; Maximilian, *Part I. Travels in the Interior of North America,* 22: 33, 34–35; *Annual Report of the Commissioner of Indian Affairs,* 16–17, 57, 66–67.

CHAPTER 4

1. For "difficult to believe," see Clifford Merrill Drury, *Marcus and Narcissa Whitman and the Opening of Old Oregon* (Glendale, CA: The Arthur H. Clark Company, 1973), 2: 211. For examples of dismissal as "superstitious," see, for instance, George Simpson, *An Overland Journey Round the World* (Philadelphia: Lea and Blanchard, 1847), 99; Joseph Neath, *Memoirs of Nisqually* (Fairfield, WA: Ye Galleon Press, 1979), 125; Principal William Isaac Marshall, *The Acquisition of Oregon and the Long Suppressed Evidence about Marcus Whitman* (Seattle: Lowman & Hanford Co., 1911), 2: 246; Ronald B. Lansing, *Juggernaut: The Whitman Massacre Trial, 1850* (Pasadena, CA: Ninth Judicial Circuit Historical Society, 1993), 9.

2. For "overreliance" quotation, see Cameron Addis, "The Whitman Massacre: Religion and Manifest Destiny on the Columbia Plateau, 1809–1858," *Journal of the Early Republic* 25, no. 2 (2005): 257. For examples of critiques aside from that in Addis, see Julie Roy Jeffrey, *Converting the West: Biography of Narcissa Whitman* (Norman: University of Oklahoma Press, 1991), 122–23, 148–49, 192–94, 212.

3. George E. Tinker, *Missionary Conquest: The Gospel and Native American Cultural Genocide* (Minneapolis: Fortress Press, 1993), 70. Tinker was speaking specifically of the Jesuit, Pier-Jean De Smet, in this section, but the observation, made throughout the text, applies generally.

4. Tinker, *Missionary Conquest,* 4–8, 21, 24, 27–31, 43–46, 65–66, 88–91, 98–99.

5. John Heckewelder, *Narrative of the Mission of the United Brethren among the Delaware and Mohegan Indians from Its Commencement, in the Year 1740, to the Close of the Year 1808* (1818; repr., New York: Arno Press, 1971), 61–62.

6. Paul A. W. Wallace, ed., *Thirty Thousand Miles with John Heckewelder* (Pittsburgh: University of Pittsburgh Press, 1958), 118, 470; Paul A. W. Wallace, *Conrad Weiser: Friend of Colonist and Mohawk* (New York: Russell & Russell, 1945), 272, 276.

7. Heckewelder, *Narrative of the Mission of the United Brethren,* 207, 217–18.

8. See discussion and examples of the Law of Innocence in Barbara Alice Mann, *George Washington's War on Native America* (Westport, CT: Praeger, 2005), 6, 53.

9. To watch this process in historical action, see Barbara Alice Mann, "'Are You Delusional?' Kandiaronk on Christianity," in *Native American Speakers of the Eastern Woodlands: Selected Speeches and Critical Analyses,* ed. Barbara Alice Mann (Westport, CT: Greenwood Press, 2001), 52–54.

10. William Clark, "1830 Report on the Fur Trade," *Oregon Historical Quarterly* 48, no. 1 (1947): 33.

11. "Delegates of the Maine Conference: The Wyandots," *Christian Advocate and Journal and Zion's Herald* 6, no. 13 (November 25, 1831): 51.

12. Joseph Rosati, Letter of December 31, 1831 from St. Louis to Editor, *Annales de l'Association de la Propagation de la Foi* (Paris: La Librairie ecclésiastique de Rusand et Cie, 1831), 5: 599.

13. Lawrence Benedict Palladino, *Indian and White in the Northwest; or, a History of Catholicity in Montana* (Baltimore: John Murphy & Company, 1894), 11.

14. George Catlin, *Letters and Notes on the Manners, Customs, and Condition of the North American Indians* (1841; repr., Edinburgh: John Grant, 1926) 2: 124, and their portraits facings, 124.

15. Rosati, Letter of December 31, 1831, *Annales de l'Association de la Propagation de la Foi,* 599, 600.

16. Rosati, Letter of December 31, 1831, *Annales de l'Association de la Propagation de la Foi,* 599.

17. Catlin, *Letters and Notes,* 2: 124, and facing portraits. Catlin drew Hee-oh'ks-te-kin and H'co-a-h'co-a-h'cotes-min in the "Sioux" regalia that the Lakotas had just given them.

18. Catlin, *Letters and Notes,* 2: 124.

19. Catlin, *Letters and Notes,* 2: 124.

20. William Walker, "The Flat-Head Indians," *Christian Advocate and Journal and Zion's Herald* 7, no. 27 (1833): 105; Catlin, *Letters and Notes,* 2: 124; Senate Executive Document 37, 41st Congress, 3rd Session (Washington, D.C.: Government Printing Office, 1871) 8–9; for "highly wrought," see Drury, *Marcus and Narcissa Whitman,* 1: 49; for Walker's inaccuracies, see Principal William Isaac Marshall, *The Acquisition of Oregon,* 2: 14.

21. Walker, "The Flat-Head Indians," 105.

22. Walker, "The Flat-Head Indians," 105.

23. Catlin, *Letters and Notes,* 2: 125.

24. Rosati, Letter, *Annales,* 599–600.

25. Rosati, Letter, *Annales,* 597.

26. Palladino, *Indian and White in the Northwest,* 9–13, *passim.*

27. Marshall, *The Acquisition of Oregon,* 2: 42.

28. Alvin C. Josephy, Jr., *The Nez Perce Indians and the Opening of the Old Northwest* (1965; repr., Boston: Houghton-Mifflin, 1997), 124–25; Marshall, *The Acquisition of Oregon,* 2: 41; Palladino, *Indian and White in the Northwest,* 12–13.

29. Marshall, *The Acquisition of Oregon,* 2: 42.

30. For Spalding's speech palmed off as originating with the so-called Four Wise Men, see "An Evening with an Old Missionary," *Chicago Advance,* December 1, 1870, reprinted in Senate Executive Document 37, 41st Congress, 3rd Session (Washington, D.C.: Government Printing Office, 1871), 8. Spalding claimed that he had been given the original text "years afterward" by the last survivor, a fairly fishy story, since the survivor, Hee-oh'ks-te-kin, a Nez Percé, was not the speaker of the group, who was Salish. Moreover, Spalding's content in no way agrees with the accounts of the purpose of the visit as given by either Clark or Rosati, who both had firsthand knowledge of the event. It is my conclusion that Spalding made up the text of the speech, as he invented so much else that he asserted about his Oregon adventure. Spalding's text reads: "I came to you with one eye partly opened; I go back with both eyes closed and both arms broken. My people sent me to obtain that Book from Heaven. You took me where your women dance as we do not allow ours to dance; and the book was not there. You took me where I saw men worship God with candles; and the Book was not there. I am not to return without it, and my people will die in darkness."

31. For 20th-century versions of Spalding's speech, see William A. Mowry, *Marcus Whitman and the Early Days of Oregon* (New York: Silver, Burdett and Company, 1901), 46; Myron Eells, *Marcus Whitman, Pathfinder and Patriot* (Seattle: The Alice Harriman Company, 1909), 26–27; for an alternate version, see Oliver W. Nixon, *How Marcus Whitman Saved Oregon* (Chicago: Star Publishing Company, 1895), 52–53.

32. Very recently, the phony speech was reproduced as authentic in Catherine Millard, "Marcus Whitman—The Preacher Who Rode for an Empire System," *Christian Heritage News,* http://www.christianheritagemins.org/articles/Marcus%20Whitman.htm (accessed December 5, 2008).

33. Eells, *Marcus Whitman,* 26–27.

34. For an acerbic Catholic commentary on the perceived competition to convert Indians, see C. Van Quickenborn, Letter of March 10, 1829, to the Editor, *Annales de l'Association de la Propagation de la Foi* (Paris: La Librairie Ecclésiastique de Rusand, 1830), 4: 586–87.

35. Most biographers and historians avoid a recital of this unseemly feud, but a rundown of it (as well as the missionaries' other feuds) can be found in Marshall, *The Acquisition of Oregon,* especially 2: 35–38, 101–18.

36. Jeffrey, *Converting the West,* as illegitimate, 30; as awkward, 54.

37. Drury, *Marcus and Narcissa Whitman,* 1: 73–75.

38. Drury, *Marcus and Narcissa Whitman,* 1: 79. In 1973, her family still maintained the tradition that the couple had been married.

39. Jeffrey, *Converting the West,* 60–61. Hints that the Prentisses were not happy about her marriage to Whitman, or at least about her going to Oregon with him as a missionary, occur in her letters home. See, for instance, Narcissa Whitman, "Letters Written by Mrs. Whitman from Oregon to Her Relatives in New York," *Transactions of the Nineteenth Annual Reunion of the Oregon Pioneer Association* (1891), complaints of never hearing from her parents, 97; that her mother did not write, 115, 130; that other relatives did not write, 116; the fact that she heard from her parents on average only about every two years, 97, 130; and especially the plaintive tone opening her letter of December 5, 1836, as she thought "of my beloved parents," the ones who seldom wrote, lingering on "the parting scene, and of the probability that I shall never see those dear faces again while I live," 86. The last sounds like a direct quotation of a sour admonition from, most probably, her

mother. Elsewhere, she actually quoted her mother's "hope" that Narcissa "did not regret the step" of becoming a missionary "in behalf of the perishing heathen," 146. Narcissa's parents did not bother to record the exact date of her marriage, a puzzling lapse.

40. Narcissa Whitman, "A Journey across the Plains in 1836: Journal of Mrs. Marcus Whitman," *Transactions of the Nineteenth Annual Reunion of the Oregon Pioneer Association* (1891): 40, 42; Whitman, "Letters Written by Mrs. Whitman," (1891), 85.

41. Drury, *Marcus and Narcissa Whitman*, 1: 376, 376 n. 19.

42. The general summary of the diagnosis was Marshall's; the internal quotation comes from Whitman's letter to ABCFM, in Marshall, *The Acquisition of Oregon,* 2: 169. Marshall took Whitman's diagnosis of Spalding seriously, contending that Spalding did, indeed, go insane later on, thus explaining Spalding's deceitful presentation of the Whitman legend. I believe, however, that Spalding was sane but dishonest, an opportunist who salved his bruised ego by controlling the telling of the Whitman legend in a way that reflected glory on himself, while covering up the disreputable spats that had actually marked his relationship with the Whitmans.

43. Whitman, "Letters Written by Mrs. Whitman," (1891) as self-supporting, 129, 131; insanity of, 144, 148; Marshall, *The Acquisition of Oregon,* 2: 40; Drury, *Marcus and Narcissa Whitman,* 1: 405; Clifford Merrill Drury, *First White Women over the Rockies* (Glendale, CA: The Arthur H. Clark Company, 1963), 3: 316; Jeffrey, *Converting the West,* 153.

44. Drury, *Marcus and Narcissa Whitman,* 1: 376.

45. Drury, *Marcus and Narcissa Whitman,* 1: 376.

46. Letter quoted in Drury, *First White Women over the Rockies,* 1: 154–55.

47. Mowry, *Marcus Whitman and the Early Days of Oregon,* 175.

48. Marshall, *The Acquisition of Oregon,* 2: 68.

49. Mowry, *Marcus Whitman and the Early Days of Oregon,* 178.

50. Marshall, *The Acquisition of Oregon,* 2: 64–67; Mowry, *Marcus Whitman and the Early Days of Oregon,* 169–72. As a researcher myself, I am astounded at what Marshall was able to pull up in those days before computers, good libraries, and easy travel. Yes, he clearly loathed Whitman and Spalding, but it was the miffed ire of someone who had started out as a Whitman fan. After seeing the actual documents and realizing just how seamy the whole Oregon affair was, Marshall resented having previously been bamboozled into buying the Whitman myth. He was angry that the public had been lied to for so long about the events in Oregon.

51. The article is reprinted in its entirety in Marshall, *The Acquisition of Oregon,* 2: 62–64.

52. Marcus Whitman, "Dr. Whitman's Bill and His Letter to the Secretary of War, Written in 1843," in *Transactions of the Nineteenth Annual Reunion of the Oregon Pioneer Association* (1891): 69–78; Mowry, *Marcus Whitman and the Early Days of Oregon,* letter and bill reprinted in their entirety, 274–84.

53. Lyon G. Tyler, *The Letters and Times of the Tylers* (Richmond, VA: Whittet & Shepperson, 1885), 2: proposal to Tyler, 438; Webster's cordiality, 439; letters, 447–50.

54. Marshall, *The Acquisition of Oregon,* no land grants, 2: 190–91; twelve months' notice, 2: 183–84.

55. J. F. Watts and Fred L. Israel, *Presidential Documents: The Speeches, Proclamations, and Policies That Have Shaped the Nation from Washington to Clinton* (New York: Routledge, 2000), 101.

56. Samuel Parker, *Journal of an Exploring Tour beyond the Rocky Mountains under the Direction of the A.B.C.F.M., Performed in the Years 1835, '36, and '37: Containing a Description of*

the Geography, Geology, Climate, and Productions; and the Number, Manners, and Customs of the Natives, with a Map of the Oregon Territory (1838; repr., Minneapolis: Ross & Haines, 1967).

57. F. O. M'Cown, "Occasional Address," *Transactions of the Twelfth Annual Re-Union of the Oregon Pioneer Association for 1884* (Salem, OR: E. M. Waite, 1885), 18.

58. Lansing, *Juggernaut,* 9.

59. Samuel Parker gave a headcount of 2,000 Cayuse, but he included 1,000 Walla Walla. In a letter of 6 February 1840, Asa Smith sent the Board an estimate of no more than 3,000 Nez Percés and Cayuses, combined, but in 1841, he revised that number downward to 2,400, in Drury, *Marcus and Narcissa Whitman,* 2: 208.

60. Federal Writers' Project, *Oregon: End of the Trail* (Portland, OR: Binfords & Mort, 1940), 47.

61. Dorothy O. Johansen, *Robert Newell's Memoranda: Travles in the Teritory of Missourie; Travle to the Kayuse War; together with A Report on the Indians South of the Columbia River* (Portland, OR: Champoeg Press, Inc., 1959), 148–49.

62. Mowry, *Marcus Whitman and the Early Days of Oregon,* 137 n. 2.

63. "Mission to Indians in the Oregon Country," *The Missionary Herald* 35, no. 1 (January 1839): 14.

64. With "Letters Written by Mrs. Whitman," (1891), 177–79.

65. Tyler, *The Letters and Times of the Tylers,* 2: 438–39.

66. Federal Writers' Project, *Oregon,* 44.

67. Marshall, *The Acquisition of Oregon,* 2: 69.

68. Board's sanction, Mowry, *Marcus Whitman and the Early Days of Oregon,* 179; Marshall, *The Acquisition of Oregon,* 2: 38.

69. Board's warning, Jeffrey, *Converting the West,* 212; Board's sanction, Mowry, *Marcus Whitman and the Early Days of Oregon,* 179; Marshall, *The Acquisition of Oregon,* 2: 38.

70. Marcus Whitman, "Oregon Indians: Report of Doct. Whiman," *The Missionary Herald* 39, no. 9 (1843): 336.

71. Whitman, "Letters Written by Mrs. Whitman," (1891), settlers, 102, 111; missionaries, 129; associates, 134; Federal Writers' Project, *Oregon,* 261.

72. Whitman, "Letters Written by Mrs. Whitman," (1891), 134.

73. Catherine Sager, "Oregon Trail Orphan," in *Seeing the Elephant: The Many Voices of the Oregon Trail,* ed. Joyce Badgley Hunsaker (Lubbock: Texas Tech University Press, 2003), 120–21.

74. Addis, "The Whitman Massacre," 242.

75. Quoted in Mowry, *Marcus Whitman and the Early Days of Oregon,* 141.

76. Marshall, *The Acquisition of Oregon,* 2: 45–46; Eells, *Marcus Whitman,* 50; Federal Writers' Project, *Oregon,* 238.

77. Eells, *Marcus Whitman,* 87.

78. Marshall, *The Acquisition of Oregon,* 2: 23.

79. Lansing, *Juggernaut,* 21–23.

80. The Mohawks have been documented, above, in notes 24 and 26–29. For the Lenape, see Drury, *First White Women over the Rockies,* 1: 226; as telling their traditions to Oregon Indians, Marshall, *The Acquisition of Oregon,* 2: 152.

81. Eells, *Marcus Whitman,* 268.

82. As versed on Iroquois, Bill Gulick, *Snake River Country* (Caldwell, ID: Caxton Printers, 1971), 77; recounting, Eells, *Marcus Whitman,* 254, 256.

83. Mann, *George Washington's War,* x, 51–110.

84. Mann, *George Washington's War,* 156–65.

85. Mann, *George Washington's War,* 123–29, 177–79.

86. For the "invitation" justification, see Whitman, "Letters Written by Mrs. Whitman," (1891), 156. For a discussion of the damage done by this continuing problem, see George E. Tinker, *American Indian Liberation: A Theology of Sovereignty* (New York: Orbis Books, 2008), 84–111.

87. Whitman, "Letters Written by Mrs. Whitman," (1891), 102.

88. Addis, "The Whitman Massacre," 241.

89. Whitman, "Letters Written by Mrs. Whitman," (1891), 134–35.

90. Whitman, "Letters Written by Mrs. Whitman," (1891), 148, 149.

91. Whitman, "Letters Written by Mrs. Whitman," (1891), 155–56.

92. Pasturing in Whitman, "Letters Written by Mrs. Whitman" (1891), 155; killing cattle, 157; burning mill, 156; melons in William Fraser Tolmie, "Letter from Dr. Tolmie," in *Transactions of the Twelfth Annual Re-Union of the Oregon Pioneer Association for 1884* (Salem, OR: E. M. Waite, 1885), 34.

93. Drury, *Marcus and Narcissa Whitman,* 1: 255.

94. Whitman, "Letters Written by Mrs. Whitman," (1891), 102; Marshall, *The Acquisition of Oregon,* 2: 152.

95. Narcissa Whitman, "A Journey across the Plains," (1891), for "hearty" welcome by clan mothers, 43; for elders' hearing, mistakenly represented as their being "anxious" for "teachers," 67.

96. Whitman, "Letters Written by Mrs. Whitman," (1891), 128, 147, 150, 155, 177, 178.

97. Whitman, "Letters Written by Mrs. Whitman," (1891), 142.

98. Whitman, "Letters Written by Mrs. Whitman," (1891), 155–56.

99. Whitman, "Letters Written by Mrs. Whitman," (1891), 157.

100. Paul Kane, *Paul Kane's Frontier, Including Wanderings of an Artist among the Indians of North America* (1859; repr., Austin: University of Texas Press, 1971), 116–17.

101. Robert Boyd, *The Coming of the Spirit of Pestilence: Introduced Infectious Diseases and Population Decline among Northwest Coast Indians, 1774–1874* (Seattle: University of Washington Press, 1999), 146–47.

102. For dysentery in 1844 and 1845, see John McLoughlin, *The Letters of John McLoughlin from Fort Vancouver to the Governor and Committee,* 3rd series, 1844–46, ed. E. E. Rich (London: The Publications of the Hudson's Bay Record Society, 1944), 6, 181; for 1847 disease combination, see Boyd, *The Coming of the Spirit of Pestilence,* 152–53.

103. Quoted in Boyd, *The Coming of the Spirit of Pestilence,* 156.

104. Nard Jones, *The Great Command: The Story of Marcus and Narcissa Whitman and the Oregon Country Pioneers* (Boston: Little, Brown and Company, 1959), 314. Beckwourth is given as "Beckwith."

105. Clarence B. Bagley, *Early Catholic Missions in Old Oregon* (Seattle: Lowman & Hanford Company, 1932), 1: 187.

106. Tolmie, "Letter from Dr. Tolmie," 37.

107. William S. Lewis and Paul C. Phillips, eds., *The Journal of John Work* (Cleveland: The Arthur H. Clark Company, 1923), 62.

108. William Fraser Tolmie, *Journals of William Fraser Tolmie, Physician and Fur Trader* (Vancouver: Mitchell Press Limited, 1963), 345.

109. As Fort Vancouver's doctor, see Tolmie, *Journals of William Fraser Tolmie,* 344; as Fort Nisqually's doctor, see Lewis and Phillips, *The Journal of John Work,* 62.

110. Tolmie "Letter from Dr. Tolmie," 33–34.

111. Tolmie, *Journals of William Fraser Tolmie,* 301.

112. Tolmie, "Letter from Dr. Tolmie," 35.

113. See, for instance, Neath, *Memoirs of Nisqually,* 125.

114. Whitman, "Letters Written by Mrs. Whitman," (1891), 93–94.

115. See, for instance, the challenge offered Lenape "superstition" by a Quaker trader attempting to show that a medicine man's poison could not affect him, in John Heckewelder, *The History, Manners, and Customs of the Indian Nations Who Once Inhabited Pennsylvania and the Neighboring States,* The First American Frontier Series (1820, 1876; repr., New York: Arno Press and *The New York Times,* 1971), 239–40.

116. Boyd, *The Coming of the Spirit of* Pestilence, as virgin soil, 146; for 50%, 159.

117. George B. Roberts, "The Round Hand of George B. Roberts: The Cowlitz Farm Journal," *Oregon Historical Quarterly* 63, no. 2 (1962): 140. Roberts added that the Indians around the settlements still took "the measles fast" because they were "so incautious and so destitute of comfort," but it is notable that the Indians in question were totally dependent upon the settlers for their goods, as Roberts also recorded, opening the way for speculation in another direction.

118. For the 1847 epidemic, see the Cayuse account in the official, 1848 statement of William Craig, in Bagley, *Early Catholic Missions in Old Oregon,* 1: 178–80; also referenced in Clifford Merrill Drury, *Marcus Whitman, M.D., Pioneer and Martyr* (Caldwell, ID: The Caxton Printers, Ltd., 1937), 394.

119. Drury, *Marcus and Narcissa Whitman,* 2: 209.

120. Report quoted in Drury, *Marcus Whitman,* 233.

121. See Whitman's July 6, 1840, report to the mission board, quoted in Drury, *Marcus Whitman,* 233.

122. For Gray as mechanic, see Marshall, *The Acquisition of Oregon,* 2: 100.

123. For laudanum in the liquor, see Charles Larpenteur, *Forty Years a Fur Trader on the Upper Missouri: The Personal Narrative of Charles Larpenteur, 1833–1872* (Chicago: The Lakeside Press, R.R. Donnelley & Sibs Co., 1933), 63–64; for gunpowder as medicine, Robert A. Rees and Alan Sandy, eds., *The Adventures of Captain Bonneville* (Boston: Twayne Publishers, 1977), 187.

124. Tolmie, "Letter from Dr. Tolmie," 34.

125. Bagley, *Early Catholic Missions in Old Oregon,* 1: 176.

126. Bagley, *Early Catholic Missions in Old Oregon,* 1: 176.

127. John Buckingham, *Bitter Nemesis: The Intimate History of Strychnine* (New York: CRC Press, 2008), 134.

128. Buckingham, *Bitter Nemesis,* 119, 151, 160.

129. Buckingham, *Bitter Nemesis,* 147.

130. Jones, *The Great Command,* 313.

131. Italics in the original. "Mission to Indians in the Oregon Country," *The Missionary Herald* 35, no. 1(January 1839): 14.

132. Marshall, *The Acquisition of Oregon,* 2: 248.

133. Addis, "The Whitman Massacre," 243.

134. Robert Thomas, *A Treatise on Domestic Medicine* (New York: Collins & Co., 1822), 452, 456.

135. Tolmie, "Letter from Dr. Tolmie," 34.

136. Tolmie, "Letter from Dr. Tolmie," 34.

137. Drury, *First White Women over the Rockies,* 2: 178.

138. Quoted in Mowry, *Marcus Whitman and the Early Days of Oregon,* 141.

139. Narcissa Whitman, "Letters Written by Mrs. Whitman," (1891), for 1837 comment, 94; for 1841 comment, 146.

140. Narcissa Whitman, "Letters Written by Mrs. Whitman," (1891), respectively, 149, 134.

141. Narcissa Whitman, "Letters Written by Mrs. Whitman," (1891), 163. This last, lurid bit came in a diary letter to Marcus, who had just departed on his showy trip east. She had not wanted him to leave, and the charge that dusky men panted after lily-white women was a commonplace of racist lore. I suspect passive-aggression on Narcissa's part, guilt-baiting an absent husband. Regardless of whether that is so, her profoundly negative attitude towards the Oregon Natives is clear in all of these passages.

142. Drury, *First White Women over the Rockies,* 288 n. 45.

143. Eugene S. Hunn with James Selam and Family, *Nch'i-Wána, the Big River: Mid-Columbia Indians and Their Land* (Seattle: University of Washington Press, 1990), 40.

144. Drury, *First White Women over the Rockies,* 3: 240.

145. Jean Baptiste Abraham Brouillet, *Blackrobe Buries Whitman,* 1853, in *Journal of a Catholic Bishop on the Oregon Trail,* ed. Edward J. Kowrach (Fairfield, WA: Ye Galleon Press, 1978), 170 n. 11.

146. J[ean] B[aptiste] A[braham] Brouillet, "House Document," in Bagley, *Early Catholic Missions,* 1: 175–76; also referenced in Drury, *Marcus and Narcissa Whitman,* 2: 210 n. 21.

147. Drury, *Marcus and Narcissa Whitman,* 2: 211.

148. For the 1836 warning, see Drury, *Marcus Whitman,* 161.

149. Drury, *Marcus Whitman,* Fort Walla Walla threat, 261; fear of Army, 287–88.

150. Drury, *Marcus and Narcissa Whitman,* 1: 255.

151. Lansing, *Juggernaut,* 33, 121 n. 74.

152. Lansing, *Juggernaut,* 57; as from Maine, Gulick, *Snake River Country,* 77.

153. Colonel Cornelius Gilliam did not believe Istacus, when he said that he had captured, but then lost Joe Lewis. Jones, *The Great Command,* 363.

154. Deposition of William Craig, in Bagley, *Early Catholic Missions,* especially, 1: 179–80.

155. Drury, *Marcus Whitman,* 393–94.

156. Brouillet, *Blackrobe Buries Whitman,* 163.

157. For Rodgers as with Spalding, Brouillet, *Blackrobe Buries Whitman,* 1853, 153; as displeased with Spalding, Marshall, *The Acquisition of Oregon,* 2: 108. His name is also sometimes spelled "Rogers."

158. For the McBean account, see *Miscellaneous Documents Printed by the House of Representatives,* 30th Congress, 1st Session, document 98, 11. See, also, Drury, *Marcus and Narcissa Whitman,* 2: 211. For descriptions of McBean and Rodgers, see Drury, *Marcus Whitman,* 377 and 364, respectively. Spalding was a fellow missionary of Whitman's. For the "half-breed" description of Finley, see Drury, *Marcus Whitman,* 387.

159. Brouillet, 163; Jones, *The Great Command,* 336.

160. *Miscellaneous Documents Printed by the House of Representatives,* 30th Congress, 1st Session, document 98, 11.

161. Quoted in Drury, *Marcus Whitman,* 393.

162. Lansing, *Juggernaut,* 45.

163. Lansing, *Juggernaut,* 63.

164. For samples of the Joe Lewis mentions, see Catherine Sager Pringle, *Across the Plains in 1844* (1905), full text at http://www.isu.edu/~trinmich/00.ar.sager1.html; Mowry,

Marcus Whitman, 228–29; Drury, *First White Women over the Rockies,* 1: 162, 2: 353; W[illiam] H[enry] Gray, *A History of Oregon, 1792–1849* (1870; repr., New York: Arno Press, 1973), 468; Jones, *The Great Command,* 242, 309, 315, 336. For Nicholas Finley, see, for instance, Drury, *First White Women over the Rockies,* 1: 162, 2: 12, 2: 335; Jones, *The Great Command,* 309. For Tom Hill, see, for example, Marshall, *The Acquisition of Oregon,* 2: 152, 159, 245, 247.

165. Jones, *The Great Command,* 313.

166. See typical dismissals of Lewis's account as a "lie," on no other evidence than racial and religious identity, Drury, *Marcus Whitman,* 393, 395; for Lewis as troublemaker, on implied racial grounds, see Eells, *Marcus Whitman,* 280. For a typical description of Nicholas Finley as a "French [i.e., Catholic] half-breed," see, Eells, *Marcus Whitman,* 280. For a similar description of not only Finley but also Joe Lewis, depicted as birds of a dirty feather, see Drury, *Marcus Whitman,* 387.

167. Those with a strong stomach who are interested in reading up on racist "science" should pull up the granddaddies of the nonsense, importantly including Johann Friedrich Blumenbach, *On the Natural Varieties of Mankind* (1795; 1865. New York: Bergman Publishers, 1969); Charles White, *An Account of the Regular Gradation in Man, and in Different Animals and Vegetables; and from the Former to the Latter* (London: C. Dilly, 1799); Samuel Morton, *Crania Americana, or a Comparatives View of the Skulls of the Carious Aboriginal Nations of North and South America, to Which Is Prefixed an Essay on the Varieties of the Human Species* (Philadelphia: J. Dobson, 1839); and the works of Francis Galton, knighted for having invented eugenics, especially *Hereditary Genius: An Inquiry into Its Laws and Consequences* (1869; repr., New York: D. Appleton, 1884), and *Natural Inheritance* (1889; repr., New York: AMS Press, 1973).

168. Drury, *Marcus Whitman,* 393.

169. Jeffries, *Converting the West,* 211; Addis, "The Whitman Massacre," 243. Yes, the Métis (from the French, meaning "half," as in "half-breed"), are a Canadian nation, considered fully Indian today, but why was Lewis's race considered important to report in terms of allegations that Whitman poisoned the Cayuses?

170. Addis, "The Whitman Massacre," 244, 244 n. 36.

171. Gray, *A History of Oregon,* 468; Pringle, *Across the Plains in 1844,* keyword search: Lewis.

172. *Miscellaneous Documents Printed by the House of Representatives,* 30th Congress, 1st Session, document 98, 11.

173. Drury, *Marcus Whitman,* 394.

174. Lansing, *Juggernaut,* 57.

175. Lansing, *Juggernaut,* 57.

176. Marshall, *The Acquisition of Oregon,* 2: 246.

177. John McLoughlin, *The Letters of John McLoughlin from Fort Vancouver to the Governor and Committee,* Second Series, 1839–44, ed. E. E. Rich (London: The Publications of the Hudson's Bay Record Society, 1943), 164 n. 1.

178. Palmer, *Journal of Travels over the Rocky Mountains,* 291–92 n. 226.

179. Marshall, *The Acquisition of Oregon,* 2: 259.

180. Marshall, *The Acquisition of Oregon,* 2: 259.

181. Quoted in Drury, *First White Women over the Rockies,* 3: 240.

182. McLoughlin, *The Letters of John McLoughlin,* Second Series, 1839–1844, 164.

183. McLoughlin, *The Letters of John McLoughlin,* Second Series, 1839–1844, 164.

184. Buckingham, *Bitter Nemesis,* xv.

185. Gray, *History of Oregon,* 493.

186. Gray, *History of Oregon,* 493.

187. Thomas, *Domestic Medicine,* primary treatment, 114; eruptions, 115.

188. Harris L. Coulter, *Science and Ethics in American Medicine: 1800–1914* (Washington, D.C.: McGrath Publishing Company, 1973), 269; Buckingham, *Bitter Nemesis,* 7. Just about anything was tried on the "grippe" (influenza), including quinine, "Dover's Powders" (opium and ipecac), calomel (mercury), morphine, and belladonna. Quinine looked like a white powder; Dover's Powders would have been brown; calomel looked white or brown; morphine was probably a brown syrup, and belladonna would have been a liquid tincture. Whitman certainly had quinine and calomel in his medicine chest, for Narcissa wrote to him on October 14, 1842, that she had taken some for what was probably the flu. Whitman, "Letters Written by Mrs. Whitman," (1891), 166. However, it was measles with dysentery that Whitman was treating.

189. Buckingham, *Bitter Nemesis.* This is a truly scary book.

190. Coulter, *Science and Ethics in American Medicine,* 404, 416, 468–71. Examples of wild experiments litter the pages of Buckingham, *Bitter Nemesis,* and I urge the reader to recall the cavalier experiments on 200 high plains Indians suffering from smallpox, in Edwin Thompson Denig, *Five Indian Tribes of the Upper Missouri: Sioux, Arickaras, Assiniboines, Crees, Crows* (Norman: University of Oklahoma Press, 1961), 428.

191. Buckingham, *Bitter Nemesis,* 67.

192. Buckingham, *Bitter Nemesis,* 69–70.

193. Buckingham, *Bitter Nemesis,* 70.

Bibliography

~

Abel, Annie Heloise, ed. *Chardon's Journal at Fort Clark, 1834–1839*. 1932. Reprint, Freeport, NY: Books for Libraries Press, 1970.

Act of June 30, 1834, CH 162, Sec. 17, 4 STAT. 735, codified as amended as 25 U.S.C. Sec. 9 (1988).

Addis, Cameron. "The Whitman Massacre: Religion and Manifest Destiny on the Columbia Plateau, 1809–1858." *Journal of the Early Republic* 25, no. 2 (Summer 2005): 221–58.

Akers, Donna L. *Living in the Land of Death: The Choctaw Nation, 1830–1860*. East Lansing: Michigan State Press, 2004.

Akers, Donna L. "Removing the Heart of the Choctaw People: Indian Removal from a Native Perspective." In *Medicine Ways: Disease, Health, and Survival among Native Americans*. Edited by Clifford E. Trafzer and Diane Weiner, 1–15. Walnut Creek, CA: Altamira Press, 2001.

Akers, Donna L. "Removing the Heart of the Choctaw People: Indian Removal from a Native Perspective." *American Indian Culture and Research Journal* 23, no. 3 (1999): 63–76.

Alter, J. Cecil. *Jim Bridger*. 1925. Norman: University of Oklahoma Press, 1962.

Annual Report of the American Historical Association for the Year 1944, Part I: 1831–1840. 3 vols. Washington, D.C.: Government Printing Office, 1945.

Annual Report of the Commissioner of Indian Affairs. For 1837–1838. Washington, D.C.: Blair and Rives, 1838.

Answers Corporation. "Biography: Jim Beckwourth." http://www.answers.com/topic/beckwourth-jim (accessed July 22, 2008).

Arendt, Hannah. *Eichmann in Jerusalem: A Report on the Banality of Evil*. London: Faber & Faber, 1963.

Arese, Francesco. *A Trip to the Prairies and in the Interior of North America [1837–1838]*. New York: The Harbor Press, 1934.

Arkansas Gazette. "The Cholera." August 15, 1832. 2. c3–4.

Arkansas Gazette. "Cholera." September 5, 1832. 4, c1.

Arkansas Gazette. "Cholera." November 14, 1832. 2, c4.

Arkansas Gazette. "CHOLERA!!!—*at last!*" October 31, 1832. 3, c4.

Arkansas Gazette. Letter Extract. November 7, 1832. 2, c6.

Arkansas Gazette. "Little Rock Gazette." October 31, 1832. 3 c1.

Arkansas Gazette. "Prevention of Cholera." November 7, 1832. 2, c5.

Arkansas Gazette. "The Progress of Cholera." August 29, 1832. 3 c2.

Arkansas Gazette. "Progress of the Cholera." September 12, 1832. 2 c5.

Arkansas Gazette. "St. Louis, (Mo.) Oct. 16, The Cholera." October 22, 1832. 2 c3.

Audubon, John James. *Writings and Drawings.* New York: The Library of America, 1999.

Audubon, Maria R. *Audubon and His Journals.* Edited by Elliott Coues. 2 vols. New York: Charles Scribner's Sons, 1897.

Bagley, Clarence B. *Early Catholic Missions in Old Oregon.* 2 vols. Seattle: Lowman & Hanford Company, 1932.

Bancroft, Hubert Howe. *The History of the Northwest Coast.* 2 vols. San Francisco: The History Company Publishing, 1886.

Bandera, Tex. "When 10,000 Indian Died of Smallpox." *Frontier Times* 15, no. 7 (1938): 319–21.

Barbeau, C. M. *Huron and Wyandot Mythology.* Memoir 80, no. 11. Anthropological series. Ottawa: Government Printing Bureau, 1915.

Barry, Louise. *The Beginning of the West: Annals of the Kansas Gateway to the American West, 1540–1854.* Topeka: Kansas State Historical Society, 1972.

Barry, Louise. "The Fort Leavenworth-Fort Gibson Military Road and the Founding of Fort Scott." *Kansas Historical Quarterlies* 11, no. 2 (1942): 115–29.

Barton, Benjamin Smith. *New Views of the Origin of the Tribes and Nations of America.* 1798. Reprint, Millwood, NY: Kraus Reprint Co., 1976.

Bieder, Robert E. *Science Encounters the Indian, 1820–1880: The Early Years of American Ethnology.* Norman: University of Oklahoma Press, 1986.

Block, Sharon. *Rape and Sexual Power in Early America.* Chapel Hill: University of North Carolina Press, 2006.

Blumenbach, Joannes Friedrich *On the Natural Varieties of Mankind.* 1795, 1865. Reprint, New York: Bergman Publishers, 1969.

Bonner, T. D. *The Life and Adventures of James P. Beckwourth, Mountaineer, Scout, and Pioneer, and Chief of the Crow Nation of Indians.* 1856. Reprint, New York: Arno Press and *New York Times,* 1969.

Bourne, Edward Gaylord. "The Legend of Marcus Whitman." *The American Historical Review* 6, no. 2 (1901): 276–300.

Boyd, Robert. *The Coming of the Spirit of Pestilence: Introduced Infectious Diseases and Population Decline among Northwest Coat Indians, 1774–1874.* Seattle: University of Washington Press, 1999.

Bradbury, John. *Travels in the Interior of America in the Years 1809, 1810, and 1811.* 2nd ed. 1819. In *Early Western Travels.* Edited by Reuben Gold Thwaites. Vol. 5. Cleveland, OH: Arthur H. Clark and Company, 1906.

Branner, John C. "Some Old French Place Names in the State of Arkansas." *Modern Language Notes* 14, no. 2 (1899): 33–40.

Brodine, Charles E., Jr. "Henry Bouquet and British Infantry Tactics on the Ohio Frontier, 1758–1764." In *The Sixty Years' War for the Great Lakes, 1754–1814.* Edited by David Curtis Skaggs and Larry L. Nelson, 43–61. East Lansing: Michigan State University Press, 2001. Brooks, Lisa. *The Common Pot: The Recovery of Native Space in the Northeast*. Minneapolis: University of Minnesota Press, 2008.

Brouillet, Jean Baptiste Abraham. *Blackrobe Buries Whitman*. 1853. In *Journal of a Catholic Bishop on the Oregon Trail*. Edited by Edward J. Kowrach, 143–69. Fairfield, WA: Ye Galleon Press, 1978.

Buckingham, John. *Bitter Nemesis: The Intimate History of Strichnine*. New York: CRC Press, 2008.

Catlin, George. *Letters and Notes on the Manners, Customs, and Condition of the North American Indians*. 2 vols. 1841. Reprint, Edinburgh: John Grant, 1926.

Chambers, J. S. *The Conquest of Cholera, America's Greatest Scourge*. New York: The Macmillan Company, 1938.

Champlain, Samuel de. *The Works of Samuel de Champlain*. Edited by H. P. Biggar. 6 vols. Toronto: The Champlain Society, 1936.

Charlevoix, Pierre de. *Journal of a Voyage to North America*. 2 vols. 1761. Reprint, Ann Arbor, MI: University Microfilms, 1966.

Chittenden, Hiram Martin. *The American Fur Trade of the Far West*. 2 vols. 1902. Reprint, New York: The Press of the Pioneers, 1935.

Chittenden, Hiram Martin. *History of Early Steamboat Navigation on the Missouri River*. 2 vols. New York: Francis P. Harper, 1903.

Claiborne, J.F.H. *Mississippi, as a Province, Territory, and State*. Jackson, MI: Power & Barksdale, Publishers and Printers, 1880.

Clark, William. "1830 Report on the Fur Trade." *Oregon Historical Quarterly* 48, no. 1 (1947): 25–33.

Coe, Pamela. "Choctaw Saga." *Indian Affairs* 34 (1959): 6.

Converse, Harriet Maxwell. *Myths and Legends of the New York State Iroquois*. Edited by Arthur C. Parker. New York State Museum Bulletin 125. Education Department Bulletin no. 437. Albany: University of the State of New York, 1908.

Cook, Frederick. *Journals of the Military expedition of Major General John sullivan against the six Nations of Indians in 1779*. 1887. Reprint, Freeport, NY: Books for Libraries, 1972.

Cooper, James Fenimore. *The Pioneers, or the Sources of the Susquehanna; A Descriptive Tale*. Edited by James Franklin Beard. 1823. Reprint, Albany, NY: State University of New York Press, 1980.

Correspondence on the Subject of the Emigration of Indians, between the 30th of November, 1831, and 27th December 1833. Document 512. 5 vols. Washington, D.C.: Duff Green, 1831–1835.

Coulter, Harris L. *Science and Ethics in American Medicine: 1800–1914*. Washington, D.C.: McGrath Publishing Company, 1973.

Council of the Citizens' Association of New York. *Report of the Council of Hygiene and Public Health of the Citizens' Association of New York upon the Sanitary Condition of the City*. New York: D. Appleton and Company, 1865.

Coventry, C. B. *Epidemic Cholera: Its History, Causes, Pathology, and Treatment*. Buffalo, NY: Geo. H. Derby, 1849.

Craighead, J. G. *The Story of Marcus Whitman. Early Protestant Missions in the Northwest*, Vol. 34. Philadelphia: Presbyterian Board of Publication and Sabbath-school Work, 1895.

Cronon, William. *Changes in the Land: Indians, Colonists, and the Ecology of New England*. New York: Hill and Wang, 1983.

Darlington, Mary Carson. *Fort Pitt and Letters from the Frontier*. Pittsburgh: J. R. Weldin, 1892.

"Delegates of the Maine Conference: The Wyandots." *Christian Advocate and Journal and Zion's Herald* 6, no. 13 (1831): 51.

Denig, Edwin Thompson. *Five Indian Tribes of the Upper Missouri: Sioux, Arickaras, Assiniboines, Crees, Crows*. Norman: University of Oklahoma Press, 1961.

Denig, Edwin Thompson. *Indian Tribes of the Upper Missouri*. 1854. In *Forty-Sixth Annual Report of the Bureau of American Ethnology to the Secretary of the Smithsonian Institution for 1928–1929*. Edited by J.N.B. Hewitt, 375–628. Washington, D.C.: Government Printing Office, 1930.

Denig, Edwin Thompson. "Of the Crow Nation." *Anthropological Papers*. Bulletin 151. Smithsonian Institution, Bureau of American Ethnography, Anthropological Papers, no. 33. Washington, D.C.: Government Printing Office, 1953.

Department of Health and Human Services. Centers for Disease Control and Prevention. "Smallpox." http://redcross.tallytown.com/library/Smallpox-Overview.pdf (accessed August 6, 2008).

DeRosier, Arthur H., Jr. "Andrew Jackson and Negotiations for the Removal of the Choctaw Indians." *The Historian* 29, no. 3 (1967): 343–62.

DeRosier, Arthur H., Jr. "Myths and Realities in Indian Westward Removal: The Choctaw Example." In *Four Centuries of Southern Indians*. Edited by Charles M. Hudson, 83–100. Athens: University of Georgia Press, 1975.

DeRosier, Arthur H., Jr. *The Removal of the Choctaw Indians*. Knoxville: The University of Tennessee Press, 1970.

d'Errico, Peter. "Jeffrey Amherst and Smallpox Blankets." Native Web Organization. http://www.nativeweb.org/pages/legal/amherst/lord_jeff.htm (accessed January 8, 2008).

De Voto, Bernard. *Across the Wide Missouri*. Boston: Houghton-Mifflin Company, the Riverside Press, 1947.

Dillard, Anthony Winston. "The Treaty of Dancing Rabbit Creek between the United States and the Choctaw Indians in 1830." *Transactions of the Alabama Historical Society* 3 (1899): 99–106.

Disosway, Gabriel P. Letter of 18 February 1833. *Christian Advocate and Journal and Zion's Herald* 7, no. 27 (March 1833): 105.

Doddridge, Joseph. "The War of 1763." In *Notes on the Settlement and Indian Wars of the Western Parts of Virginia and Pennsylvania*. 1824. Reprint, New York: Garland Publishing, 1977. 214–24.

Dollar, Clyde D. "The High Plains Smallpox Epidemic of 1837–38." *Western Historical Quarterly* (January 1977): 15–38.

Donck, Adriaen Cornelissen van der. "Description of New Netherland." 1653. In *Mohawk Country: Early Narrative about a Native People*. Edited by Dean R. Snow, Charles T. Gehring, and William A. Starna. Syracuse: Syracuse University Press, 1996, 104–30.

Drake, Samuel Gardner, ed. "Alexander Henry's Captivity." In *Indian Captivities, or Life in the Wigwam*. 1851. Reprint, New York: AMS Press, 1975. 286–332.

Drury, Clifford Merrill. *First White Women over the Rockies*. Vol. 2. Glendale, CA: The Arthur H. Clark Company, 1963.

Drury, Clifford Merrill. *Marcus and Narcissa Whitman and the Opening of Old Oregon*. 2 vols. Glendale, CA: The Arthur H. Clark Company, 1973.

Drury, Clifford Merrill. *Marcus Whitman, M.D., Pioneer and Martyr*. Caldwell, ID: The Caxton Printers, 1937.

Duffy, John. "Smallpox and the Indians in the American Colonies." In *Biological Consequences of European Expansion, 1450–1800.* Edited by Kenneth F. Kiple and Stephen V. Beck. 1951. Reprint, Brookfield, VT: Ashgate Publishing Company, 1997. 233–50.

Edwards, Jonathan, ed. *David Brainerd: His Life and Journal.* 1749. Edingburgh: H.S. Baynes, 1826.

Eells, Myron. *Marcus Whitman, Pathfinder and Patriot.* Seattle: The Alice Harriman Company, 1909.

Emerson, Ralph Waldo. *Essays by Ralph Waldo Emerson.* New York: Thomas Y. Crowell, 1926.

"An Evening with an Old Missionary." *Chicago Advance.* December 1, 1870.

Farnham, Thomas Jefferson. *Farnham's Travels, Part I.* 1843. In *Early Western Travels.* Edited by Reuben Gold Thwaites. Vol. 28. Cleveland, OH: Arthur H. Clark Company, 1906.

Fenn, Elizabeth A. "Biological Warfare in Eighteenth-Century North America: Beyond Jeffery Amherst." *The Journal of American History* 86, no. 4 (2000): 1552–80.

Fenn, Elizabeth A. *Pox Americana: The Great Smallpox Epidemic of 1775–82.* New York: Hill and Wang, 2001.

Ferch, D.L. "Fighting the Smallpox Epidemic of 1837–1838: The Response of the American Fur Company Traders." *Museum of the Fur Trade Quarterly* 19, no. 4 (1983): 2–7.

Ferguson, Robert B. "Treaties between the United States and the Choctaw Nation." In *The Choctaw before Removal.* Edited by Carolyn Keller Reeves, 214–30. Jackson: University Press of Mississippi, 1985.

Flavin, Francis E. "A Pox on Amherst: Smallpox, Sir Jeffrey, and a Town Named Amherst." *Historical Journal of Massachusetts* (Winter 2002): 1–20.

Fletcher, Alice C., and Francis La Flesche. *The Omaha Tribe.* 2 vols. 1911. Reprint, Lincoln: University of Nebraska Press, 1972.

Foreman, Grant. *Indian Removal: The Emigration off the Five Civilized Tribes of Indians.* 1932. Reprint, Norman: The University of Oklahoma Press, 1972.

Franklin, Wayne. *James Fenimore Cooper: The Early Years.* New Haven, CT: Yale University Press, 2007.

Galton, Francis. *Hereditary Genius: An Inquiry into Its Laws and Consequences.* 1869. Reprint, New York: D. Appleton, 1884.

Galton, Francis. *Natural Inheritance.* 1889. Reprint, New York: AMS Press, 1973.

Gray, W[illiam] H[enry]. *A History of Oregon, 1792–1849.* 1870. Reprint, New York: Arno Press, 1973.

Gregory, George. *Lectures on the Eruptive Fevers.* New York: S.S. & W. Wood, Publishers, 1851.

Gulick, Bill. *Snake River Country.* Caldwell, ID: Caxton Printers, 1971.

Guthrie, Chester L., and Leo L. Gerald. "Upper Missouri Agency: An Account of Indian Administration on the Frontier." *The Pacific Historical Review* 10, no. 1 (1941): 47–56.

Hafen, LeRoy R. *The Life of Thomas Fitspatrick: Mountain Man, Guide and Indian Agent.* 1931. Reprint, Lincoln: University of Nebraska Press, 1973.

Haines, Aubrey L., ed. *Osborne Russell's Journal of a Trapper.* Lincoln: University of Nebraska Press, 1965.

Hamilton, Milton W., ed. *The Papers of Sir William Johnson.* 14 vols. Albany: The University of the State of New York Press, 1921–1965.

Handbook of Texas. "Gaines, Edmund Pendleton (1777–1849)," http://tshaonline.org/hand
book/online/articles/GG/fga3.html (accessed August 21, 2008).

Heagerty, John J. *Four Centuries of Medical History in Canada.* 2 vols. Toronto: The Macmillan Company of Canada, 1928.

Heaton, Herbert. "Benjamin Gott and the Anglo-American Cloth Trade." *Journal of Economic and Business History* 2, no. 1 (1929): 146–62.

Heckewelder, John. *Narrative of the Mission of the United Brethren among the Delaware
and Mohegan Indians from Its Commencement, in the Year 1740, to the Close of the Year
1808.* 1818. Reprint, New York: Arno Press, 1971.

Heckewelder, John. *The History, Manners, and Customs of the Indian Nations Who Once Inhabited Pennsylvania and the Neighboring States.* The First American Frontier Series.
1820, 1876. Reprint, New York: Arno Press and *New York Times,* 1971.

Herring, Elbert. "Report from the Office of Indian Affairs." 22nd Cong., 2nd sess. House
Document 2, 1832. 159–77.

Hill, Edward E. *Office of Indian Affairs, 1824–1880: Historical Sketches.* New York: Clearwa-
ter Publishing, 1974.

Hopkins, Donald R. *Princes and Peasants: Smallpox and History.* Chicago: University of Chicago Press, 1983.

Hunn, Eugene S., with James Selam and Family. *Nch'i-Wána, the Big River: Mid-Columbia
Indians and Their Land.* Seattle: University of Washington Press, 1990.

Jacobs, Wilbur J., ed. *The Letters of Francis Parkman.* 2 vols. Norman: University of Oklahoma Press, 1960.

Jeffrey, Julie Roy. *Converting the West: Biography of Narcissa Whitman.* Norman: University
of Oklahoma Press, 1991.

Johansen, Bruce E. *Shapers of the Great Debate on Native Americans: Land, Spirit, and Power.*
Westport, CT: Greenwood Press, 2000.

Johansen, Dorothy O. *Robert Newell's Memoranda: Travles in the Teritory of Missourie; Travle
to the Kayuse War; together with A Report on the Indians South of the Columbia River.*
Portland, OR: Champoeg Press, 1959.

Jones, David S. *Rationalizing Epidemics: Meanings and Uses of American Indian Mortality
since 1600.* Cambridge, MA: Harvard University Press, 2004.

Jones, Landon Y. *William Clark and the Shaping of the West.* New York: Hill and Wang,
2004.

Jones, Nard. *The Great Command: The Story of Marcus and Narcissa Whitman and the Oregon
Country Pioneers.* Boston: Little, Brown and Company, 1959.

Josephy, Alvin C. Jr. *The Nez Perce Indians and the Opening of the Old Northwest.* 1965. Reprint, Boston: Houghton-Mifflin, 1997.

"The Journal of Pontiac's Conspiracy." In *The Siege of Detroit in 1763.* 3–206. Chicago:
R. R. Donnelley & Sons, 1958.

Jung, Patrick J. *The Black Hawk War of 1832.* Norman: University of Oklahoma Press, 2007.

Kane, Paul. *Paul Kane's Frontier, Including Wanderings of an Artist among the Indians of North
America.* 1859. Austin: University of Texas Press, 1971.

Kappler, Charles J., ed. "Treaty Made and Concluded at Prairie du Chien, in the Territory
of Michigan, between the United States of America, by their Commissioners, General John McNeil, Colonel Pierre Menard, and Caleb Atwater, Esq. and the United
Nations of Chippewa, Ottawa, and Potawatamie Indians, of the Waters of the Illinois, Milwaukee, and Manitoouck Rivers, 29 July 1829." Vol. 2: 297–300. Washington, D.C.: Government Printing Office, 1904.

Kappler, Charles J., ed. "Treaty Made and Concluded at the Village of Prairie du Chien, Michigan Territory, on This First Day of August, in the Year One Thousand Eight Hundred and Twenty-nine, between the United States of America, by Their Commissioner, General John M'Neil, Colonel Pierre Menard, and Caleb Atwater, Esq., for and on Behalf of Said States, of the One Part, and the Nation of Winnebaygo Indians of the Other Part." Vol. 2: 300–303. Washington: Government Printing Office, 1904.

Kappler, Charles J., ed. "Treaty Made and Concluded by William Clark Superintendent of Indian Affairs and Willoughby Morgan, Col. of the United States 1st Regt. Infantry, Commissioners on Behalf of the United States on the One Part, and the Undersigned Deputations of the Confederated Tribes of the Sacs and Foxes; the Medawah-Kanton, Wahpacoota, Wahpeton and Sissetong Bands or Tribes of Sioux; the Omahas, Ioways, Ottoes and Missourias on the Other Part, July 15, 1830. Vol. 2: 305–10. Washington, D.C.: Government Printing Office, 1904.

Kappler, Charles J., ed. "Treaty of Dancing Rabbit Creek." In *Indian Affairs: Laws and Treaties*. Vol. 2: 310–19. Washington: Government Printing Office, 1904.

Kappler, Charles J., ed. "Treaty with the Sioux and Chippewa, Sacs and Fox, Menominie, Ioway, Sioux, Winnebago, and a Portion of the Ottawa, Chippewa, and Potawattomie Tribes, August 19, 1825." Vol. 2: 250–55. Washington: Government Printing Office, 1904.

Kiernan, Ben. *Blood and Soil: A World History of Genocide and Extermination from Sparta to Darfur.* New Haven, CT: Yale University Press, 2007.

Killoren, John J. *"Come, Blackrobe": De Smet and the Indian Tragedy.* Norman: University of Oklahoma Press, 1994.

Kiple, Kenneth E., and Stephen V. Beck. *Biological Consequences of the European Expansion, 1450–1800.* Aldershot: Ashgate Publishing, 1997.

Knollenberg, Bernhard. "General Amherst and Germ Warfare." *Mississippi Historical Review* 41 (1954): 489–94.

Kurz, Rudolph Friedrich. *Journal of Rudolph Friederich Kurz.* Edited by J.N.B. Hewitt. Lincoln: University of Nebraska Press, 1970.

Lafitau, Joseph Francois. *Customs of the American Indians Compared with the Customs of Primitive Times.* Edited by William N. Fenton and Elizabeth L. Moore. 2 vols. 1724. Reprint, Toronto: The Champlain Society, 1974.

Lahontan, Louis Armand, Baron de. *New Voyages to North America.* Edited by Reuben Gold Thwaites. 2 vols. 1703. Reprint, Chicago: A. C. McClure, 1905.

Lansing, Ronald B. *Juggernaut: The Whitman Massacre Trial, 1850.* Pasadena, CA: Ninth Judicial Circuit Historical Society, 1993.

Larpenteur, Charles. *Forty Years a Fur Trader on the Upper Missouri: The Personal Narrative of Charles Larpenteur, 1833–1872.* Chicago: The Lakeside Press, R. R. Donnelley & Sibs Co., 1933.

Larpenteur, Charles. "White Man Bear (mato Washejoe), Upper Missouri Trader: Journals and Notes of Charles Larpenteur between 1834 and 1872." Transcribed by Edwin T. Thompson. National Park Service Library. Denver, CO. Photocopy.

Lawrence, Jane. "The Indian Health Service and the Sterilization of Native American Women." *American Indian Quarterly* 24, no. 3 (2000): 400–19.

Lemkin, Raphael. *Axis Rule in Occupied Europe: Laws of Occupation, Analysis of Government, Proposals for Redress.* Washington, D.C.: Carnegie Endowment for International Peace, 1944.

Letters Received by the Office of Indian Affairs, 1824–1876. Roll 170. Choctaw Agency, 1824–1876. The National Archives and Records Service, General Services Administration, 1959. Microcopy No. 234.

Letters Received by the Office of Indian Affairs, 1824–1881. Roll 184. Choctaw Agency, 1824–1876. The National Archives and Records Service, General Services Administration, 1959. Microcopy No. 234.

Letters Received by the Office of Indian Affairs, 1824–1881. Roll 185. Choctaw Agency, 1824–1876. The National Archives and Records Service, General Services Administration, 1959. Microcopy No. 234.

Letters Received by the Office of Indian Affairs, 1824–1881. Roll 884. The National Archives and Records Service, General Services Administration, 1959. Microcopy No. 234.

Lewis, William S., and Paul C. Phillips, eds. The Journal of John Work. Cleveland: The Arthur H. Clark Company, 1923.

Lighthouse Friends. "Larzaretto Point Lighthouse, MD." http://www.lighthousefriends.com/light.asp?ID=421 (accessed July 30, 2008).

Linneaeus, Carolus. A General System of Nature. 1758, 1806. Reprint, Ann Arbor: University Microfilms, 1968.

Long, J[ohn] C[uthbert]. Lord Jeffrey Amherst, A Solider of the King. New York: The Macmillan Company, 1933.

Mann, Barbara Alice. "'Are You Delusional?' Kandiaronk on Christianity." In Native American Speakers of the Eastern Woodlands: Selected Speeches and Critical Analyses. Edited by Barbara Alice Mann, 35–81. Westport, CT: Greenwood Press, 2001.

Mann, Barbara Alice. George Washington's War on Native America. Westport, CT: Praeger, 2005.

Mann, Barbara Alice. "The Greenville Treaty of 1795: Pen-and-Ink Witchcraft in the Struggle for the Old Northwest." In Enduring Legacies: Native American Treaties and Contemporary Controversies. Edited by Bruce E. Johansen, 135–202. Westport, CT: Praeger Press, 2004.

Mann, Barbara Alice. Iroquoian Women: The Gantowisas. New York: Peter Lang Publishing, 2006.

Mann, Barbara Alice. Native Americans, Archaeologists, and the Mounds, New York: Peter Lang Publishing, 2003.

Mante, Thomas. The History of the Late War in North America, and the Islands of the West Indies. London: W. Strahan and T. Cadell, 1772.

Marshall, Principal William Isaac. The Acquisition of Oregon and the Long Suppressed Evidence about Marcus Whitman. 2 vols. Seattle: Lowman & Hanford, 1911.

Maslow, Abraham H. "A Theory of Human Motivation." Psychological Review 50 (1943): 370–96.

Maximilian, Prince of Wied. Part I. Travels in the Interior of North America. 1843. In Early Western Travels. Edited by Reuben Gold Thwaites. Vol. 22. Cleveland, OH: Arthur H. Clark and Company, 1906.

Mayor, Adrienne. "The Nessus Shirt in the New World: Smallpox Blankets in History and Legend." The Journal of American Folklore 108, no. 427 (1995): 54–77.

M'Cown, F. O. Transactions of the Twelfth Annual Re-Union of the Oregon Pioneer Association for 1884. Salem, OR: E.M. Waite, 1885.

McCoy, Isaac. The Annual Register of Indian Affairs in the Western (or Indian) Territory, 1835–1838. 1835–1838. Reprint, Springfield, MO: Particular Baptist Press, 1998.

McCoy, Isaac. *History of Baptist Indian Missions*. 1840. Reprint, Springfield, MO: Particular Baptist Press, 2003.

McKee, Alexander. "Minutes of Debates in Council on the Banks of the Ottawa River, (Commonly Called the Miami of the lake), November, 1791." Philadelphia: William Young, Bookseller, 1792.

McKee, Alexander. "Report of Speeches of the Delaware Indians." Fort Pitt, June 24, 1763. In *The Papers of Col. Henry Bouquet*. Series 21655. Edited by Sylvester K. Stevens, et al., 208–10. B.M., Add. MSS 21655, f. 216, D. 1943. Ohio Valley-Great Lakes Ethnohistory Archives: The Miami Collection.

McLoughlin, John. *The Letters of John McLoughlin from Fort Vancouver to the Governor and Committee*. Second Series, 1839–44. Edited by E. E. Rich. London: The Publications of the Hudson's Bay Record Society, 1943.

McLoughlin, John. *The Letters of John McLoughlin from Fort Vancouver to the Governor and Committee*. Third Series, 1844–46. Edited by E. E. Rich. London: The Publications of the Hudson's Bay Record Society, 1944.

Meline, Mary M., and Edward F. X. McSweeny. *The Story of the Mountain: Mount St. Mary's College and Seminary, Emmitsburg, Maryland*. Emmitsburg, MD: *Weekly Chronicle*, 1911.

Miles, Edwin A. "Andrew Jackson and Senator George Poindexter." *The Journal of Southern History* 24, no. 1 (1958): 51–56.

Millard, Catherine. "Marcus Whitman—The Preacher Who Rode for an Empire System." *Christian Heritage News*, http://www.christianheritagemins.org/articles/Marcus%20 Whitman.htm (accessed December 5, 2008).

Miller, Robert J. *Native America, Discovered and Conquered: Thomas Jefferson, Lewis & Clark, and Manifest Destiny*. Westport, CT: Praeger, 2006.

Miscellaneous Documents Printed by the House of Representatives. 30th Congress, 1st Session. Document 98. Washington, D.C.: Tippen & Streeper, 1848.

"Mission to Indians in the Oregon Country." *The Missionary Herald* 35, no. 1 (1839): 14.

Missouri Historical Society. "Reports of the Fur Trade and Inland Trade to Mexico." *Glimpses of the Past* 9 (January–September 1941): 3–39.

Missouri Republican. "Dinner to General Gaines." January 25, 1838.

Missouri Republican. "The Dinner to Gen. Gaines." January 24, 1838.

Missouri Republican. "Old Times: An Interview with Gen. Bernard Pratte." November 24, 1879.

Montaigne, Michel Eyquem de. "*Des cannibales*." *Essais*. 2 vols. 1580. Paris: Éditions Garnier Frères, 1962.

Montaigne, Michel Eyquem de. "*Des cannibales*." *Essais*. 2 vols. 1580. Reprint, Paris: Éditions Garnier Frères, 1962.

Montgomery, Thomas Lynch, ed. *Frontier Forts of Pennsylvania*. 2 vols. Harrisburg, PA: William Stanley Ray, State Printer, 1916.

Morgan, Henry Lewis. *League of the Haudenosaunee, or Iroquois*. 2 vols. 1851. Reprint, New York: Burt Franklin, 1901.

Morris, R. J. *Cholera 1832: The Social Response to an Epidemic*. London: Croom Helm, 1976.

Morris, Robert D. *The Blue Death: Disease, Disaster, and the Water We Drink*. New York: HarperCollins, 2007.

Morton, Samuel George. *Crania Americana*. Philadelphia: J. Dobson, 1839.

Morton, Samuel. *Crania Americana, or a Comparatives View of the Skulls of the Various Aboriginal Nations of North and South America, to Which Is Prefixed an Essay on the Varieties of the Human Species*. Philadelphia: J. Dobson, 1839.

Moulton, Gary E., ed. *The Journals of the Lewis and Clark Expedition.* Lincoln: University of Nebraska-Lincoln, 2003. http://lewisandclarkjournals.unl.edu/index.html (accessed July 30, 2008).

Mowry, William A. *Marcus Whitman and the Early Days of Oregon.* New York: Silver, Burdett and Company, 1901.

Mumey, Nolie. *James Pierson Beckwourth: An Enigmatic Figure of the West, 1856–1866.* Denver: Old West Publishing, 1957.

Neath, Joseph. *Memoirs of Nisqually.* Fairfield, WA: Ye Galleon Press, 1979.

Nelson, Larry L. *A Man of Distinction among Them: Alexander McKee and British-Indian Affairs along the Ohio Country Frontier, 1754–1799.* Kent, OH: Kent State University Press, 1999.

New York Observer. "Domestic." November 18, 1837.

Nixon, Oliver W. *How Marcus Whitman Saved Oregon.* Chicago: Star Publishing Company, 1895.

O'Callaghan, E. B., ed. *Documents Relative to the Colonial History of the State of New York.* Vol. 7. Albany: Weed, Parsons, Printers, 1853–1887.

Osborn, Charles S., and Stellanova. *Schoolcraft→Longfellow→Hiawatha.* Lancaster, PA: The Jaques Cattell Press, 1942.

Owen, Thomas McAdory, ed. *Publications of the Transactions of the Alabama Historical Society, 1898–1899.* Vol. 3. Tuscaloosa: Alabama Historical Society, 1899.

Palladino, Lawrence Benedict. *Indian and White in the Northwest; or, a History of Catholicity in Montana.* Baltimore: John Murphy & Company, 1894.

Palmer, Joel. *Journal of Travels over the Rocky Mountains to the Mouth of the Columbia River in the Years 1845 and 1846. In Early Western Travels.* Edited by Reuben Gold Thwaites. Vol. 30. Cleveland, OH: Arthur H. Clark Company, 1906.

Papers of the St. Louis Fur Trade, Part 1: The Chouteau Collection, 1752–1925. Roll 24. Bethesda, MD: University Publications of America, 1991.

Papers of the St. Louis Fur Trade, Part 1: The Chouteau Collection, 1752–1925. Roll 25. Bethesda, MD: University Publications of America, 1991.

Parker, Arthur Caswell. "The Constitution of the Five Nations, or the Iroquois Book of the Great Law." *New York State Museum Bulletin* 184 (April 1916): 1–155.

Parker, Arthur Caswell. *The Iroquois Uses of Maize and Other Food Plants. In Parker on the Iroquois.* Edited by William N. Fenton. 1913. Reprint, Syracuse, NY: Syracuse University Press, 1968. 5–119.

Parker, Arthur Caswell. *The Life of General Ely S. Parker: Last Grand Sachem of the Iroquois and General Grant's Military Secretary.* Buffalo, NY: The Buffalo Historical Society, 1919.

Parker, Samuel. *Journal of an Exploring Tour beyond the Rocky Mountains under the Direction of the A.B.C.F.M., Performed in the Years 1835, '36, and '37: Containing a Description of the Geography, Geology, Climate, and Productions; and the Number, Manners, and Customs of the Natives, with a Map of the Oregon Territory.* 1838. Reprint, Minneapolis, MN: Ross & Haines, 1967.

Parkman, Francis. *The Conspiracy of Pontiac and the Indian War after the Conquest of Canada.* 2 vols. 1851, 1870. Reprint, Lincoln: University of Nebraska Press, 1994.

Pearson, J. Diane. "Lewis Cass and the Politics of Disease: The Indian Vaccination Act of 1832." *Wacazo-Sa Review* 18, no. 2 (2003): 9–35.

Pearson, J. Diane. "Medical Diplomacy and the American Indian: Thomas Jefferson, the Lewis and Clark Expedition, and the Subsequent Effects on American Indian Health and Public Policy." *Wacazo-Sa Review* 19, no. 1 (2004): 105–30.

Peckham, Howard. *Pontiac and the Indian Uprising.* 1947. Reprint, Princeton: Princeton University Press, 1994.

Phillips, Paul Chrisler. *The Fur Trade.* 2 vols. Norman: University of Oklahoma Press, 1961.

Pouchot, Pierre. *Memoirs on the Late War in North America between France and England.* Edited by Brian Leigh Dunnigan. Translated by Michael Cardy. 1781. Reprint, Youngstown, NY: Old Fort Niagara Association, 1994.

Pringle, Catherine Sager. *Across the Plains in 1844.* 1905. http://www.isu.edu/~trinmich/00.ar.sager1.html.

Pritts, Joseph, comp. "Review.—The Great West." In *Incidents of Border Life.* 465–511. Chambersburg, PA: J. Pritts, 1839.

Rees, Robert A., and Alan Sandy, eds. *The Adventures of Captain Bonneville.* Boston: Twayne Publishers, 1977.

Richardson, James D., ed. *A Compilation of the Messages and Papers of the Presidents.* 10 vols. Washington, D.C.: Bureau of National Literature, 1897.

Roberts, George B. "The Round Hand of George B. Roberts: The Cowlitz Farm Journal." *Oregon Historical Quarterly* 63, no. 2 (1962): 101–72.

Robertson, R. G. *Rotting Face: Smallpox and the American Indian.* Caldwell, ID: Caxton Press, 2001.

Rosati, Joseph. Letter of 31 December 1831 from St. Louis to Editor. *Annales de l'Association de la Propagation de la Foi.* Vol. 5, 597–600. Paris: La Librairie ecclésiastique de Rusand et Cie, 1831.

Rosenberg, Charles E. *The Cholera Bulletin Conducted by an Association of Physicians, Volume I, Numbers 1–24.* 1832. Reprint, New York: Arno Press and *New York Times,* 1972.

Rosenberg, Charles E. *The Cholera Years: The United States in 1832, 1849, and 1866.* Chicago: University of Chicago Press, 1962.

Ross, C., Rev. M. Eells, and W. H. Gray, eds. *The Whitman Controversy.* Portland: Geo. H. Himes, Book and Job Printer, 1885.

Ross, Marvin G. *The West of Alfred Jacob Miller (1837).* Norman: University of Oklahoma Press, 1951.

Rutherfurd, John. "John Rutherfurd's Captivity Narrative." In *The Siege of Detroit in 1763.* Chicago: R. R. Donnelley & Sons, 1958. 219–74.

Sagard, Gabriel. *The Long Journey to the Country of the Hurons.* Edited by George M. Wrong. 1632. Reprint, Toronto: The Champlain Society, 1939.

Sager, Catherine. "Oregon Trail Orphan." In *Seeing the Elephant: The Many Voices of the Oregon Trail.* Edited by Joyce Badgley Hunsaker, 110–22. Lubbock: Texas Tech University Press, 2003.

Satz, Ronald N. "Rhetoric Versus Reality: The Indian Policy of Andrew Jackson." In *Cherokee Removal, Before and After.* Edited by William L. Anderson, 29–54. Athens: The University of Georgia Press, 1991.

Schoolcraft, Henry Rowe. *Information Respecting the History, Condition, and Prospects of the Indian tribes of the United States.* 6 vols. Philadelphia: Lippincott, Grambo, & Co., 1853–1857.

Schoolcraft, Henry Rowe. *Outlines of the Life and Character of Gen. Lewis Cass.* Albany: J. Munsell, Printer, 1848.

Senate Executive Document 37. 41st Congress, 3rd Session. Washington, D.C.: Government Printing Office, 1871.

Seton, Ernest Thompson. *The Gospel of the Red Man: An Indian Bible.* Garden City, NY: Doubleday, Doran & Company, 1936.

Shurkin, Joel. *The Invisible Fire: The Story of Mankind's Triumph over the Ancient Scourge of Smallpox*. New York: Putnam's, 1979.

Simpson, George. *An Overland Journey Round the World*. Philadelphia: Lea and Blanchard, 1847.

Sipe, C. Hale. *The Indian Wars of Pennsylvania*. Harrisburg, PA: The Telegraph Press, 1929.

Smith, J. David. *The Eugenic Assault on America: Scenes in Red, White, and Black*. Fairfax, VA: George Mason University Press, 1993.

Spalding, Henry H. "Oregon Indians." *Missionary Herald* 44, no. 7 (1848): 237–41.

Spalding, Henry H. "Recent Intelligence: Oregon Indians." *Missionary Herald* 39, no. 9 (September, 1843): 367.

Stearn, Wagner, and Allen E. Stern. *The Effects of Smallpox on the Destiny of the Amerindian*. Boston: Bruce Humphries, 1945.

Stern, Bernhard Joseph. *Society and Medical Progress*. Princeton, NJ: Princeton University Press, 1941.

Stone, William, ed. *The Life and Times of Sir William Johnson, Bart*. 2 vols. Albany: J Munsell, 1865.

Sunder, John Edward. *Joshua Pilcher: Fur Trader and Indian Agent*. Norman: University of Oklahoma Press, 1968.

Sundstrom, Linea. "Smallpox Used Them Up: References to Epidemic Disease in Northern Plains Winter Counts, 1714–1920." *Ethnohistory* 44, no. 2 (1997): 305–43.

Sutter, John A. *New Helvetia Diary*. San Francisco: The Grabhorn Press, 1939.

Thomas, David Hurst. *Skull Wars: Kennewick Man, Archaeology, and the Battle for Native American Identity*. New York: Basic Books, 2000.

Thomas, Robert. *A Treatise on Domestic Medicine*. New York: Collins & Co., 1822.

Thornton, Russell. *American Indian Holocaust and Survival: A Population History since 1492*. Norman: University of Oklahoma Press, 1987.

Thwaites, Reuben Gold, ed. *Early Western Travels*. 32 vols. Cleveland, OH: Arthur H. Clark and Company, 1906.

Thwaites, Reuben Gold, ed. *The Jesuit Relations: Travels and Explorations of the Jesuit Missionaries in New France, 1610–1791*. 73 vols. New York: Pageant Book Company, 1959.

Timbrook, Mark J. "An Extended Interpretation of the Smallpox Epidemic of 1837." M.A. Thesis. Northfield: Vermont College of Norwich University, 2001.

Tinker, George E. *American Indian Liberation: A Theology of Sovereignty*. New York: Orbis Books, 2008.

Tinker, George E. *Missionary Conquest: The Gospel and Native American Cultural Genocide*. Minneapolis: Fortress Press, 1993.

Tolmie, William Fraser. "Letter from Dr. Tolmie." In *Transactions of the Twelfth Annual Re-Union of the Oregon Pioneer Association for 1884*. Salem, OR: E. M. Waite, 1885. 25–37.

Tolmie, William Fraser. *Journals of William Fraser Tolmie, Physician and Fur Trader*. Vancouver: Mitchell Press, 1963.

Tracey, Ebenezer Carter. *Memoir of the Life of Jeremiah Evarts, Esq*. Boston: Crocker and Brewster, 1845.

Trimble, Michael K. "Epidemiology on the Northern Plains: A Cultural Perspective." PhD Diss. University of Missouri-Columbia, 1985.

Trimble, Michael K. *An Ethnohistorical Interpretation of the Spread of Smallpox in the Northern Plains Utilizing Concepts of Disease Ecology*. Reprints in Anthropology. Vol. 33. Lincoln, NB: J&L Reprint Company, 1986.

Tucker, Jonathan B. *Scourge: The Once and Future Threat of Smallpox.* New York: Atlantic Monthly Press, 2003.

Tyler, Lyon G. *The Letters and Times of the Tylers.* 2 vols. Richmond, VA: Whittet & Shepperson, 1885.

United States Senate. *Report of the Select Committee of the Senate of the United State on the Sickness and Mortality on Board Emigrant Ships.* Washington, D.C.: Beverley Tucker, Senate Printer, 1854.

United States. *U.S. Statutes at Large.* Boston: Charles C. Little and James Brown.

U.S. House of Representatives. *American State Papers: Public Lands.* 24th Cong., 1st sess. Washington, D.C.: Gales and Seaton, 1832–1861.

Van Quickenborn, C. Letter of 10 March 1829 to the Editor. *Annales de l'Association de la Propagation de la Foi.* Vol. 4, 572–89. Paris: La Librairie Ecclésiastique de Rusand, 1830.

Varner, John Grier, and Jennette Johnson Varner. *Dogs of Conquest.* Norman: University of Oklahoma Press, 1983.

Vaughn, Genevieve, ed. *Women and the Gift Economy: A Radically Different Worldview Is Possible.* Toronto: Inanna Publications and Education, 2007.

Vestal, Stanley. *Jim Bridger: Mountain Man, A Biography.* New York: William Morrow & Company, 1946.

Vestal, Stanley. *Joe Meek: The Merry Mountain Man, A Biography.* Lincoln: University of Nebraska Press, 1952.

Victor, Frances Fuller. *The River of the West.* 1870. Reprint, Oakland, CA: Brooks-Sterling Company, 1974.

Waddell, Louis M., ed. *The Papers of Henry Bouquet.* Vol. 6. Harrisburg: The Pennsylvania Historical and Museum Commission, 1994.

Wade, Mason, ed. *The Journals of Francis Parkman.* 2 vols. New York: Harper & Brothers Publishers, 1947.

Walker, William. "The Flat-Head Indians." *Christian Advocate and Journal and Zion's Herald* 7, no. 27 (1833): 105.

Wallace, Paul A. W. *Conrad Weiser: Friend of Colonist and Mohawk.* New York: Russell & Russell, 1945.

Wallace, Paul A. W., ed. *Thirty Thousand Miles with John Heckewelder.* Pittsburgh: University of Pittsburgh Press, 1958.

Ward, Matthew C. "The Microbes of War: The British Army and Epidemic Disease among the Ohio Indians, 1758–1765." In *The Sixty Year's War for the Great Lakes, 1754–1814.* Edited by David Curtis Skaggs and Larry L. Nelson, 63–78. East Lansing: Michigan State University Press, 2001.

Watkins, Albert, ed. *Publications of the Nebraska State Historical Society.* Vol. 20. Lincoln: Nebraska State Historical Society, 1922.

Watts, J. F., and Fred L. Israel. *Presidential Documents: The Speeches, Proclamations, and Policies That Have Shaped the Nation from Washington to Clinton.* New York: Routledge, 2000.

Wedel, Waldo R. *The Dunbar-Allis Letters on the Pawnee.* New York: Garland Publishing, 1985.

White, Charles. *An Account of the Regular Gradation in Man, and in Different Animals and Vegetables; and from the Former to the Latter.* London: C. Dilly, 1799.

White, Richard. *The Middle Ground: Indians, Empires, and Republics in the Great Lakes Region, 1650–1815.* Cambridge, MA: Cambridge University Press, 1991.

Whitman, Marcus. "Dr. Whitman's Bill and His Letter to the Secretary of War, Written in 1843." *Transactions of the Nineteenth Annual Re-Union of the Oregon Pioneer Association* (1891): 69–78.

Whitman, Marcus. "Oregon Indians: Report of Doct. Whitman." *The Missionary Herald* 39, no. 9 (September, 1843): 336–39.

Whitman, Narcissa. "A Journey across the Plains in 1836: Journal of Mrs. Marcus Whitman." *Transactions of the Nineteenth Annual Re-Union of the Oregon Pioneer Association* (1891): 40–68.

Whitman, Narcissa. "Letters Written by Mrs. Whitman from Oregon to Her Relatives in New York." *Transactions of the Nineteenth Annual Re-Union of the Oregon Pioneer Association* (1891): 79–179.

Whitman, Narcissa. "Mrs. Whitman's Letters." *Transactions of the Twenty-first Annual Re-Union of the Oregon Pioneer Association* (1893): 53–219.

Williams, G. Edward. *The Orderly Book of Colonel Henry Bouquet's Expedition against the Ohio Indians, 1764.* Pittsburgh: Mayer Press, 1960.

"William Trent's Journal at Fort Pitt, 1763: Notes and Documents." *Mississippi Valley Historical Review* 11 (1924): 390–413.

Wilson, Elinor. *Jim Beckwourth: Black Mountain Man and War Chief of the Crows.* Norman: University of Oklahoma Press, 1972.

Wilson, James Grant. *The Life and Letters of Fitz-Greene Halleck.* New York: D. Appleton and Company, 1869.

Withers, Alexander Scott. *Chronicles of Border Warfare, or, a History of the Settlement by the Whites, of Northwestern Virginia, and of the Indian Wars and Massacres in that Section of the State.* 1895. Reprint, New York: Arno Press, 1971.

Wright, Muriel L. "The Removal of the Choctaws to the Indian Territory, 1830–1833." *Chronicles of Oklahoma* 2 (1928): 103–28.

Wright, Robert E., and David J. Cowen. *Financial Founding Fathers: The Men Who Made America Rich.* Chicago: University of Chicago Press, 2006.

Index

❧

About the Author

BARBARA ALICE MANN is a PhD scholar working heavily in Native American Studies, as well as in women's studies and nineteenth-century American literature. An Ohio bear-clan, community-recognized Seneca, she has authored eight previous books along with dozens of chapters and articles. She has also written on James Fenimore Cooper and Jane Austen, in addition to working for indigenous rights as an elder in Ohio.